African-American Who's Who™

Past & Present Greater Rochester Area
Second Edition

Mike F. Molaire, Editor/Publisher

Marsha Jones, Copy Editor

Introduction by Mayor William A. Johnson, Jr.

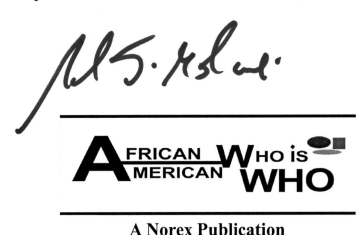

A Norex Publication

<u>Front cover photographs</u>*: (clockwise, from left): The Honorable William A. Johnson, Jr.; The Greater Bethlehem Temple Pentecospal Church (historic landmark, the old AME Zion Church at 42 Favor St.); Mary-Frances Winters; Kenneth W. Woodward, MD; James and Carolyne Blount; The Honorable Ruth Scott; Dr. Frederick C. Jefferson, Jr.; The Frederick Douglass Memorial Statue at Highland park.

<u>Back cover photographs</u>*: (clockwise, from left): Dr. David A. Anderson/Sanfoka, 1997 Kwanzaa celebration at the Phillis Wheatley Library; The entrance of the Monroe County Community Hospital, designed by Thomas Boyde, Rochester's first Black architect; Rodric Cox-Cooper in front of the Norton St. NET, Neighborhood Empowerment Team; Dr. Walter Cooper; Armenta Adams Hummings; Essie Calhoun (photo, courtesy Essie Calhoun); Kathryn Terrell; Almeta Whitis; Garth Fagan; Mike F. Molaire (photo, Fred Tanskley).

* All photographs by Mike F. Molaire, and Copyright 1998, Norex Publications, unless otherwise indicated.

Published by Norex Publications.

ISBN: 0-9649390-4-5

Printed in the United States of America

098765432

"The people that take no pride in the noble achievements of remote ancestors will never achieve anything worthy to be remembered with pride by remote generations."

Macaulay, English historian

Dedicated to my lovely wife Tulienne, my wonderful daughters, Alexandra and Melissa, my mother Marie Therese Cherubin, my late father Marcel Molaire.

and to...

All unrecognized African Americans across the U.S.A.

Introduction

Rochester has had a long-standing history of producing innovative African-American publications. Frederick Douglass published the infamous *North Star* here, and Howard Coles printed the *Frederick Douglass Voice* for nearly fifty years. For the past twenty-five years, Jim and Carolyne Blount have overcome tremendous odds, yet they have successfully published *about...time Magazine.*

Mike Molaire can now be added to the illustrious list of Rochester's African-American publishers, with the release of this second edition of the *African-American Who's Who™ Greater Rochester Area*. This publication contains a wealth of information on the contributions and accomplishments of successful African-American business, social, community and political leaders in the Greater Rochester Area, both past and present.

Having had the privilege of seeing the draft manuscript prior to printing, it was evident that this publication is the result of many long and painstaking hours of research and editing. Obviously space limitations could not allow for the inclusion of every individual who may deserve to be included, but Mike Molaire has compiled a vast amount of information into the *African-American Who's Who™ Greater Rochester Area*. This publication represents an important "second step" in documenting the positive impact African Americans have had on the entire region. I believe it can serve as an important reference tool for anyone who is interested in knowing more about the many contributions African Americans have made, and continue to make locally.

I want to personally commend Mike Molaire for his exhaustive effort and meticulous attention to detail, in his quest to produce an accurate and comprehensive publication such as the *African-American Who's Who™ Greater Rochester Area*. I encourage every Rochesterian to keep a copy on their desk and bookshelf.

William A. Johnson, Jr.
Mayor, Rochester, New York

Contents

Preface

Demographics

African-American Who's Who

African-American Who's Who

Contents

*
**

Who's Who Politics & Government

Who's Who Churches & Religion

Who's Who Churches & Religion

Illustrations

Illustrations

Contents

PREFACE

African-American Who's Who™ is a new concept. There exist many biographical directories, including *Who's Who Among Black Americans*. However those directories are national, and as such, are restrictive for information published on any given individual.

African-American Who's Who™ by design, has a local focus. We intend to provide comprehensive information about the individuals listed. The goals of this publication include:

- First, to provide a means of documenting the contributions of African Americans to the Greater Rochester Area.

- Second, to identify and reinforce positive role models for African-American children and children of other backgrounds.

- Third, to provide a unique networking forum, for Greater Rochester Area African Americans. By understanding the accomplishments of their associates, Rochester area leaders can play a more positive role in developing new associations for mutual growth throughout all our communities.

Individuals' reference value is a key factor for their inclusion. Many individuals are eligible because of their position. We nominate others because of notable achievements in their fields. Decisions for inclusion are solely and independently made by Norex Publications. This project is funded in his entirety by Norex Publications. Inclusion is absolutely free of charge.

The first edition of the *African-American Who's Who™ Greater Rochester Area*, for several reasons was not as complete as intended. Because of the scope of information published on each individual, our policy requires full entrants' corroboration. Many nominees regrettably had failed to return the corroborated information.

We had missed many deserving candidates. Nevertheless we made the decision to publish the first edition, with the goal of immediately updating it within a year. Since then, we have decided to extend the scope of the publication by including notables of the past. It took us more than a year to complete this new edition. Four years to be exact!

In our quest to increase participation, we assembled an advisory committee. We solicited nominations from community organizations, churches, news organizations and past nominees. Over 500 hundred nominations were sent out. Two follow-up letters were mailed to the non-respondents. Still direct telephone calls were placed to many important notables. Lastly, we issued press releases, appealing to the general community for nominations. We gathered information on notables of the past through research in newspaper articles, obituaries, books, magazines and periodicals.

Our efforts have paid off. This edition is definitively more complete. Yet we are still missing many deserving candidates in our biographical section. We have added two new sections, *African-American Who's ,Who™ Politics & Government,* and *African-American Who's Who™ Churches & Religion,* Greater Rochester Area. *For* these two sections, entrant's corroboration was not sought. We strictly relied on published information. Thus many individuals who have made historic contributions and perhaps chose not to, or neglected to provide the biographical information, are represented in those new sections. Wherever possible published biographical information is included along with the appropriate reference.

We have made every effort possible to ensure the accuracy and currency of all information.However, readers may find some errors. The editors and/or Norex Publications cannot assume any responsibility for errors or omissions in the *African-American Who's Who™ Greater Rochester Area,* whether such errors or omissions are the result of accident, negligence, or any other cause. In case of publication error or omissions, the sole responsibility of the editors and/or Norex Publications will be to correct the information in succeeding editions. Please send all such information to:

Mike F. Molaire

Norex Publications

16 Cardogan Square

P.O. Box 25333

Rochester, New York 14625

Tel/Fax: (716) 671-5164 Email: NOREXpub@ix.Netcom.com

We are very grateful for the excellent help of the Rundel Library staff, especially the local history crew. We pay special tribute to our copy editor, Mrs. Marsha Jones, and to the members of our advisory committee, the honorable William A. Johnson Jr., Dr. Walter Cooper, Dr. Thomas Smith, Mr. Rufus Agnew, Ms. Essie Calhoun, Dr. Frederick C. Jefferson, Jr., and Dr. William A. Nowlin. We salute the nominees who have used their valuable time corroborating, and supplying the information for this publication. Their gracious collaboration is indeed one more testimony why we are honoring them.

Mike F. Molaire, Editor

Using This Book

NAME

Last names are printed first and capitalized. Pseudonyms are included in parentheses. We also include professional titles such as Ph.D., MD, and DDS. For notables of the past, birth and death years are indicated. Example:

JORDAN, Sr., Isaac L. (Ike), 1934-1994

BIRTH DATES AND PLACES

Date and place of birth are listed, including the city and state. The year the individual moved to the Greater Rochester Area also is included. Dates of birth in particular are kept optional; thus, in many cases birth information may be missing.

PARENTS

Father and mother's names are listed. In the case of married couples, only the husband's last name is shown, unless a maiden name was voluntary provided for the mother. In some cases, a note is made of parents' professions and of any other noteworthy information. Examples:

Lewis E. and Aurelia L. Allen

Florence L. Davis and George H. Bell (deceased)

FAMILY

Marital status is listed, along with the name of the spouse. The names of children and grandchildren are listed. In some cases a note is made of spouses and children' professions and any other noteworthy information. Examples:

Married to Moussa Bagate, Ph.D., Civil Engineering; one daughter, Maimouna Fields Bagate.

EDUCATION

The highest degree earned by the individual is listed first. The field of the degree, the institution name, and the state also are listed.

CAREER

The present position is listed first and highlighted in italics, with the company/institution name, followed by the year started in that position. The entire career of the individual (when known), is listed in reverse chronological order. For notables of the past, career information is most likely in chronological order.

PROFESSIONAL/COMMUNITY INVOLVEMENT

Current and past memberships in Professional Societies, Board of Directors, Nonprofit Organizations, Committees are listed. The period of involvement when known, also is included.

AWARDS/RECOGNITION

All known awards and recognition received by the individual are listed. Dates and granting institutions are always mentioned when known.

PATENTS/PUBLICATIONS

The numbers of U.S. patents held by the individual are listed. The subject matters of these patents when known also are reported. Titles of published books are listed, along with the year of publication. The number of published articles is mentioned; the names of the publications where these articles appear are mentioned.

EULOGIES/QUOTATIONS

All quotations are fully referenced, with the source of the information and the complete date of publication.

PHOTOGRAPHS

All photographs are fully identified with the subject matter, the photographer's name if known, the copyright owner and/or the permission grantor.

Demographics

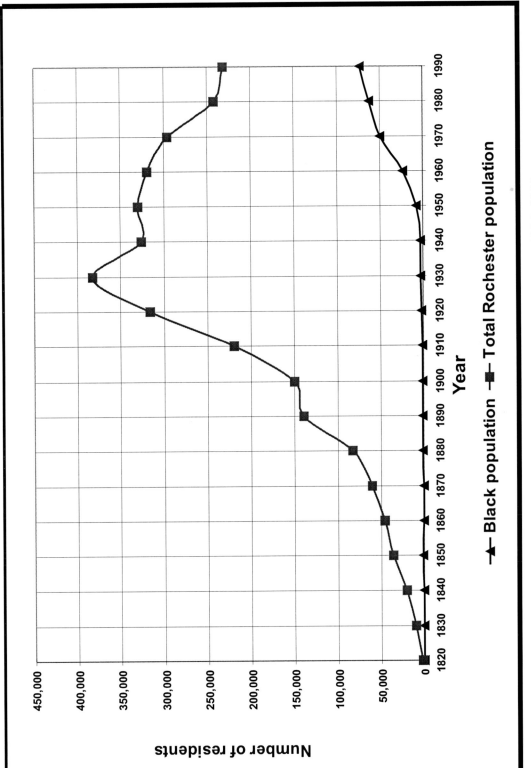

Chart-1   Black population in the City of Rochester, 1820-1990.

Artwork, Mike F. Molaire. Copyright 1998, Norex Publications.

The NeW<u>M</u>illenium Edition™

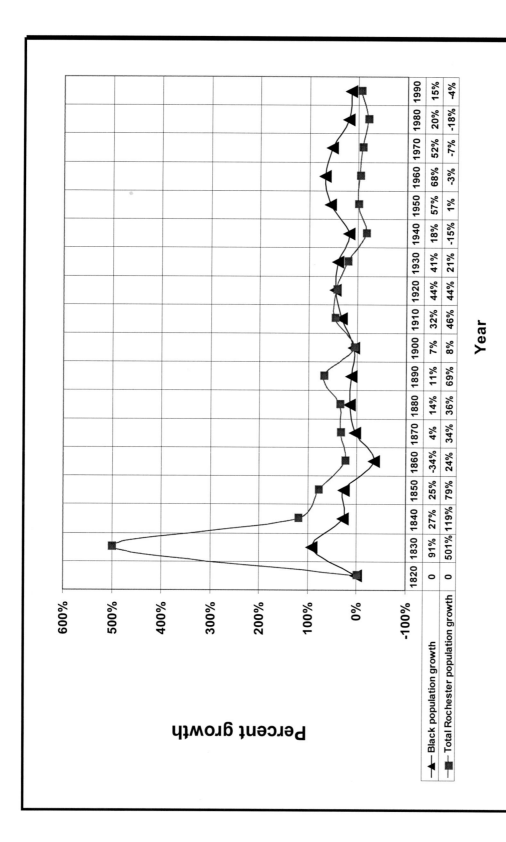

	1820	1830	1840	1850	1860	1870	1880	1890	1900	1910	1920	1930	1940	1950	1960	1970	1980	1990
Black population growth	0	91%	27%	25%	-34%	4%	14%	11%	7%	32%	44%	41%	18%	57%	68%	52%	20%	15%
Total Rochester population growth	0	501%	119%	79%	24%	34%	36%	69%	8%	46%	44%	21%	-15%	1%	-3%	-7%	-18%	-4%

Year

Percent growth

— Black population growth
— Total Rochester population growth

Chart-2   Black population growth in Rochester, 1820-1990.

Artwork, Mike F. Molaire. Copyright 1998, Norex Publications.

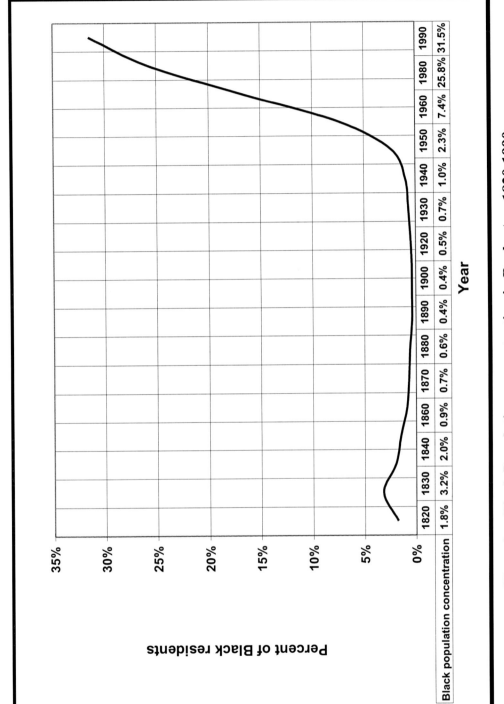

| Black population concentration | 1.8% | 3.2% | 2.0% | 0.9% | 0.7% | 0.6% | 0.4% | 0.4% | 0.5% | 0.7% | 1.0% | 2.3% | 7.4% | 25.8% | 31.5% |

Year

Percent of Black residents

Chart-3   Black Population concentration in Rochester, 1820-1990.

Artwork, Mike F. Molaire. Copyright 1998, Norex Publications.

The NeWMillenium Edition™

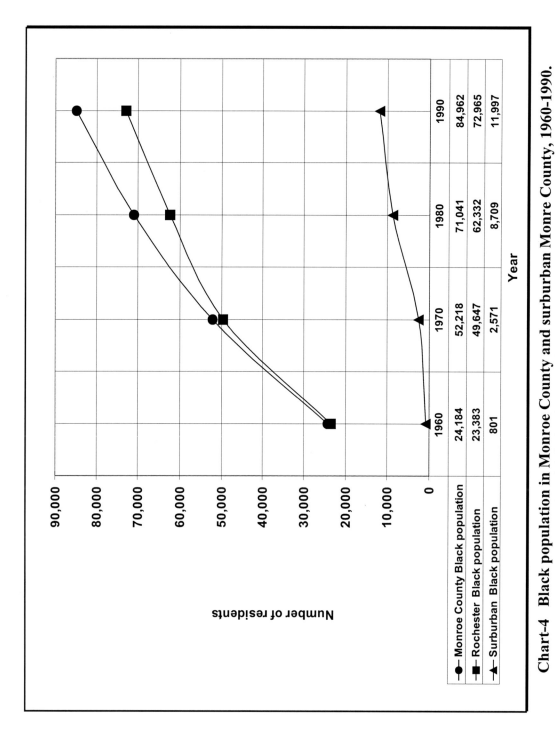

	1960	1970	1980	1990
Monroe County Black population	24,184	52,218	71,041	84,962
Rochester Black population	23,383	49,647	62,332	72,965
Surburban Black population	801	2,571	8,709	11,997

Year

Number of residents

Chart-4 Black population in Monroe County and surburban Monre County, 1960-1990.

Artwork, Mike F. Molaire Copyright 1998, Norex Publications.

**African-American Who's Who™
Past & Present Greater Rochester Area**

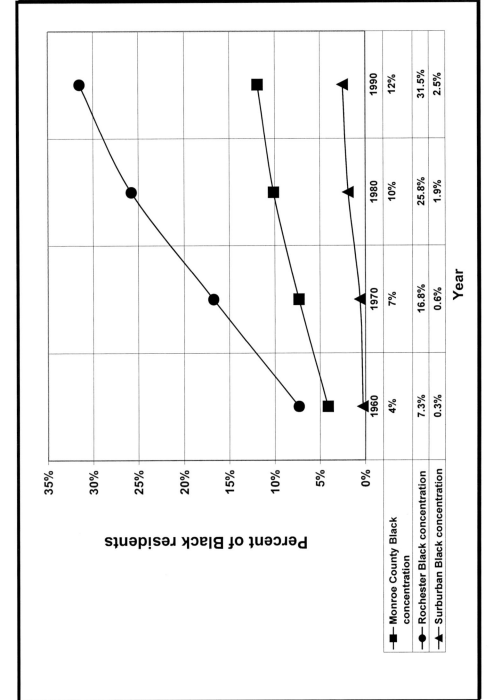

	1960	1970	1980	1990
Monroe County Black concentration	4%	7%	10%	12%
Rochester Black concentration	7.3%	16.8%	25.8%	31.5%
Surburban Black concentration	0.3%	0.6%	1.9%	2.5%

Year

Percent of Black residents

Chart-5 Black population concentration in Monroe County and surburban Monroe County, 1960-1990.

Artwork, Mike F. Molaire. Copyright 1998, Norex Publications.

The NeWMillenium Edition™

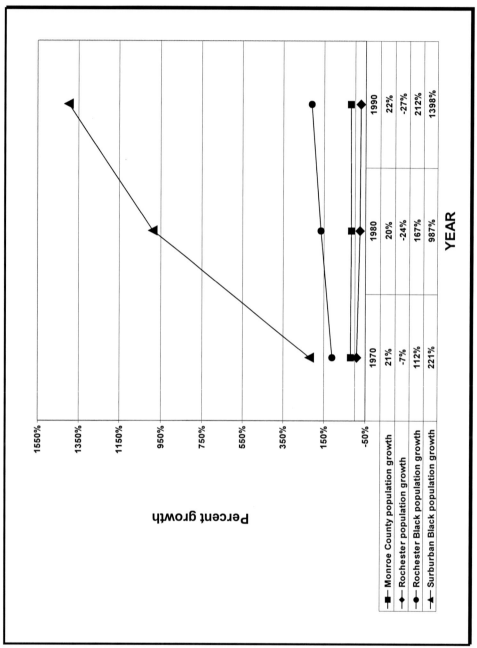

	1970	1980	1990
Monroe County population growth	21%	20%	22%
Rochester population growth	-7%	-24%	-27%
Rochester Black population growth	112%	167%	212%
Surburban Black population growth	221%	987%	1398%

YEAR

Chart-6   **Black population growth in Rochester and surburban Monroe County, 1960-1990.**

Artwork, Mike F. Molaire. Copyright 1998, Norex Publications.

28   **African-American Who's Who™**
          Past & Present Greater Rochester Area

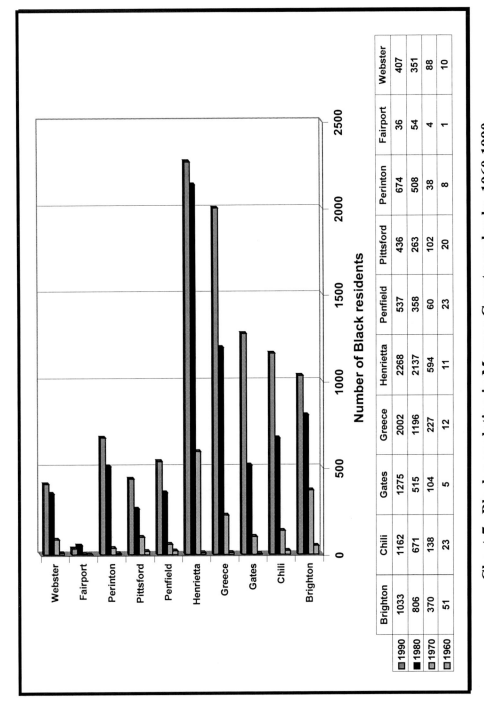

	Brighton	Chili	Gates	Greece	Henrietta	Penfield	Pittsford	Perinton	Fairport	Webster
1990	1033	1162	1275	2002	2268	537	436	674	36	407
1980	806	671	515	1196	2137	358	263	508	54	351
1970	370	138	104	227	594	60	102	38	4	88
1960	51	23	5	12	11	23	20	8	1	10

Number of Black residents

Chart-7 Black population in Monroe County surburbs, 1960-1990.

Artwork, Mike F. Molaire. Copyright 1998, Norex Publications.

The NeWMillenium Edition™

29

African-American Who's Who

ABERNETHY, Alexis, Ph.D.

Moved to Rochester, 1986.
Parents: Reverend Rufus Abernethy and Mrs. Agnes T. Abernethy
Family: Single
Education: Ph.D., Clinical Psychology, University of California, Berkeley, 1985; MA, Clinical Psychology, University of California, Berkeley, 1982; B.S., Psychology, Howard University, 1980; Licensed in New York State, 1987.

Career: *Clinical Associate Professor, Department of Psychiatry (Psychology); Assistant Professor Department of Psychiatry (Psychology), and Psychologist, Department of Psychiatry, Adult Ambulatory Services, University of Rochester School of Medicine and Dentistry, and Strong Memorial Hospital since 1988*; Psychological Consultant, Occupational Health, University of Rochester since 1990; Research Consultant, Rochester Police Department since 1986; Senior Instructor in Psychology and Psychologist, Department of Psychiatry, Adult Ambulatory Services, University of Rochester School of Medicine and Dentistry, and Strong Memorial Hospital, 1986-88; Post-doctoral Fellow, D.C. General Hospital/Howard University Hospital, Washington, D.C., 1985-86; Psychology Intern, Howard University Hospital, Washington, D.C., 1984-1985; Psychology Intern, Alameda Mental Health Clinic, Alameda, CA., 1983- 84; Psychology Intern, Psychology Clinic, University of California, Berkeley; Psychology Extern, San Francisco VA Hospital, San Francisco, CA., 1981; Lecturer, Biopsychosocial Medicine and Psychiatry Clerkship, University of Rochester School of Medicine and Dentistry since 1992; Teacher, Seminar on Ethnicity and the Psychotherapeutic Process, Division of Psychology, Department of Psychiatry, University of Rochester School of Medicine since 1990; Teacher, Clinical Psychology, Howard University, Graduate Seminar on Psychopathology, 1986.

Professional/Community Involvement: Member, Board of Directors, Ralph Bunche Scholarship Fund since 1991; International Society of Traumatic Stress Studies, Division of Industrial & Organizational Psychology, American Psychology Association, (APA); Division of Psychologists in Public Service, (APA); Association of Black Psychologists, American Group Psychotherapy Association, American Psychological Association, Association of Black Cardiologists, 1987-89; Student Representative for the Bay Area Association of Black Psychologists, 1982-84; Coordinator of Psychology Training in Adult Ambulatory Services, Department of Psychiatry, Strong Memorial Hospital since 1990; Chairperson, Quality Assurance and Utilization Review Committee, Ambulatory Services, Department of Psychiatry, Strong Memorial Hospital, 1991-92.

Awards/Recognition: NIMH Fellowship, 1983-84; Graduate Minority Program Fellowship, 1980-83; APA Minority Program Fellowship, 1980-83; James A. Bayton Award for Distinguished Undergraduate Achievement in Psychology, 1980; elected to Beta Kappa Chi, 1980; Psi Chi, 1979; Phi Beta Kappa, 1979; National Competitive Scholarship, 1976-80.

Patents/Publications: Publications and presentations in the areas of anger management, cultural competency training, law enforcement personnel, and spirituality.

Residence: Brighton, New York.

AGNEW, Rufus

Moved to Rochester, 1978.
Parents: William C. Agnew, Sr.; Mother deceased.
Family: Single
Education: Master's Degree, Social Work with

concentration in Community Organization, University of North Carolina at Chapel Hill, North Carolina; Bachelor's Degree, Sociology, Livingston College, Salisbury, North Carolina; Learn to Lead Program, United Way of America; Human Services Executive Management Program, Harvard Business School Faculty; Management Skills Program, United Way of America; Finance for Non-Financial Managers, United way of America; Allocations I and II, United Way of America; Community Problem Solving, United Way of America; United Way System, United Way of America; Computer Applications, MIS Department, United Way of Greater Rochester.

Career: *Senior Vice President, and Allocations Director, United Way of Greater Rochester, Rochester New York (Metro I) since 1978*; Current responsibilities include oversight of Board, Campaign Communications in six counties; also responsible for the African-American Leadership Development Program & Hispanic Leadership Development Program; Planning Associate, United Way Community Services of Metropolitan Detroit, Michigan (Metro I), 1975-78; Project Director, United Way of Delaware, Wilmington, Delaware (Metro I), 1972-74; Delinquency Prevention Specialist, State of Delaware, Wilmington, Delaware, 1971-72.

Professional/Community Involvement: Member, 1996 Conference Planning Committee, United Way of New York State; Treasurer and Board Member, Leadership Rochester; Advisory Committee Member, African-American Who's Who™, Greater Rochester Area; President, Manhattan Golf Club of Rochester, New York; Golf Instructor for Inner City Youth & Adults.

Hussain Ahmed
Photo, Mike F. Molaire. Copyright 1998, Norex Publications.

AHMED, Hussain, Baba

Born: Calabar, Nigeria, West Africa, 1954; Moved to Rochester, 1983.
Parents: Hajia Nana Fatimah and Alhaji Ahmadu Dan-Nufawa.
Family: Married to Hannah Ahmed; Three children, Nana-Fatimah, Ahmadu, and Ali Junaid.
Education: Ed. D, Medical and Health Professions Education, University of Rochester, expected May 1999; MA Education, University of Rochester, 1998; MS, Career and Human Resource Development, Rochester Institute of Technology, 1993; MS, Health Education, SUNY Cortland, 1984; B.S., Biological Sciences, SUNY Cortland, 1982; West African School Certificate, General Science, Sardauna Memorial College, Kawo, Kaduna, Nigeria, West Africa,

1974; Certificate in Hypnotherapy training, Halcyon College, Santa Cruz, CA, 1990; Certificates, Higher Education Opportunity Program, and Counseling/Cross-Counseling Training, New York State Department of Education, 1987; Certificate, Communication for Professionals, Upstate Center for Neuro-linguistic Programming, 1990.

Career: *Founder and President, Dan-NuFawa African Imports/Book store. since 1991*; Senior Counselor/Assistant Professor, Rochester Institute of Technology, Higher Education Opportunity Program, Rochester, NY, 1986-1994; Community Education Specialist, Planned Parenthood of Rochester and the Genesee Valley, 1985-1986; Counselor/Job Developer, Urban League of Rochester, Inc., Rochester, NY, 1985; Assistant Administrator, Memorial Health Center, ABU Teaching Hospital, Kaduna, Nigeria, 1974-1976; Personnel Officer, Kaduna Local Government Census Board, Kaduna, Nigeria, 1972-73; Special Assistant to Managing Director, Dan-NuFawa and Sons, Inc., Lagos, Nigeria, 1973-1974.

Professional/Community Involvement: Former RIT Resident Assistants Training, "Self-Knowledge and Spirituality", 1990; Member, HEOP Director Search Committee, RIT Student Affairs, 1988; RIT First Annual Advisors' Luncheon, Spring 1988; RIT Student Affairs Division, Minority Professional Staff Support, 1983; RIT, OSMA Hispanic Heritage Week Planning Committee, 1989; Director, Youth Programs, Islamic Center of Rochester, New York; Board Member, Islamic Center of Rochester, Inc. Rochester, NY; Advisor, Muslim Student Association, RIT; Advisor, Society of African-American Business Students, RIT; Advisor, Phi Beta Sigma Fraternity; Member, Educational Development Faculty Grievance; Executive Committee Member, RIT Chapter, AAUP.

Residence: Rochester, New York.

ALFORD, Natalie P., Reverend

Born: Newark, New Jersey; Moved to Rochester, 1993.
Parents: Christeen I. E. Alford and Lawrence, Sr.
Family: Single; No children.
Education: E.D.D., Counseling, University of Rochester, Candidate 2000; Master of Divinity, Theology, Harvard Divinity School, MA, 1992; B.S., Management Sciences, Rutgers University, 1976; African-American Leadership Development Program, Class of 1993.

Career: *Vice President for Program Operations, Urban League of Rochester, NY, Inc. since 1996*; Pastor, St. James African Methodist Episcopal Church, Utica, NY, 1996-97; Director of Program Initiatives, Colgate Rochester Divinity School, Rochester, NY, 1993-96; Assistant Pastor, Baber African Methodist Episcopal Church, Rochester, NY, 1993-1996; President's Administrative Fellow, The Divinity School, Harvard University, Cambridge, MA, 1992-93; Director, St. Matthew African Methodist Episcopal Church, 1989; Student Staff Assistant, Harvard University, The Divinity School, 1989-92; Associate Minister, Bethel African Methodist Episcopal Church, Jamaica Plains, NY, 1991-93; Minister of Family Life, Bridge Street African Methodist Episcopal Church, Brooklyn, NY, 1990-91; Associate Minister/Enrichment Program Coordinator, Charles Street African Methodist Episcopal Church, Roxbury, MA, 1989-90; Director, Information Services Administration, Tupperware Home Parties, World Headquarters, Kissimmee, Fl., 1987-89; Administrative Plant Manager, Boise Cascade, Orlando Fl, & St. Louis, MO, 1983-84, Assistant to Manufacturing Manager, 1983-84; Manager, AT&T Long Lines, New York, NY & Bedminster, NJ, 1982; Manager of Manpower Planning 1979-82, Operations Supervisors, 1978-79; Manager of Manpower 1977-78.

Professional/Community Involvement: Member, National Association of Black Seminarians, 1989-92; Black Women Ministry, New York Mission Society, 1990; Delta Sigma Theta Sorority, Inc., Lifetime Member; President, Harambee (Pan African Student Organization), Harvard Divinity School, 1990-91; Lifetime Member of NAACP; Board Member, New York State Head Injury Association, 1994-95; Member, "High School Redesign & Revitalization" Committee, Rochester City School District, 1993-94; Board Member, Rochester/Monroe County Private Industry Council, 1996-99; Board Member, Economic Community Zone Enterprise, City of Rochester, 1996-97; Member, American Counseling Association, 1996; Appointed Member, Committee for Academic Programs, Harvard Divinity School, 1991-92; Black History Month Student Coordinator, Harvard Divinity School, 1990-91; Volunteer Advisor to Junior Achievement of Mississippi Valley, Inc., Missouri, 1983-83.

Awards/Recognition: The Benjamin E. Mays Fellowship (FTE), 1989-92; Delta Sigma Theta Sorority, Inc., Scholarship, 1989-91; The Barton Scholarship, 1990-91; The Hopkins Share Scholarship, Harvard Divinity School, 1991.

Patents/Publications: "Can't Just Pray for Those Who Prey," *Democrat & Chronicle*, Rochester, NY, March 20, 1994, pp. 13A; "The Divine Counselor," in *Sister to Sister: Devotions for and From African American Women*, Ed. Susan D. Johnson Cook, Judson Press, Valley Forge, PA, 1995, pp 4; *Sisters of the Spirit: A Journal of Reflections and Workshops*, Contributing Editor, Rochester, NY, 1996.

Residence: Rochester, New York.

ALLEN, Lewis E., Ph.D.

Born: Monroe, Louisiana, 1937; Moved to Rochester, 1970.
Parents: Lewis E. and Aurelia L. Allen.
Family: Married to Diane Ferguson; Three children, Adrienne, G. Erica, Gregory.
Education: PH.D., Physical Organic Chemistry, Syracuse University, 1970; B.S. Chemistry, Queens College of the State University of New York (SUNY), 1958.

Career: *Presently Visiting Assistant Professor, Empire State College (SUNY), Genesee Valley Regional Center*; Eastman Kodak Company: unit director, Environmental Analytical Services, 1983-1992; Analytical Coordinator, 1981-1983; Problem Solving and Decision Analysis instructor, Training Department, 1979-81; Environmental Coordinator, Consultant to Marketing Organizations, 1975-79; Senior Research Chemist, Photographic Emulsions Laboratory, 1970-1975; Associate Professor, Organic, General, and Analytical Chemistry, Florida A & M University, 1963-1970.

Professional/Community Involvement: National Science Foundation Faculty Fellow, Florida State University, 1967-68; Chairman of the Rochester Chapter of the American Chemical Society, 1987; Treasurer of the same organization, 1984-85; currently an associate member of the National Committee on Project SEED, an ACS committee which promotes educational experiences for the disadvantaged; volunteer in the Kodak 21st Century Learning Challenge; member of the National Organization of Black Chemists and Chemical Engineers, New York Association of Approved Environmental Laboratories, and the Center for Environmental Information.

Awards/Recognition: 1993 Rochester Section Award, American Chemical Society.

Residence: Penfield, New York.

ALLEN, Shirley Jeanne , Ph.D.

Born: Tyler, Texas, 1941; Moved to Rochester, 1973.
Parents: Ralph C. Allen & Theresa McDonald.
Family: Single.
Education: PH.D., Education, University of Rochester, 1992; MA Counseling, Howard University, 1972; BA, English, Gallaudet University, 1966.

Career: *Associate Professor, Human Development, National Technical Institute for the Deaf, Rochester Institute of Technology (RIT) since 1980*; Assistant Professor, Human Development, RIT, 1973-80; Residence Hall Supervisor, Gallaudet University 1967-73; Editorial Clerk/U.S. Internal Revenue Service, Distribution Clerk/U.S. Post Office/Classification Clerk, U.S. Peace Corps, 1965-67.

Professional/Community Involvement: Member of the National Black Deaf Advocates Board of Directors, and the Consumer Advisory Board of the National Captioning Institute.

Awards/Recognition: Listed in *Who's Who in Black America,* and *Who's Who Among American Women*; Believed to be the first Black Female Deaf Ph.D. in the world.

Patents/Publications: Over 15 appearances as panelist, presenter, keynote speaker, and session leader at various conferences and workshops since 1975.

Residence: Rochester, New York.

ANDERSON, Betty Marian

Born: Rochester, New York; Raised in Leroy, New York.
Parents: Minnie Lee and Williams A. Majors; Judd and Betty Nelson of Leroy, New York, grandparents.
Family: Married to Moses McKinley Anderson; Two children, Mark McKinley, and Mia Loriat; Four grandchildren, Renada, Casmera, Mark McKinley, Jr., and Hans McKinley.
Education:Bachelor of Science, SUNY Oswego; MS, Educational Administration, SUNY Brockport; B.S., Vocational Technical Education, SUNY Oswego.

Career: *Rochester City School District since 1965.*

Professional/Community Involvement: New York State Examiner; New York State Curriculum Evaluation Committee; Group Leader, Instructional Service Occupation; Advisor, National Honor Society; Advisor, Vocational Industrial Clubs of America; Coordinator, International Day Student Exchange (country-wide); Member, Rochester Teachers Association, National Education Association, American Vocational Association, New York State Teachers Association; Member, Ministerial Review Committee, Diocesan Pastoral Council, Diocese of Rochester; Past Vice and Chairperson, Office of Black Ministries; Secretary/Historian Black Lay Catholic Caucus, Diocese of Rochester; Past President of the Immaculate Conception Parish Council; Past Representative, Southwest Regional Assembly; Past president, A Club Against Discrimination; Past Branch President, National Association for the Advancement of Colored People; Past Member of Youth Board, YWCA; Member and Past Chairperson, American Business Women's Club; Student Selection Committee, Sister City Bamako, Mali; Member, Professional Women's Exchange Program; Northeast Re-

Betty Marian Anderson
Photo, Mike F. Molaire. Copyright 1998, Norex Publications.

gional Contact Person, National Board of Black Lay Catholic Conference Advisory Council; Member, American History Club; President, Negro Club History; Member and Past Vice President of Membership, Partners of America; President, Metropolitan Women's Network of the National Council of Negro Women; City of Rochester and County of Monroe Coordinator, Adolescent Pregnancy Child Watch Project of the Children's Defense Fund, Washington, D.C.; Counselor of the College Bound, Teen Pregnancy Group; Commissioner, Martin L. King, Jr. (MLK) Commission; MLK Nonviolence Institute Coordinator, Member Church and Worship Committee; Volunteer Grocery Shopping Service for Senior Citizens; Member, Greater Rochester Black Catholic Women's Association of the Rochester Diocese; Member, Urban League of Rochester; Board Member, Educational Opportunity Center, SUNY College at Brockport; Chairperson for Churches, Agencies and Industries, We Care Committee of the Jane Pittman Fountain Committee; Telephone Committee, National Women's Hall of Fame, Inc.; Past President and current Chaplain, Rochester Genesee Valley Club of the National Association of Negro Business and Professional Women's Club, Inc.; Advisor and Steering Committee Member, African-American Leadership Development Program, United Way.

Awards/Recognition: Sojourner Truth Award, National Association of Negro Business and Professional Women; Girl Scouts Genesee Valley Award; Partners of Americas, Rochester, Coal Pot Award; Susan B. Anthony, and Martin Luther King (MLK) Volunteer Award; Immaculate Conception Church Award; MLK Center Award; Sibley Professional Award; Edison Class of 85, Meritorious Awards; North East District President of the Year; Eureka Lodge # 36 F&AM (Prince Hall Masons); United Way Education Award; United Negro College Fund Award; Golden Service Award, Urban League.

Residence: Rochester, New York.

ANDERSON, David A., Ph.D.

Born: Cincinnati, Ohio, April 28, 1930; Moved to Rochester, 1956 for undergraduate studies; Permanent resident since 1965.
Family: Married to Ruth Brown Anderson; Three children, David M., Kenwood M., and Joanine C. Anderson.
Education: Ph.D., Educational Administration, Union Institute, Cincinnati, Ohio, 1975; MA,

Education, Syracuse University, Syracuse N.Y., 1962; B.F.A., Photography, Rochester Institute of Technology, Rochester, N.Y., 1960.

Career: *Professional Teller and Writer of Stories, and Educational Consultant*; Lecturer in Humanities, St. John Fisher College, and State University of New York College at Brockport; Taught at Rochester Institute of Technology; Colgate Rochester Divinity School, 1984-88; The Department of Preventive Medecine and Community Health of the University of Rochester Medical School,1970-82; The State University of New York at Geneseo; Rochester NY City School District Administrator, 1970-1992; Deputy Executive Director, Urban League of Rochester Inc., 1967-70; Associate Director, Action for a Better Community, 1965-67; Manager, Curriculum Materials Development Center, City School District, 1962-65.

Professional/Community Involvement: Director, "Family Histories + Community Elders Histories = Heritage Project; Founder, Black Storytelling League; Convener of the Rochester Kwanzaa Coalition; Board Member, Frederick Douglass Museum & Cultural Center Foundation, Inc.; Consultant, Arts & Cultural Council of Greater Rochester; Member, National Association of Black Storytellers, National Storytelling Association; Past Trustee, Memorial Art Gallery, University of Rochester, Writers & Books, and Rochester Museum & Science Center; Consultant to United Way (African-American Leadership Development Program and Hispanic Leadership development Program).

Awards/Recognition: "Culture & Arts Award", Rochester Metro Chamber of Commerce, 1998; "Elder Award", African-American Leadership Development Program (AALDP) Alumni Association,1996; Special Citation Award for Outstanding Contributions to the Arts, Arts & Cultural Council of Greater Rochester, 1996; Featured on National Public Radio's "Celebrating African American Storytelling," WGBH, Boston, 1995; *The Origin of Life on Earth: An African Creation* Myth book was named the "Outstanding Children's Book on Africa", the African Studies Association, 1992; Coretta Scott King Award for Illustration *The Origin of Life on Earth: An African Creation Myth*, Sights Productions, 1992, received the Coretta Scott King Award for Illustration, American Library Association (1993), and the Outstanding Children's Book on Africa Award, African Studies Association, 1993; Honored by Hampton University Museum during the exhibit, "The River Never Rests: Yoruba Art and Story," January 23-March 15,1993; The paintings/illustration for *The Origin of Life on Earth*, formed the core of that exhibit; Self-Esteem Award, Mental Health Association of Rochester, 1992; Distinguished Volunteer Service Award, Mental Health Association of Rochester, 1986; Outstanding Community Service Award, Mental Health Association of Rochester, 1984; Lewis Scott Community Award, Project Head Start, Monroe County, 1985; Father of the Year and King of the Pan African Cultural Exposition Royal Family, Rochester, NY, 1969; Community Leadership Award, 1982; Man of The Year, Urban League of Rochester, 1969; Invited Workshop Presenter, "Africa to African America: Storytelling and Storybook," United States Information Agency, Accra, Ghana, 1993.

Patents/Publications: *Kwanzaa: An Everyday Resource and Instructional Guide*, Gumbs and Thomas, 1992; *The Origin of Life on Earth: An African Creation Myth*, illustrated by Kathleen Atkins Wilson, Mount Airy, Maryland, Sights Productions, 1991; *The Rebellion of Humans: An African Journey*, illustrated by Claude Rassoul Joachim, Mount Airy, Maryland, Sights Productions, 1994; "Feet in Water, Song in the Heart," and, "Nzambi and the Earth Connection," in *Jump Up and Say*, Linda and Clay Goss ed., New York, Touchstone, Simon & Schuster, 1995;

David Anderson/Sankofa, Ph.D., at the Corn Hill Festival, July 1997.

Photo, Mike F. Molaire. Copyright 1998, Norex Publications.

Under What Name Shall We Collect Our Identity," Introduction to Images *Afro-Rochester 1910-1935*, Rochester Museum & Science Center, 1996; "Traveler on the River of Life.", *Genesee Country*, Vol. 2, No 3, Aug/Sept., 1994, pp. 58-59; "Kwanzaa: a Rededication to Traditional African American Values," *Genesee Country*, Vol. 1, No 5, Dec/Jan, 1993-94, pp. 18-19; "Kwanzaa: A Resource for Resourceful Educators," *Multicultural Review*, Vol.2, No 4, Dec., 1993, pp. 36-38; "The Changing Relevant Intermediary: *The Role of Mental Health Professionals in the Community," in The Paraprofessional: Selected Readings*, Nash, Lifton and Smith, ed., National Institute of Mental Health, 1980, pp. 48-59; "Public Institutions: Their War Against the Development of Black Youth," *American Journal of Orthopsychiatry*, Vol. 41, No. 1, January, 1971, pp. 65-73.

Residence: Rochester, New York.

ANDERSON, Sr., Joe L.

Born: Washington, Georgia.
Parents: Mr. and Mrs. Leroy Anderson.
Family: Married to Angie Anderson.
Education: B.S., Economics, Cum Laude, North Carolina A & T State University, Greensboro, North Carolina.

Career: *Eastman Kodak Company: Manager, Workforce Excellence, Apparatus Division, Rochester New York since December 1992*; Strategic Human Resource Partner, Chemical Manufacturing/Photochemical, Polymer, and Recovery Divisions, Kodak Park, Rochester, New York, 1991-92; Manager, Personnel Relations, Western Region-North, Walnut Creek, California, 1988-91; Various Positions in Human Resources (Placement Services, Equal Opportunity, Compensation, Personnel Relations supporting Marketing, Distribution, and Corporate Staffs) in Rochester, New York; Arlington, Virginia; and Cranbury, New Jersey, 1970-88; First Lieutenant, U.S. Army active duty, Fort Benning, Georgia, 1971-73; U.S. Army Reserves, Lieutenant Colonel-Strength Management Officer, 98th Division, 1973-present.

Professional/Community Involvement: Chairman, Board of Directors, Network North Star, an Eastman Kodak Employee Network for African-American employees; President, Rochester Chapter, N.C. A&T State University Alumni Association; Member/Past President, Board of Directors of Baden Street Settlement; Past Member, Advisory Board, Bay Area Urban League, San Francisco, California; Board of Directors, Interface Institute, Oakland, California (an after-school math and science tutorial program); Mayor's Committee on the Handicapped, Washington, D.C.; Advisory Board, Virginia Employment Commission, Arlington, VA; Eastman Kodak Company Representative, Business/Industry Cluster, N.C. A&T State University; member, Omega Psi Phi Fraternity; Reserve Officers Association; Planning Committee/1992 Loftus C. Carson Human Relations Commission; Deacon, Mount Vernon Baptist Church, Rochester, New York.

Awards/Recognition: Distinguished Service Award, A&T State University, 1996.

Residence: Pittsford, New York.

ATKINS, Carl J., Ph.D.

Born: Birmingham, Alabama, 1945; Moved to Rochester, 1978.
Parents: Robert F. and Kathryn W. Woods.
Family: Married to Deborah Little Atkins; Two daughters, Kathryn-Louise Atkins, and Leslie McKnight; Two grandsons, Albert, and Michael McKnight.

Education: Ph.D., Musical Arts Conducting, Eastman School of Music, University of Rochester, 1982; MA, Music Conducting, with Honors, New England Conservatory, Boston Massachusetts, 1975; BS, Music, Woodwinds, Indiana University, Bloomington, Indiana, 1967; Music Education, Central State College, Wilberforce, Ohio, 1962-63; Professional Training in Conducting with Frank Battisti, Donald Hunsberger, David Effron, Samuel Adler, and Gunther Schuller; Theory and Composition: with David Baker, George Russell, Robert Cogan, and Samuel Adler; Woodwinds, with Eugene Rousseau, Joseph Allard, James Pellerite, Harry Houdeshel, Leonard Sharrow, David Carrol and Jerry Sirucek.

Career: *President, Carl Atkins & Associates, (A Management Consultant Firm to the Nonprofit Sector), since 1993*; President and Chief Operating Officer, Rochester Philharmonic Orchestra, 1991-93; Part-time Assistant Professor of Music, Conductor, University Symphony, Chamber Orchestra, Wind Ensemble, University of Rochester since 1984; Director, David Hochstein Memorial Music School, 1984-91; Registrar and Dean of Students, Hochstein Music School, 1979-1984; Guest conductor, Rochester Philharmonic Orchestra, 1981; Music Director and Principal Director, Genesee Symphony Orchestra, Batavia, 1980-82; Registrar and Dean of Students, David Hochstein Memorial Music School, 1979-83; Teaching Associate, Conducting and Musicology, Eastman School of Music, 1978-82; Associate Conductor, Boston Festival Orchestra, 1977-78; Music Director, New England Wind Sinfonia, 1976-78; Assistant Conductor, Massachusetts Youth Wind Ensemble, Boston Massachusetts, 1974-78; Lecturer in Afro-American Music History, Wellesley College, Wellesley, Massachusetts, 1971-73; Instructor of Woodwinds, Wind Ensemble Conductor, Chairman, Afro-American and Jazz Studies Department, New England Conservatory of Music, Boston, Massachusetts, 1968-78; Clarinet, Saxophone

Carl J. Atkins, Ph.D.
Photo, Fred Tanksley. Copyright 1993, Norex Publications.

and Flute Player, American National Opera Company, Boston Opera Company, Boston Pops, Boston Symphony Orchestra, and Colonial and Schubert Theaters, 1967-78.

Awards/Recognition: Who's Who Among Black Americans, 1992; Recipient of the first University Fellowship in Conducting, Eastman School of Music, University of Rochester, 1978.

Patents/Publications: Film Score, NEH Documentary, "We Are Universal," 1972; Script Research, NEH Documentary, "Didn't We Ramble On, A History of African and African-American Marching Music," 1977; Book of the same title to be published in 1994.

Residence: Rochester, New York.

Quotations:

"I used to see the white kids on Saturdays leaving with their horn cases and violin cases, and I passed the building with longing...I guess unconsciously or subconsciously-I didn't deliberately set out to do this-I don't want any other black child to walk by a music school and 'long' to get in."

Carl Atkins, about...time *Magazine, p22, Dec. 1988.*

AUGUSTINE, Matthew

Born: Macon, GA, Nov. 11, 1944; Moved to Rochester, 1976.

Family: Married to the former Rita V. Guillory since 1968; Two sons, Malcolm, a marketing manager for Eltrex, and Karanja, sophomore at Duke University (1994).

Education: MBA, Business Administration, Harvard University; B.S. Degree, Southwestern University.

Career: *President and CEO Eltrex Industries since 1976*; Former Director of Management Information Systems, and Materials Manager, Adage of Boston, Massachusetts; Production Manager, Polaroid Corporation; also served in the U.S. Marine Corps.

Professional/Community Involvement: Past President, Black Business Association of Greater Rochester, 1994; Board Member of Rochester Community Savings Bank since 1994; Chairman, SUNY Brockport's Business & Industry Center; President, Baden Street Settlement; Immediate Past President, Rochester Business Opportunity Corporation; Board Member of Boys Scouts, Rochester Area Foundation, Urban League, M&T Bank, Central Trust Division, Industrial Management Council, Chamber of Commerce, YMCA and Wilson Commencement Park, and Blue Cross/Blue Shield; Frederick H. Minett Professor at Rochester Institute of Technology's College of Continuing Education, 1992-93; former Chairman of the Private Industry Council; Former Board Member of Upstate Small Business Development Center, Junior Achievement, Boys & Girls Club, Rochester Downtown Development Corporation, United Way of Greater Rochester, Buffalo Federal Reserve Bank of New York, Hochstein Music School, and COMPEER.

Awards/Recognition: Recipients of numerous awards, both on a local and national basis; Greater Rochester Area Chamber of Commerce Medal for Education Award; Black Family Award, Niagara University's Center for the Study and Stability of the Black Family, 1996.

Residence: Pittsford, New York.

AUGUSTINE, Rita G.

Born: Eunice, Louisiana, 1945; Moved to Rochester, 1977.

Parents: Rose Guillory and Lucius Guillory (both deceased).

Family: Married to Matthew Augustine; Two children, Malcolm Lee and Karanja Atim Augustine.

Education: MS Social Work, Simmons College, Boston, MA, 1972; BA, Social Welfare, University of Southwestern Louisiana, 1967; Executive Leadership Training Program, National Urban League, National Urban League Headquarters, New York, NY, 1986; Certified Social Worker, Association of Certified Social Workers.

Career: *Vice President, Program Services, Catholic Family Center since 1994*; President, Rochester New Futures Initiatives, Inc., 1990-1993; Senior Staff Assistant to County Executive, Monroe County, Rochester, New York, 1988-1990; Vice President for Program Operations, Urban League of Rochester (URL), 1986-1988; Manager of Family Services Division,

URL, 1983-1986; Director of Intensive Family Support Service, Hillside Children's Center, Preventive Services, 1979-1983; Primary Therapist for Children and Families, Senior Program Planner and Public Welfare Social Worker, 1967-1977.

Professional/Community Involvement: Immediate Past Chair, Board of Directors, Brockport College Foundation; First Vice President, Board of Directors, Girl Scouts of Genesee Valley; Former Board Member, United Way of Greater Rochester, Women's Foundation of Genesee Valley, Inc., State-Wide Youth Advocacy, Hillside Children's Center, Center for Youth Services, YWCA,; Former Member, Board of Trustees, St. John Fisher College; Former Member, National Forum for Black Public Administrators, New York State Developmental Disabilities Planning Council; New York State Governor's Task Force on Teen Pregnancy; Monroe County Department of Social Services, Three-Year Consolidated Service Plan, Monroe County Department of Social Services, Children's Services Subcommittee, Monroe County Office of the Aging Task Force on Services to Elderly Minorities, Monroe County Council on Teen Pregnancy-Member Steering Committee, Monroe County Public Defenders Office Advisory Board, The Rochester-Monroe County Youth Bureau, Persons In Need of Supervision (PINS) Adjustment Advisory Board, Rochester and Monroe County Early Childhood Education Steering Committee, Goals For a Greater Rochester Education & Human Services Issues Committee.

Awards/Recognition: Community Leadership Award, Urban League of Rochester, 1991; Black Family Award, Niagara University's Center for the Study and Stability of the Black Family, 1996.

Residence: Pittsford, New York.

AZODO, Ada Uzoamaka, Ph.D.

Born: Oba Anambra, Nigeria; Moved to Rochester, 1978.
Parents: Bertram Enuma and Bessie Chineze.
Family: Married to Michael Valentine Udennaka, MD; three sons, Uchendu I.C., Chijioke U., Okechukwu A.; one daughter, Queen Ijeoma
Education: Ph.D., African Literature in French, University of Lagos, Nigeria; MA French, University of Lagos, Nigeria; BA (Hons) French, University of Ife, Nigeria.

Career: *Professor and Director of International Studies, St. John Fisher College*; Former part-time Lecturer, University of Lagos; Assistant Personnel Manager, Nigerian Telecommunications Limited (NITEL), Mainland Territory, Lagos, Nigeria.

Awards/Recognition: Ada Di Edube of Amawbia (an honorary title); National Award and Open Scholarship for Academic Excellence, at University of Ife, Nigeria.

Patents/Publications: Author of *L'imaginaire dans les Romans de Camara Laye* ("The Imaginary in the Novels of Camara Laye," a book about African Culture, Traditions, and Civilizations), Peter Lang Publishing Inc., New York, 1993; "The African Child," in *Journal of Religion in Africa*, the Netherlands, 1993; "The Menage of Spirits and Humans in Africa: An Inquiry into Its Origins, Relevance and Survival in Society," in *Spirit Possession in Social Spaces* (forthcoming early 1994), by a German Publisher.

Residence: Rochester, New York.

BAIYINA, Askia (Edward R. Walker)

Born: Rochester, New York, Sept. 1949.
Parents: Delbert and Virginia Walker.

Family: Married to Jameelah (AKA Idella Frazier); Three sons, Varick, Tariq, & Aquil.
Education: Attended SUNY College at Brockport.

Career: **Publisher of *The Rise Journal, The Smart Shopper Guide, The Message, and Black History Briefs*; Fire Fighter with the Rochester Fire Dept; First Vice President of the Montgomery Neighborhood Center Inc.

Awards/Recognition: Distinguished Service Award; Masjid Taqwa Coach's Award, Southwest Colts-Monroe County Pop Warner Youth Football.

Patents/Publications: Articles published in the above-mentioned publications.

Residence: Rochester, New York.

Iris Jean Sulcer Banister
Photo, Fred Tanksley. Copyright 1993, Norex Publications.

BANISTER, Iris Jean Sulcer

Born: Oklahoma, 1947; Moved to Rochester, 1969.
Parents: Iris and Mable Sulcer.
Family: Married to Thomas A. Banister, Jr.; Three sons, Thomas, Simeon, and Ethan.

Education: MS, Education Administration, SUNY Brockport, 1979; MS, Urban Education, SUNY Geneseo, 1970; B.S., Education, Cum Laude, Jarvis Christian College, Texas, 1969; Multicultural Trainer Certification, University of Rochester; New York State Teacher Certification, Elementary School N-6 and Reading K-12; New York State School Administration Certification, Secondary Dean, Principal & Superintendent; New York State School Guidance and Counseling Certification; currently a Doctoral Candidate in Education and Human Development at the University of Rochester.

Career: *Rochester City School District Administrator; Program Administrator, S.H.A.P.E. Program; Program Administrator, Tutoring Services, 1995-97;* Secondary Specialist, Office of Student Equity and Placement, since 1989; Counselor, 1987-1989; In House Suspension Teacher/Manager, 1985-86; Remedial Reading Teacher, 1982-85; Secondary Teacher Trainer, 1978-1980; Reading Teacher, 1976-78; Transition Facilitator, Secondary School Restructuring, 1987-1989; Founder and Senior Consultant of Darcus Inc., a consulting firm that provides training, facilitation and presentation on a variety of topics in the areas of Cultural Diversity, Parent Empowerment, and Early Childhood Education.

Professional/Community Involvement: Former Board Member, Jefferson Avenue Day Care Center, Urban League of Rochester, and Marketview Heights Neighborhood Association; Chairperson, International Exchange Committee;

member, United Nations Committee; Women In Industry Committee; Youth Motivation Through Careers Program; Young Men's Christian Association; Parent Leadership Coalition; United Negro College Fund Planning Committee; Chairperson, Concerned Citizens Committee of RoAction For a Better Community Steering Committee; Coalition for Downtown; the Window Project; the United Way of Rochester Board of Directors; Member of the National Association of Black Social Workers; President, Board of Directors, Center For Dispute Settlement, Grapevine, Black Women United for Change and Zion Hill Foundation.

Awards/Recognition: Enstooled as Queen Mother Nan Ama Ankwanda, Winneba, Giba, 1998; Volunteer Appreciation Citation, Urban League of Rochester; Board Appreciation Certificate, Action For a Better Community; International Service Award, Links of Rochester Chapter; United Negro College Fund Recognition, Rochester UNCF Committee; Recognition for Volunteerism, Center for the Study and Stabilization of the Black Family; *Who's Who in American Education*, 1994-95; Outstanding African-American Woman Award 1993; Alpha Kappa Mu Honor Society; *Who's Who in American Colleges and Universities*; Alpha Kappa Alpha Sorority Inc., Miss Jarvis 1969.

Patents/Publications: *The Fifth Ace*, GNT Press, 1995; "Why Johnny Really Can't Read", *International Reading Association Magazine,* Vol. III, Page 4, 1982; "Multiculturalism In the Arts", *Art Scene Magazine* of Arts for Greater Rochester.

Residence: Rochester, New York

Charles Cecil Barrentine
Photo Courtesy Charles Barrentine.

BARRENTINE, Charles Cecil

Born: Millington, Tennessee, 1946; Moved to Rochester, 1972.
Parents: Catherine and Henry Barrentine.
Family: Married to Anne Barrentine; Three children, Rashard, Tameka, and Patrick.
Education: B.S., Chemistry, LeMoyne-Owen, 1972; Advanced Degree Courses, Chemistry; Kodak Internal Business and Technical Training; Certificate, Management, Berkeley, Executive Management Development Program, 1996.

Career: *Operations Manager for Color Paper Manufacturing, Kodak Park, Eastman Kodak Company, 1994-1997*; Unit Manager, Consumer Film Sensitizing Manufacturing, Melting and Coating Operations, 1992-1994; Assistant to the General Managers/Vice Presidents of Kodak Park, 1991-1992; Unit Manager, Black & White Film Manufacturing, 1988-1991; Unit Manager,

Solution Preparation, Film Sensitizing, 1986-1988.

Professional/Community Involvement: Member, Board of Directors, United Way of Rochester; Chairman, Kodak Park United Way Campaign, 1994; Kodak Park United Way Leadership Chair, 1993; Member, Network North Star, Manhattan Golf Club and Mt. Olivet Baptist Church.

Award/Recognition: Bronze Star Medal, Vietnam; Outstanding Jaycee Award; A variety of Special Recognition Awards for Community Service and within Kodak; First Recipient of the Annual Network Northstar Manager Award, 1997.

BELL, Archie, Reverend, 1892-1984

Born: 1892, McCormick, S.C.; Moved to Rochester, 1940; Died Friday, Dec. 28, 1984, at his Lake Towers apartment in Rochester.
Family: Survived by his wife, Julie Bell; A son, Henry Bell; Five daughters, Elizabeth Smith, Lena Jones, Samantha Miller, Edith Carlson, Audrey Frazier; A brother, Willie Bell; A sister, Essie Robinson; 16 grandchildren and 28 great-grandchildren.
Education: Self-taught; Never went beyond the eighth grade.

Career: *Pastor of the AME Zion Church, 1949-1961;* Preached in Ohio, Pennsylvania, Virginia during the depression and World War II before coming to Rochester; Left Rochester to pastor in Buffalo, Binghamton and Charlotte, N.C.; Returned to Rochester in 1974, to retire.

Professional/Community Involvement: Member, Urban League of Rochester, the NAACP, and the Rochester Chamber of Commerce.

Eulogies/Quotations:

"He was probably one of the most wonderful persons I have ever known…He was a warm, understanding, caring person…You could go to him with a problem. He would listen and you felt comfortable talking to him."

Reuben K. Davis, NY. State Supreme Court Justice
Times Union, Dec 31, 1984

"He was known as a builder…He was a planner and organizer and administrator. When he was given an assignment, usually it was a place that had need of a person who would come in and plan and get things in focus."

Audrey Frazier, Bell's daughter
Times Union, Dec 31, 1984

"He was a good pastor and a businessman…He was the one who started the building fund program at the church. Originally, he envisioned it was a way to add a wing to the old church. When the urban renewal came along and said the church had to go, that was what helped us get a new building."

Robert Hodge, AME Zion Church's steward.
Times Union, Dec. 31, 1984

"Young men and young women have always been drawn to him…He could tell a joke. He could pray. He could use simple words to express profound thoughts.

Audrey Frazier, Bell's daughter
Times Union, Dec 31, 1984

BELL, Fred J..

Born: Pittsburgh, Pennsylvania, 1943; Moved to Rochester, 1965.
Parents: Florence L. Davis, and George H. Bell (deceased).
Family: Married to Grace Mollis-Bell.
Education: A.A.S., Criminal Justice, Monroe Community College, Rochester, New York, 1973; Managing Change, Rochester Institute of Technology, 1996; Cultural Diversity Training, Community Relations Service, U.S. Dept. of Justice, 1995; Contemporary Issues For Police, Regional Criminal Training Center, 1992;

BELL, Maurice L.

Executive Training Seminar, NOBLE Training Institute, 1986, 1988; Management Development Program, City of Rochester, 1988; Advanced Supervision and Management, City of Rochester, 1981; Total Immersion Conversational Spanish, SUNY Brockport, 1981; Advanced Police Supervision, City of Rochester, 1981; Supervision and Management, City of Rochester, 1980 and Standard Supervision, City of Rochester, 1978.

Career: *Rochester Police Department: Patrol Section Commander*, supervising three lieutenants, six sergeants, 40 patrol officers, and one civilian; Commander of Management Services Division ($4 million annual budget), supervised two lieutenants, five sergeants, 19 patrol officers, and 40 civilians; Promoted to Captain, 1987; Lieutenant-supervised two sergeants, three investigators, and 15 patrol officers, 1982-1986; Sergeant, 1979-82; Investigator, 1972-79; Patrol Officer, 1967-72; Rochester Police Department, since 1967.

Professional/Community Involvement: Member, Montgomery Neighborhood Center Board of Directors, YMCA Minority Achievers Program Steering Committee, and Action For A Better Community Project Re-Direct; Community Advisory Board Member, St Mary's Hospital Mental Health Services, and Depaul Mental Health Services; District Chairman, Boy Scouts of America; Volunteer, Boys and Girls Club of Rochester, Big Brothers and Big Sisters, and Baden Street Settlement; Member, National Organization of Black Law Enforcement Executives, National Forum for Black Public Administrators, American Society for Public Administrators, and Rochester Safety Council; Consultant to City of Rochester Civil Service Commission, 1983, 1986, 1987; Examination Assessor, Rochester Police Department (1980, 1984), Detroit Police Department, Detroit, Michigan (1985), Hartford Police Department, Hartford, Connecticut (1990, 1994), Toledo Police Department, Toledo, Ohio, 1990.

Awards/Recognition: Honorable Discharge, U.S. Navy, 1961-1965.

Residence: Rochester, New York.

BELL, Maurice L.

Born: Smithfield, North Carolina, 1947; Moved to Rochester, 1970.
Parents: Joseph and Louise Bell.
Family: Married to Rosa, a Vice-Principal at the City's Edison Technical High School; Two daughters, Maureen, and Monique.
Education: CAS, SUNY Brockport University, 1977; MS, Microbiology, North Carolina Central University, 1970; B.S., Biology, North Carolina University, 1969.

Career: *Assistant Superintendent, Rochester City School District since 1985*; Supervises 14 city schools and programs; Served for 23 years in the City School District as a teacher and administrator; Principal, Frederick Douglass Junior High, 1981-1985; Vice Principal, East High School, 1979-81; Dean, East High School, 1977-1979; Teacher, Madison High School, 1970-77.

Professional/Community Involvement: Member, Omega Psi Phi Fraternity; member, Board of Directors, Red Cross, Boy Scouts, Rochester Jobs Inc., and Center for Educational Development, (CED); listed in the *Diversity Resource Directory of Rochester Area Volunteers: 1993-1994*, Published by the Philanthropic Diversity Consortium of the Rochester (NY) Region.

Awards/Recognition: Notable Americans, 1976; Outstanding Leader in Secondary Education Award; Certificate of Merit, Monroe County District Attorney; Certificate of Outstanding Service, Urban League Rochester, 1977, 1983; Action For a Better Community

Service Certificate; Tyme for a Change Outstanding Community Service Award, 1992.

Residence: Rochester, New York.

BILSON, Carole Abena

Born: Washington, D.C., 1959; Moved to Rochester, 1980.
Family: Married to T. Andrew Brown, Esq.
Education: B.F.A., Industrial Engineering, University of Michigan, Ann Arbor, Michigan, 1980; Strategic Marketing, Amos Tuck, Dartmouth College, 1996.

Career: *Eastman Kodak Company since 1981*; Worldwide Product Marketing Manager, Consumer Imaging since 1995; Consumer Digital Business Representative to the Kodak Branded Retail Team (KBRT), since 1995; Kodak Loaned Executive-Rochester Coordinator for the New York Statewide Systematic Initiative, a $10 million National Science Foundation grant project, to move systemic change from State-level policy and activity to school implementation, 1994-1995; Project Industrial Designer, Design Resource Center, Equipment and Software Platform Center, 1993; Senior Industrial Designer, Design Resource Center, 1987-93; Project Leader, Future Products Concepts, 1989-90; Industrial Designer, Consumer Products Engineering, 1981-87; College Recruiter Volunteer, Eastman Kodak Company, 1983-88.

Professional/Community Involvement: Board Member, Rochester Chapter of the Links, Inc., since 1996; World Design Foundation 1992-96; Montgomery Neighborhood Center 1992-94; Board Chair and Founder, National Science Foundation/SSI Urban Network Partnership (to support local education initiatives in math, science and technology), since 1995; President, Rochester Women's Network, the largest women's network in the U.S. with a membership of 850 professional, executive and business owners and two paid staff, 1997-98; Chair, Women's Forum of Kodak Employees, 1994; President and Co-Founder, Network North Star, Inc. (Kodak Black Employees Network), 1988-1990; Member, Total Youth Development Seminar Series Team of Network North Star, 1989-92; Mentor, Kodak Academy of 1,000 Stars for Middle School Students, 1993-95; Appointed to City of Rochester's Preservation Board by Mayor Johnson, 1992-1996.

Patents/Publications: Holder of two patents; *U.S. 358,602*, "Removable Sorter Bin For Collating Sheet Material," May, 1995; *U.S. 5,270,839*, "Dual Imaging Station Photoprint Scanner," Dec., 1993; "Just Think-Problem Solving Through Inquiry" in Math, Science & Technology Professional Development publication and Video Series for Teachers (Team Member).

Awards/Recognition: 40 Under 40 Award, Rochester Business Journal, 1996; Chief Technical Officer Award for receipt of two patents, Eastman Kodak Company, 1996; Award from the University of Rochester, Center for Work & Career Development, 1994; Leadership America, Among 100 women selected to participate in a national leadership program, 1993; Recognition as team leader of the Portable Image Handler Project, Design Resource Center, Eastman Kodak Company, 1991; Recognition for contributions as Co-Founder and President of Eastman Kodak Company's first Recognized Employee Network, Network North Star, Inc., 1990; Recognition as Board Chair, Women's Forum of Kodak Employees, 1994; Selected to Participate in a National Broadcast, "Futures" (a Peabody award-winning show about Industrial Engineering), 1992.

Residence: Rochester, New York.

BLAKE Jr., John L., 1921-1993

Born: Providence RI, 1921; Died of cancer at Strong Memorial Hospital, September 7, 1993.
Family: Wife, Marie Blake; Two sons, Edward M. Blake, and John Jr.; Four daughters, Peggy Courtney, Kim Blake-Wilcox, Barbara Benford, and Delores Dorsey; Nine grandchildren; Two great-grandchildren.
Education: Bachelor of arts Degree, Business and Public Service, Michigan State University.

Career: *Owner of John L. Blake and Associates*, 1983-1993 (seven employees and $1-3 million in sales in 1992); National Director of the Job Corps and Deputy Manpower Administrator for employment security at the U.S. Department of Labor in the Nixon administration; former Assistant Vice President, Marine Midland Bank; First General Manager of Rochester Business Opportunities Corporation (RBOC), 1968; Taught for five years at West High; Served in the Marine Corps as a Combat Instructor with the rank of Sergeant.

Professional/Community Involvement: One of the founders of the Black Business Association and its first president; A Ttrustee at Rochester Institute of Technology; Former President, Board of Directors, Seat House Corporation; former Board Member, Strong Memorial Hospital; General Chairman, United Negro College Fund of Rochester; Vice Chairman, Ralph Bunche Scholarship Committee; Deputy Director, Monroe Human Relations Commission; President, Board of Directors, Montgomery Neighborhood Center.

Awards/Recognition: Delegate to the White House Conference on Small Business, 1986; One of the Finalists, Small Business Council's Business of the Year, 1989.

Eulogies/Quotations:

John L. Blake, Jr., 1921-1993
Reprinted with permission of <u>about...time</u> Magazine, Inc.

"I would look at him as a pioneer in the struggle of minority business enterprise"

> Clarence Ingram, former general manager, Rochester Business Opportunities Corp.
> <u>D&C</u>, Sept. 10, 1993

"He worked tirelessly in the area of corporate development ... he always wanted to call it a partnership. He never wanted it to be us and them."

> Mary-Frances Winters, president, Black Business Association.
> <u>D&C</u>, Sept. 10, 1993

"The program will show that the Negro can succeed in his own business and industry... It will give the young people a model to show that they too can be successful."

> John L. Blake Jr., referring to Rochester Business Opportunities Corporation
> <u>Times Union</u>, March 9, 1968

"When I came here, I had already said to hell with America and was on my way to Africa. I had a five-year plan; disposing of all my property, obtaining the necessary education courses for a teaching Certificate, and spending three years in the teaching field...then off to Africa."

John L. Blake Jr.
<u>about...time</u> Magazine, p14, March 1974.

BLOUNT, Carolyne S.

Born: Richmond, Virginia, March 21, 1943; Moved to Rochester, 1970.

Family: Married to James M. Blount; Three children, James U., Christina E. and Cheryl E. Blount.

Education: MS, Library Science, Drexel Institute of Technology, Philadelphia, PA, 1964; B.S., Liberal Arts, Virginia State University, Petersburg, VA, 1963.

Career: *Editor, about...time Magazine, Inc., Rochester, NY since 1974;* Associate Librarian, Glendale Laboratory Engineering Library, IBM Corporation, Systems Development Division, Endicott, NY; Assistant Librarian, Technical Reports Center, IBM Corporation, Federal Systems Division, Owego, NY; Instructor, Morgan State College, Baltimore, MD.

Professional/Community Involvement: Board Member, Montgomery Neighborhood Center; Alpha Kappa Alpha Sorority, Delta Nu Omega Chapter, Rochester, NY; Virginia State University Alumni Association, Rochester Chapter; Urban League of Rochester, New York, Inc., The Ad Council of Rochester; The Greater Rochester Martin Luther King Holiday Commission; Frederick Douglass Museum Development Committee; The Friends of Frederick Douglass; Gateway Music Festival Planning Committee; Past Member of Kappa Delta Phi National Honor Fraternity; Strong Museum's African-American History Initiative, Community Advisory Commit-

Carolyne S. Blount
Photo, Mike F. Molaire, Copyright 1998, Norex Publications.

tee; Goals for Greater Rochester Cultural Resources Issues Committee; American Library Association; Board of Advisors, Montgomery Neighborhood Center; Board Member, Community Child Care Center.

Awards/Recognition: Women's History Month Award, Rochester Board of Education, 1997; Journalism Award, Revelation Choir, 1992; Community Choice Award, Western New York Hospitality Committee's 3rd Annual Gospel Music and Community Achievement Awards, 1991-92; "Bigger and Better Business Award", Phi Beta Sigma Fraternity, Theta Upsilon Sigma Chapter, 1991; Business Award, Arts for Greater Roches-

BLOUNT, James M.

ter, 1991; Community Service Award, Prison Family Bus Service, 1991; Certificate of Appreciation, Northeast District of the National Association of Negro Business and Professional Women's Clubs, Inc., 1990; Arbor Day Award, Friends of Frederick Douglass, 1990; "Excellence" Award for American Heart Association Reporting, New York State Heart Association, 1990; Communicator of the Year Award, Pennington-Moye VFW Post # 9251, 1990; Special Tribute in the *Freedom's Journal* Exhibit, Strong Museum, 1990; Business of the Year Award, Phi Beta Sigma, Iota Phi Chapter, 1990; Dr. Martin Luther King Civic Service Award, Colgate-Rochester Divinity School, 1990; Distinguished Alumni Citation of the Year Award, National Association for Equal Opportunity in Higher Education, 1990; Communications Excellence to Black Audiences (CEBA) Award of Merit, The World Institute of Black Communinations, Inc., 1989; Media Achievement, Virginia State University National Alumni Association, 1989; Certificate of Appreciation, Advertising Council of Rochester, 1988; Certificate of Excellence in Education, Rochester Brainpower Program, 1988; Appreciation Award, Delta Sigma Theta Sorority, Rochester Chapter, 1988; Appreciation Award, International F&AM Masons, Beehive Lodge, 1988; Community Service Award, Omega Psi Phi, Theta Omicron Chapter, 1987; Matrix Award, Women in Communications Incorporated, 1987; Certificate of Recognition, Minority Enterprise Development Week, 1985; Certificate of Recognition, United Church Ministry, 1985; Certificate of Recognition, Minority Enterprise Development Week, 1985, 1990; Certificate Appreciation, Rochester City School District, 1984; Business Award, Metropolitan Women's Network, National Council of Negro Women, 1984; Howard Coles Communications Award, Rochester Association of Black Communicators, 1983, 1985.

Patents/Publications: Numerous articles, over the years in *about..time.* Magazine.

Residence: Rochester, New York.

BLOUNT, James M.

Born: Newport News, Virginia, June 5, 1943; Moved to Rochester, 1970.
Family: Married to Carolyne Blount; Three children, James U., Christina E, and Cheryl E. Blount.
Education: Graduate Studies, Business Administration, University of Scranton, Scranton, PA, 1969-1970; Management and Technical Courses, IBM Corporation, 1967-1970; B.S., Industrial Management, Virginia State University, Petersburg, VA, 1965.

Career: *President and Publisher, about...time Magazine, Inc., Rochester NY* since 1974; Sales Representative, Office Products Division, IBM Corporation, Rochester, NY, 1970-1973; Marketing and Proposal Developer, Federal Systems Division, IBM Corporation, Owego, NY, 1966-1970.

Professional/Community Involvement: Board Member, Rochester Business Opportunities Corporation; Community Advisory Board Member, SUNY Brockport; Urban League of Rochester, The Ad Council; Former Member, Goals for Greater Rochester Communications Committee; Montage 93, International Festival of the Image, Marketing and Communications Committee; Board of Education, Rush Henrietta Central School District (served two 3-year terms, 1981-1987); Board Member, Program to Interest Rochester Students in Science and Mathematics, Industrial Management Council; Board Member, Arts Council of Rochester; Board Member, Otetiana Council, Inc., Boy Scouts of America.

James Blount
Photo, Mike F. Molaire, Copyright 1998, Norex Publications.

Awards/Recognition: U. S. Postal Service Black History Committee Award, 1997; Empire State Federation of Women's Clubs State Award, 1994; Hall of Fame, First Church Divine, 1993; Homecoming Parade Marshals, Virginia State University, 1993; Journalism Award, Revelation Choir, 1992; Community Choice Award, Western New York Hospitality Committee's 3rd Annual Gospel Music and Community Achievement Awards, 1991-92; "Bigger and Better Business Award," Phi Beta Sigma Fraternity, Theta Upsilon Sigma Chapter, 1991; Business Award, Arts for Greater Rochester, 1991; Community Service Award, Prison Family Bus Service, 1991; Certificate of Appreciation, Northeast District of the National Association of Negro Business and Professional Women's Clubs, Inc., 1990; Arbor Day Award, Friends of Frederick Douglass, 1990; "Excellence" Award for American Heart Association Reporting, New York State Heart Association, 1990; Communicator of the Year Award, Pennington-Moye VFW Post # 9251, 1990; Special Tribute in the *Freedom's Journal* Exhibit, Strong Museum, 1990; Business of the Year Award, Phi Beta Sigma, Iota Phi Chapter, 1990; Dr. Martin Luther King Jr. Civic Service Award, Colgate-Rochester Divinity School, 1990; Distinguished Alumni Citation of the Year Award, National Association for Equal Opportunity in Higher Education, 1990; Communications Excellence to Black Audiences (CEBA) Award of Merit, The World Institute of Black Communications, Inc., 1989; Media Achievement, Virginia State University National Alumni Association, 1989; Certificate of Appreciation, Advertising Council of Rochester, 1988; Certificate of Excellence in Education, Rochester Brainpower Program, 1988; Appreciation Award, Delta Sigma Theta, Rochester Chapter, 1988; Appreciation Award, International F&AM Masons, Beehive Lodge,

Residence: Rochester, New York.

BODDIE, Bertrand M., Dr., 1924-1990

Born: New Rochelle, Westchester County, New York, September 21,1924; 19th child of 20 siblings; Died, October 13, 1990 of complications from heart surgery.
Family: Married Elizabeth Catherine Schery, a former nurse at Genesee Hospital (February 20, 1954)...a pioneering interracial couple; Three daughters, Lydia Athea Boddie-Neal, Carol Elizabeth Boddie-Graham, and Kathryn Loiuse Boddie-Lomb; A son, Bertrand M. Boddie II; Eight grandchildren, Leah, Amber, Jacob, Ray, Sara, James, Samantha and Trystan; many rela-

tives.

Education: Doctor of Medicine, University of Rochester, 1951; Internship and residency at Genesee Hospital, 1951-1954; Graduate of Virginia Union University.

Career: Retired from Eastman Kodak Company Industrial Medical Staff, 1973-1988; General Practitioner in Rochester for almost 20 years; United States Army/WWII veteran and recognized sharpshooter, 1945-1947; Private Practice (Joseph Avenue and 220 Alexander Street) until 1973.

Professional/Community Involvement: Devoted Member of the Heart Association for over twenty years; First Black President of the New York State Heart Association, 1983-1984; President, Genesee Valley Chapter, Heart Association, 1985-1986; Member of the Lake Avenue Baptist Church choir; Member and first Black president, Rochester Oratorio Society; Advisory Board, University of Rochester School of Medicine; Charter Member, Theta Omicron Chapter, Omega Psi Phi Fraternity, Inc,, 1955.

Awards/Recognition: Recipient of the first Lewis Stark Award for distinguished service, New York State Heart Association, 1981.

Eulogies/Quotations:

"He was a very caring person...I guess what struck me most about him was his compassion."

> Judith Bopp, executive director of the Genesee Valley Region of the Heart Association.
> *Times Union*, Oct. 15, 1990

"I remember he often wouldn't take their money, or he would take whatever they could give...He is a man of compassion, dedicated to serving humanity."

> Lydia Boddie-Neal, Dr. Boddie's daughter
> *Times Union*, Oct. 15, 1990

"We were in a situation where we felt nothing in the world was more important to each other than each

Dr. Bertrand McClenden Boddie
Photo Courtesy Kathryn Boddie-Lomb.

other...Whatever else came along was a reasonable price to pay for this kind of relationship."

> Dr. Bertrand Boddie, referring to his interracial marriage. 1978 article, *Upstate Magazine*

"I knew him as a very compassionate, community-oriented individual with...a great belief in humanity...He was definitely a link in bridging communities in a very positive way."

> Dr. Walter Cooper, retired chemist, Eastman Kodak Company; regents Emeritus
> *D&C*, October 15, 1990

"His principle was, people were respected for themselves, whatever they could offer and bring...He made no distinctions because of race or ethnic background."

> Dr. Kenneth Woodward
> *D&C*, October 15, 1990

BODDIE-NEAL, Lydia

Born: Rochester, NY, 1954.

Parents: Elizabeth S. Boddie and Dr. Bertrand M. Boddie.

Family: Single mother; Two children, Leah Michele Neal and Amber Celeste Neal.

Education: BA, Art with Psychology minor, Brown University, 1976; Teaching Certificate (grade k-12), Rhode Island School of Design, 1976; MA, Agency Counseling, Rhode Island College, 1980.

Career: *Director of Community Relations, Rochester Gas and Electric since October, 1996*; *Commissioner of Schools, Rochester City School District since January 1996*; Director of the Center of High Falls 1992-96; Communications Assistant, Interpretive Center/Urban Cultural Park Director 1987-92; Assistant Manager/Officer, Citibank, Rochester, NY, 1986-87; Personnel Administrator, Case-Hoyt Corp., Rochester, NY, 1985-86; Personnel Assistant, Case-Hoyt Corp. 1984-85; Personnel Assistant, Gannett Co., Inc., 1983-84; Graphics Consultant/Free Lance Artist (Self-employed), 1982-83; Previously employed in Rhode Island in the areas of communications and education, 1974-1983.

Professional/Community Involvement: Board of Governors Member, Genesee Hospital since 1993; Board Member, Genesee Health Service since 1987; President, Board of Directors, Genesee Health Center since 1991; Board Member, Fair Business Council; Board Member, Seneca Park Zoo Society; Board Member, Arts & Cultural Council; Publicity Chair, Urban League of Rochester Black Scholars Program since 1987; Advisory Board, Frederick Douglass Museum & Cultural Center, 1995.

Awards/Recognition: Volunteer Service Award (10 years), Urban League of Rochester, Inc.,

Lydia Boddie-Neal

Photo Courtesy Lydia Boddie-Neal. Reprinted with permission of Leichtner Studios, Inc.

1998; Leadership Award, Anthony L. Jordan Health Center, 1997; Women's Foundation of Gennesee of Genesee Valley, *In Celebration of Women Tribute Book*, 1997; Woman of Greatness Award, New Life Fellowship, 1995; Volunteerism Award, City of Rochester, 1991; Employee of the Year Commissioner's Award, Department of Parks, Recreation & Human Services, City of Rochester, 1989; Certificate of Distinguished Volunteer Service, Urban League of Rochester, Inc., 1987-90; Appointed to the Minority Advisory Committee, Congress by Claudine Scheiner, Rhode Island, 1982; *Who's Who Among American Colleges & Universities*, 1980; Certificate for Outstanding Volunteer Service, Foster Grandparent Program, Rhode Island, 1980; Senior Year Exchange Program, Education Department of Brown University, and Rhode Island School of Design, 1975-76.

Residence: Rochester, New York

BOYD, Maggie Y., Reverend

Born: Chester County, South Carolina, 1948; Moved to Rochester, 1979.
Parents: Rev. James W. and Cassie Boyd.
Family: Two sons, Samuel Fitzgerald, and Cambridge Imen Boyd.

Education: MS, Divinity, Colgate Rochester Divinity, Rochester, New York, 1985; B.S., Winthrop College, Rock Hill, South Carolina, 1976; Graduate, Community Actions Secretarial/General Business Project, York Technical College, Rock Hill, South Carolina, 1966; Business major, Barber Scotia College, Concord, North Carolina; Leadership Rochester, 1992; Total Quality Management (TQM) Training, Rochester Convention Center, 1992.

Career: *Pastor, Graves Christian Methodist (CME) Church*, Rochester, New York since 1984; Director of Baden Street Settlement's Dollar Day Care Operation, since 1986; Director, City of Rochester's Summer Youth Program, Baden Street Settlement, 1981-85; Interim Secretary and Switchboard Operator, Administration, Baden Street Settlement, 1980-81; Assistant Director for Baden Street Family Services Department, 1979-80; Coordinator, Public Housing Social Services Department, Rock Hill, South Carolina, 1970-78; Business Manager, Rock Hill Masonry Inc., Rock Hill, South Carolina, 1971-78; Writer for Commercial Advertising, WRCG Radio Station, Columbus, Georgia, 1969-70; Intake Counselor, Satellite Office for Community Actions Program, Demonstration Project, Columbus, Georgia, 1968-69; Program Development Aide, Program Development, Lower Chattacho-

chee Community Actions, Inc., Columbus Georgia, 1967-69; Payroll Clerk, Rock Hill Community Actions Agency, Inc., Rock Hill, South Carolina, 1966-67.

Professional/Community Involvement
NAACP, Inc. Rochester, New York, 1992; Board Member, Norman Howard School, Rochester New York, 1992; Association for the Academy of University Women, 1992; Member Board of Directors, Habitat for Humanity, 1992; Treasurer, National Honor Society Parent Association, 1991; Organizer, South West Anti-Drug Task Force, 1988; Founding Pastor in Full Connection/Graves C.M.E. Church/New York/Washington Annual Conference, Rochester, New York, 1985; Organizer, Neighborhood Action Council for the Genesee-Jefferson Conservation Area; Convener, Martin Luther King City-Wide Celebration in conjunction with Colgate-Rochester Divinity Schools, 1982-83; Founding Member, Sickle Cell Anemia Foundation in South Carolina, 1970-73; Delegate/General Conference of C.M.E. Church, Arlington, Texas, 1990; YMCA's Steering Committee for the Construction of a Women's Resource Center, 1989-90; New York/Washington Annual Conference, Board of Personnel Services, 1988; Advisory Board, Center for Youth Services, 1988; Board of Director, Wellsprings Ecumenical Resource Center, 1989-90; Advisory Board, St Mary's Hospital Revitalization Task Force, 1989-90; Advisory Board, Project Excellence for Revitalization Task Force, 1989-90; Advisory Board, Police Interaction Committee Southwest Precinct, 1989-90; Advisory Board, Alumni Association, Colgate-Rochester Divinity Schools since 1987; Co-Treasurer, Concerned Citizens Committee of Rochester since 1985; Delegate, Black Theology U.S. Ecumenical Tour of Cuba, 1986-87; Member, Board of Education Secondary Restructuring Committee, 1987-88; Member, Minority Task Force Development for The Health Associa-

Thomas Boyde Jr.
Reprinted with permission of __about...time__ Magazine, Inc.

tion, 1988-89; member, Urban League of Rochester since 1984.

Awards/Recognition: Nominee, *Oxford Who's Who*, New York, New York, 1993; White Rose Friendship, The Links of Rochester, 1993; Pastor's Appreciation Award, Zone III Laity, Buffalo, New York, 1992; Membership Drive Plaque, Urban League of Rochester, 1989-92; Manager of The Year, Baden Street Settlement, 1988; Distinguished Service Award, Baden Street Settlement, 1988; Fund-raising Campaign Christmas Food Project, Baden Street Settlement, 1988; Certificate for Meritorious Services, City of Rochester, 1987; Excellence in Program Administration Award, City of Rochester, 1986; Benjamin E. Mays Fellowship, Princeton, New Jersey, 1983-85; Nominee, *Outstanding Young Women of America*, New York, 1986; Outstanding Adult Scholar, Monroe County Adult Educa-

tion Committee, 1985; Elaine Sands Memorial Scholarship Award, Winthrop College, Rock Hill, South Carolina, 1976; Fifth Avenue Community Service Awards, Muscogee County, Georgia, 1968.

Residence: Rochester, New York.

BOYDE, Wendy J.

Born: Rochester, New York, 1960
Parents: Marie J., and Thomas W. Boyde.
Family: Shares life with Andre Langston, Program Director of his family-owned radio station WDKX-104; One daughter, Andrea.
Education: B.S., Psychology, University of Houston; Graduate of the Rochester Dental Assistant School; Graduate of St. Agnes High School; Five years of intense training in the area of Construction Management, Specification Writing, Bidding Logic, Bidding Strategies, Commercial Renovation, Property Problem Solving, and Code Violation Work.

Career: *Owner and President of MIC Contracting Services Inc. since 1986*; The first Black Female to be a New York State Certified Minority General Contractor.

Professional/Community Involvement: Former Member, Board of Directors of the Community Child Care of the Third Ward, and the Rochester Women's Network.

Awards/Recognition: National Association of Negro Business and Professional Women's Club Business Award, 1990; American Business Women's Association Boss of the Year Award, 1990; nominated for the Minority Business Person of the Year Award by the Minority Business Enterprise Development Committee.

Residence: Brighton, New York.

BOYDE Jr., Thomas, 1907-1981

Born: Washington, D.C., 1907; Moved to Rochester, 1930; Died in his home on Winterroth Street after a long illness, Sept. 13, 1981.

Family: Survived by wife Jennie; a son, Thomas Boyde III; Two daughters, Dolores R. Boyde and Barbara M. Boyde; A brother, William U. Boyde; A sister, Mrs. Mildred Gray; Two grandchildren.

Education: Undergraduate Degree in Architecture, Syracuse University, 1929; Master's Degree, Civil Engineering, Brown University; Studied in the Lombardy region of northern Italy; First Black Architecture graduate at Syracuse University; First Black Graduate in Civil Engineering at Brown University.

Career: *First Black Architect in Rochester, Siegmund Firestone Architectural Firm, 1930-*

1947; Opened Private Office in his home, 1947; Moved to an office at 104 East Ave., 1957-1981; Chief Architect for the Monroe Community Home and Infirmary; contributed to the design of the Rundel Memorial Library; Built 13 Star Market and several Big N grocery stores, the Great Lake Press Building; designed the Lexington Hotel in New York City (a landmark building), Franklin High School, The Triangle Building, The Strathallan, the former Rochester Fire Department headquarters, Kennedy Towers apartments, and St. Joseph's Villa.

Professional/Community Involvement: Member, American Institute of Architects and the Rochester Society of Architects.

Awards/Recognition: His thesis from Syracuse University was an award-winning design of the State Tower Building in Syracuse ($1,500 in gold), 1929; Recognized for the design of Monroe County Hospital at a ceremony commemorating the Hospital 60th anniversary; A plaque was unveiled and placed in the hospital's lobby, Feb, 24, 1995.

Eulogies/Quotations:

"If he were here today, he would be very proud and honored... Dad, no matter where you are, I love you very much."

Dolores Boyde, Boyde's daughter, accepting the honor for her father, Feb. 24, 1995 at the Monroe Hospital Ceremony

Evelyn Brandon, 1917-1995

*Reprinted with permission of **about...time** Magazine, Inc.*

recognizing Boyde as the designer of the Hospital.
D&C, Feb. 25, 1995

"Mr. Firestone, you advertised for an architect."

> *Thomas W, Boyde Jr., responding to the surprised Firestone of the architectural firm Siegmund Firestone, seeing that he was a black man at their first face to face meeting.*
> *D&C, Feb. 25, 1995*

"I think he wanted to be praised, but he never was because of the times he lived in... As a black professional, he had to work twice as hard as anyone else to get the recognition he deserved."

> *Dolores Boyde, Boyde's daughter.*
> *D&C, Feb. 25, 1995*

BRANDON, Nancy Evelyn, 1917-1995

Born: South Carolina, 1917; Moved to Rochester, 1921; Died at Park Ridge Hospital, April 27, 1995.

Parents: Golden O. and Abbie Jeter Brandon, a native of Carlyle, S.C.; Came to Rochester, in 1921; died, March 31, 1962; Was a deaconess at the A.M.E. Zion Church; Organized the Howard University Mothers Club in 1939.

Family: Single; Survived by a brother, Robert Brandon, sisters Abbie Johnson, and Phyllis Thompson; Several nieces and nephews.

Education: B.S., 1938 and MS, 1939, Psychology, Howard University; studied Human Development at the University of Chicago.

Evelyn Brandon Health Center, 81 Lake Avenue.
Photo, Mike F. Molaire.Copyright 1998, Norex Publications.

Career: *Retired, Professor Emeritus, Rochester Institute of Technology (RIT), 1985*; Assistant Professor, Psychology, RIT, 1966-1985; Director of Adult Programs, YWCA; Psychology Instructor, University of Alabama, Montgomery, Alabama; Assistant Professor of Psychology, Hampton University, Virginia.

Professional/Community Involvement: Board Member, former Park Avenue Hospital; Board Member, Park Ridge Hospital for more than 20 years (appointed in 1973); Board Member, Rochester Public Library, 1973-1995; Member of Book Lovers Club, Church Women United, Alpha Kappa Alpha Sorority, The Federation of Negro Women's Club, and Memorial A.M.E. Zion Church.

Awards/Recognition: Park Ridge Health System Satellite at 81 Lake Ave, Rochester, NY, is named the Evelyn Brandon Health Center, Oct., 1995; A Alpha Kappa Alpha Sorority Scholarship is named in her honor.

Eulogies/Quotations:

"Her interest in learning and libraries goes way back... Libraries played a big part in her life."

Dick Panz, director, Rochester Public Library
<u>Times Union</u>, May 10, 1995

"The one thing I wanted them to be aware of is that living in this world they are going to be living with elderly people... They are going to be with elderly people on their jobs and their neighborhoods, in their social interactions. I wanted them to have a feeling that growing old was not growing useless."

Evelyn Brandon, in a 1986 interview.
<u>D&C</u>, May 10, 1995

"She was an incredible woman... She never had a bad thing to say about anybody. She always was articulate and spoke very positively about things."

Dick Panz, director, Rochester Public Library.
D&C, May 10, 1995

BRANDON, Julia, 1919-1982

Born: South Carolina, 1919; Moved to Rochester, 1921.
Parents: Golden O. and Abbie Jeter Brandon, a native of Carlyle, S.C.; Came to Rochester, in 1921; Died, March 31, 1962; Was a deaconess at the A.M.E. Zion Church; Organized the Howard University Mothers Club in 1939.
Family: Single; Survived by sisters Evelyn Brandon, Mrs. Phyllis Johnson and Mrs. Abbie Johnson; A daughter, Mrs. Nancy Scott; Two brothers, Dr. Donald G. Brandon and Robert A. Brandon; a grandson.
Education: B.S. Dietetics, Howard University, 1942; Graduate Studies, Social Work, Atlanta University, and drug dependence at Cornell and Yale Universities; Urban Development at Rochester Institute of Technology.

Career: Appointed Assistant Project Coordinator in the Bureau of Redevelopment and Relocation, Department of Urban Renewal and Economic Development, May, 1965; Program Director, Montgomery Neighborhood Center, for 25 years; Teacher's Assistant, Rochester Institute of Technology; Dietician, YWCA of Rochester; Dietitian at a Chicago hospital; taught public school in Alabama and North Carolina.

Professional/Community Involvement: Member, Alpha Kappa Alpha Sorority, Black Political Caucus, Church Women United, Community School Council, Jack and Jill Clubs of America, Judicial Process Commission, National Council of Negro Women, National Association for the Advancement of Colored People, Job Corps, Urban League of Rochester, Women's Coalition for Downtown, Women in Community Service, YWCA; Board Member, Girl Scouts of America, United Church Ministries, St. Joseph Villa, Hillside Children's Center, and Genesee Ecumenical Ministries; Financial Secretary, Memorial A.M.E. Zion Church; President, Women's Human Relations Council and Genesee Valley Camping Associations.

Awards/Recognition: "Woman of the Year," Monroe County Human Relations Commission, 1970.

BRAY Jr., Robert 1914-1989

Born: Birmingham, Alabama, 1914; Moved to Rochester, 1919
Parents: Predeceased by wife of 44 years, Mildred Bray; Survived by sisters, Jessie Clark, and Virginia Bundy; A brother, Harry Bray (former Executive Director of Montgomery Neighborhood Center); Several nieces and nephews.
Education: Graduated from Franklin High School and Brockport Normal School (now SUNY College at Brockport).

Career*: Retired in 1981; Columbia Banking Federal Savings and Loan Associations' Mortgage Department, 1973-1981*; Assistant Treasurer, Finance Department of Monroe County, 1961-1973; Appointed Head of the Anti-Discriminatory Office by County Manager Gordon Howe, 1960; Monroe County Department of Finance, 1945-1960; Enlisted in the Army, 1943; Discharged with the rank of Staff Sergeant, 1945; Monroe County Finance Department, 1942-1943; Customer and Factory Service Liaison, Fincher Motors, 1939-1942; Taught and coached baseball and basketball at Holy Redemer School, after college and until 1939; Army Reserve, 1945-1973; Retired a Master Sergeant; A semi-professional basketball player in Rochester for a few seasons.

Professional/Community Involvement: Trustee, Republican Presidential Task Force; Member, Green Hills Golf Club in Mendon and United States Golf Association; Marshal, Ladies Professional Golf Association (LPGA) Rochester International and the Seniors Tournament; Member, Rochester Community Players, Muscular Dystrophy Association, Cystic Fibrosis Foundation and the Webster's Lions Club; Board Member, Genesee Settlement House.

Awards/Recognition: Received three battle stars and a Legion of Merit for his liaisons work with the French.

Eulogies/Quotations::

"He was chosen liaison to the French because of his knowledge of the French language... He was very proud of the awards he received while in the service."
> *Jessie Clark, Bray's Sister*
> *D&C, Apr. 25, 1989*

"I can't think of anybody who wanted to be more helpful to his fellow man than Bob Bray... I'll best remember him as a man who was always willing to give a helping hand to anyone who asked."
> *Reuben K. Davis, Appellate Division Justice, a friend of Bray for 34 years.*
> *D&C, Apr. 25, 1989*

"He had a real zest for life and enjoyed being active... His philosophy was live every day as fully as you could."
> *Jessie Clark, Bray's Sister*
> *D&C, Apr. 25, 1989*

"He just loves golf... He had served as marshal for the LPGA Rochester International and the Seniors Tournaments and was hoping to serve at the PGA's U.S. Open at Oak Hill this year."
> *Jessie Clark, Bray's Sister*
> *D&C, Apr. 25, 1989*

BRIGHAM, Willa D.

Born: in Tuskegee, Alabama; Moved to Rochester, 1991.

Parents: Louise W. Nall.

Family: Married to Ronald Brigham; two sons, Jason, and Jarett.

Education: MS, Health Science, Indiana University, Bloomington, Indiana; B.S., Health and Physical Education, Alabama State University, Montgomery, Alabama.

Career: Independent Professional Beauty Consultant; Storyteller; Avid writer of short stories, poetry and songs; Former Kindergarten Elementary and Secondary School teacher; Former Coach for the Special Olympics in Illinois, and former High School Track and Field, Softball, and Tennis Coach.

Professional/Community Involvement: Past President, Marklund Children's Home Clown Club; Board Member, Wilmington Public Service Television, Wilmington, Massachusetts; presently, Member of the Executive Committee of Fairport Parent/Teacher/Student Association; the Rochester Kwanzaa Committee; Boys Scouts USA, and Toastmasters International; Speaker at Phillis Wheatley Library, Arnett Library, Rochester Institute of Technology, University of Rochester, Rochester Public School #36, Dudley Elementary School, Montgomery Community Center, Jack and Jill of Rochester, A Different View (UAVC Production), The Drug and Rehabilitation Center of Monroe County, and Community Child-Care Center.

Awards/Recognition: Winner of the Area and Division Humorous Speech Contest, Toastmaster International, 1992; Placed second in District Contest.

Patents/Publications: Produced and directed multiple Public Service Television Programs in Wilmington, Massachusetts.

Residence: Fairport, New York.

BROOKS, Alfreda

Born: Rochester, New York.
Parents: Lillie M. Chaney and James Weldon Brumfield (Deceased).
Family: Divorced; three children, April Shantell, Vincent Stuart, and Crystal Raquel.
Education: MS, Career & Human Resource Development, Rochester Institute of Technology (RIT), 1995; B.S., Management of Organizational Development, Roberts Wesleyan College, Rochester, NY, 1994; Leadership Rochester Class of 1995; African-American Leadership Development Program, United Way of Greater Rochester, 1995.

Career: *Director, Commission for Promoting Pluralism, RIT since 1994*; Assistant to the Dean, Administrative and External Support, College of Applied Science and Technology, RIT, 1990-94; Assistant to the Director of the School of Photographic Arts & Sciences, College of Graphic Arts & Photography, RIT, 1989-90; Secretary to the Director of the School of Photographic Arts & Sciences, College of Graphic Arts & Photography, 1987-89; TAD Technical Services, Rochester, NY, Temporary positions, 1986-87; Office Manager, Instamation, Inc., Rochester, NY, 1985-86; Executive Secretary, Sales & Marketing Department, Sykes Datatronics, Inc., Rochester, NY, 1984-85; TAD Technical Services, Rochester NY, 1983-84; Homemaker, 1981-83; Medical Secretary, Eastman Kodak Company, Rochester, NY, 1971-81.

Professional/Community Involvement: Board Member, Women's Foundation, Pre-Trial Serv-

Alfreda Brooks
Photo, Mike F. Molaire, Copyright 1998, Norex Publications.

ices; Past Board Member, Campfire Boys & Girls; Past Chair, Staff Council, RIT; Member, Black Business Association, Rochester Women's Network, ; Secretary, African-American Leadership Development Program Alumni Association; Past Member, Women's Advisory Board, Colgate Divinity, Rochester 2010 Committee, Philanthropic Diversity Consortium, National Association for the Advancement of Colored People.

Awards/Recognition: Inducted into Kodak Brainpower Hall of Fame; Professional Woman of the Year, 1997.

Residence: Henrietta, New York.

BROOKS, Wilfred S.

Born: Washington, DC, 1924.
Parents: Ruth and Arthur E. Brooks.
Family: Married Juanita A. Brooks; Four children, Craige, Brad, Linne Hopkins and Haeter Welch Brooks.
Education: Graduate of Leroy High School, 1942.

Career: Retired; Formerly employed at Lapp Insulator, Leroy, New York; Genesee County Legislator since 1990; Chairman of Public Service Committee and member of Ways & Means Committee, Genesee County Legislator, 1996; Supervisor, Town of Oakfield, New York, for four years; Councilman, Town of Oakfield, New York, for six years.

Professional/Community Involvement: President, V.F.W. Western New York Council, Commander, 7th District V.F.W; Recording Secretary, Federal Labor Union 22485; Vice President, IUE Union 22485; Secretary, Oakfield republican Party; Chairman, Oakfield Republican Party; Board Member, Genesee/Leroy United Way, Pavilion State Bank Advisory, Greater Rochester Area United Way; Chairman, GLOW Solid Waste Management Committee; Chairman, Genesee Finger Lakes Regional Planning Council; Lay Leader, Oakfield United Methodist Church; Dean, Annual Retreat of Camp Asbury United Methodist; President, Oakfield/Alabama Lions Club; Chairman, Genesee Area Men's Prayer Breakfast; Chairman, DCOM United Methodist Batavia District, and Cub Master Boy Scouts.

Residence: Oakfield, New York.

BRANT, Jacqueline

Born: October, 1950.
Parents: Clyde and Mattie Dixon.
Family: Married to Eddie Bryant; Two children, Erica, and Tiffany.
Education: B.S., Mathematics, New York University, 1972; MS, Education, Nazareth College, 1990.

Career: *Co-owner of Visions Research; Co-creator of the African-American Bingo Game*; More than 10,000 have been sold since 1990; An educator, Conducts workshops at schools, church groups, recreation centers and professional conferences; Former Manager Computer Business Systems, Xerox Corporation.

Residence: Pittsford, New York.

BULLARD, H. Todd, The Honorable

Born: York, Pennsylvania, 1961; Moved to Rochester, 1963.
Parents: Christeen and Herbert Bullard.
Family: Married to Darnelle Bullard; One child, Bianca Bullard.
Education: JD, Law, (State and Local Government concentration), State University of New York at Buffalo, 1987; BA, Political Science, Allegheny College, 1984; Admission to New York State Bar, 1988; U.S. District Court, Western District of New York, 1988; U.S. Bankruptcy Court, Western District of New York, 1990.

Career: Monroe County Legislator, 27th Legislative District; Assistant Minority Leader, (1993-1995)-Ranking Member of Public Safety Committee; Principal, H. Todd Bullard, Esq., P.C. since 1993; Associate Attorney, Fiz, Spindelman, Brovitx, Turk, Himelein & Shukoff, P.C., 1991-1993; Associate Attorney, Harris, Beach & Wilcox, 1987-1990.

Professional/Community Involvement: Member, American Bar Association-Young Lawyers Section; New York Bar Association-Young Lawyers Section; Monroe County Bar Association-Minorities Affairs Committee since 1988; Chair (1991-92) Judiciary Committee (1988-1991); Arbitration Program, Seventh Judicial District since 1988; The Association of Trial Lawyers of America since 1989; Monroe County Bar Foundation since 1995; Board Member, American Heart Association, 1989-1991; Corresponding Secretary, Austin Steward Professional Society, 1989-1994; Chairman, Advisory Committee, Southwest Area Neighborhood, Inc., 1988-1993; Board Member, Center For Dispute Settlement, (1988-1992);Secretary, 1990-91; Board Member, Urban League of Rochester since 1990; Cor porate Counsel since 1995; Legal Aid Society, 1990-1991; Rochester Preservation Board, 1990-1991; Executive Board, Boy Scouts of America, Inc., 1991-1995; Rochester Area Foundation since 1995; Board Member, University of Buffalo Law School Alumni Association-Treasurer, 1989; President, 1991-1992.

Awards/Recognition: *Who's Who in American Law*, 1992; Man of The Year, Rochester Genesee Valley Club of the National Association of Negro Business and Professional Women's Clubs, Inc., 1993.

Residence: Rochester, New York.

BURNS, Ursula M.

Parents: Olga and Terrance Burns.
Family: Married Lloyd Bean; Two children, Melissa R. and Malkom K. Bean.
Education: Master of Science, Mechanical Engineering with Honors, Columbia University, NY, NY, 1981; B.S., Mechanical Engineering with Honors, Polytechnic Institute of New York, 1980.

Career: *Vice President, Xerox Corporation since Oct 13, 199*7; Vice President and General Manager, Departmental Copier Unit, Xerox Corp., Rochester, NY, responsible for all aspects of the value chain (design development, manufacturing, marketing, planning, finance, logistics, distribution) of the worldwide mid-range analog and digital copier business with total revenues of $3B, 200+ direct employees, $70M worldwide R&D budget and $600M+ cost of production since 1997; Vice President and General Manager, Workgroup Copier Business Unit, located in London, England, Xerox Corp. With total revenues of $1.8B, 350+ direct employees, $40M worldwide R&D Budget and $500M+ cost of production, 1995-1997; Vice President and General Manager, Office Network Copying Business, located in Rochester, NY, Xerox Corp. With 200+ direct employees, $150M engineering worldwide budget, 1993-1995; Vice President and General Manager, Office Color & Facsimile Business, located in Rochester, NY, Xerox Corp., 1992-1993; Executive Assistant to the Chairman and CEO, Xerox Corp., Stamford Ct., 1991-1992; Executive Assistant to The Executive Vice President of Marketing and Customer Operations, Xerox Corp., Stamford Ct., 1990-1991; Various positions in Engineering and Business Planning, Xerox Corp., Rochester, NY, 1982-1990.

Professional/Community Involvement: Board Member, PQ Corporation, a Pennsylvania medium sized chemical company since 1994; Dames and Moore Inc., the largest publicly traded environmental engineering/consulting firm in the US. since 1997.

BYRD, Anna Lee

Born: New Rochelle, NY, 1929; Moved to Rochester,1956.
Parents Anna and Irvin Lybrand

Family: Widow; A son, James A. Byrd, Jr.
Education: Graduate of Isaac E. Young High School, 1948; Graduate, Rochester Business Institute, 1965.

Career: *Urban League of Rochester since 1967*; Special Assistant to the President/Education Division Manager, 1993-1997; Vice President for Program Operations/Education Division Manager, 1988-1991; Executive Director Manager, 1972; Training Division, 1967-1988; Executive Secretary, 1965-1967.

Professional/Community Involvement: Member, Board of Directors, Liberty Partnership; Advisory Committee, Rochester Gas & Electric, and Rochester Telephone; Former Member, Finance Committee, Mt. Olivet Baptist Church; Former Ministries Coordinator, American Baptist Women Church.

CALHOUN, Essie L.

Family: Single .
Education: MS, Administration & Supervision, Bowie State University, Bowie, MD.; B. Ed., Social Science, University of Toledo, Toledo, Ohio.

Career: *Eastman Kodak Company: Director of Community Relations and Public Affairs since 1989*; Director of Public Affairs Planning, Communications & Public Affairs, responsible for minority-focused outreach efforts, 1988; Sales Manager for Copy Product Division, 1987-89; Marketing Specialist, Copy Product Division, 1984-87; Resource Specialist for Talented & Gifted Program, Coordinator for Junior High School Cross-Age Tutorial Program and Curriculum Coordinator, Prince George County School, Prince George, MD., 1974-81; Coordinator, Programs for the Disadvantaged, Washtenaw Country Schools, Ann Arbor, MI, 1971-73; Instructor,

Essie L. Calhoun
Photo Courtesy Essie Calhoun

South Bend Skills Center, South Bend, Indiana, 1970-71.

Professional/Community Involvement
Serves on the Board of Directors of Rochester Brainpower Learning Alliance, Network North Star (a Kodak African-American Networking Group, she chaired in 1993), the Urban League of Rochester, The American Red Cross, Rochester Grantmakers Forum, Young Audiences of Rochester, and United Way of Greater Rochester; Member of Business Policy Review Council, the Center for Community Relations Advisory Board, National Corporate Women's Network, Public Relations Society of America, Rochester Women's Network, Martin Luther King Jr. Greater Rochester Commission, NAACP-

ACTSO Industry Advisory Council; Vice-Chair of the Urban League Black Scholars Steering Committee; Past Member of the Writers & Books Board of Directors; Led the initiative, and is the first chairperson of the Greater Rochester Area United Way's *African-American Leadership Development Program*; Co-chair of the Minority Achievers Program, YMCA of Rochester, 1993; A member of the Aenon Baptist Church.

Awards/Recognition: National Urban League's Volunteer Award for the Eastern Region; 1998 Nominee, Athena Award, Rochester Chamber of Commerce; Women's History Month Award, 1997.

Residence: Fairport, New York.

CALLOWAY, Cabell (Cab), 1907-1994

Born: Rochester, NY, December 25, 1907; Lived in Rochester for five years; Died November 18, 1994, in a Delaware nursing home.
Family: Married Nuffie Calloway; Five daughters, Chris Calloway, Cecelia "Lael" Calloway Tyson, Cabella Calloway Langsam, and Camay Calloway Murphy.
Education: Attended Baltimore's Frederick Douglass High School; Studied law for two years at Crane College, in Chicago.

Career: Started moonlighting as master of ceremonies at a Chicago South Side nightclub, while attending Law School; Met Louis Armstrong and learned his loose, jivey scat-singing style; Became a regular at the Cotton Club in Harlem; had two hit records; By 1978, his 1931 recording of *"Minnie the Moocher"* sold 2.5 million copies over 47 years; Performed a rousing version of Minie the Moocher in the John Belushi and Dan Akroyd film` *The Blues Brothers (1980).*

Cabell (Cab) Calloway, 1907-1994
Photo Courtesy Columbia records/Reprinted with permission of **about...time** *Magazine Inc.*

Film: *"The Singing Kid"* with Al Jolson, *"St. Louis Blues"* with Nat King Cole, *The Cincinnati Kid* with Steve McQueen, *"Stormy Weather"* (1943) with Lena Horne and Bill "Bojangles" Robinson, *The Big Broadcast* (1932); *International House* (1933), *The Cotton Club* (1984).

Theater: George Gershwin's Porky and Bess (portrayed the cocaine-dealing Sportin' Life), 1953; Hello Dolly (all-black version with Pearl Bailey, 1967), *The Pajama Game, Bubbling Brown Sugar.*

Recordings: *Kicking the Gong Around (1931), Reefer Man* (1932), *The Scat Song* (1933),

Mama, I Want To Make Rhythm (1937), *A Chicken Ain't Nothin' But a Bird* (1945), *Hi-De-Ho Man* (1947).

Patents/Publications: Mr. Hepster's Jive Talk ictionary, a collection of phrases he coined that originated in jazz musicians' banter, 1938; examples include "beat" (tired), "chick" (girl), "pad" {apartment), "jam" (musical improvisation), "square" (unhip); *Of Minnie the Moocher and Me*, an autobiography; *Rhythm and Soul Series* (a collection of 22 Cab Calloway recordings, 1993), Legacy Recording, Columbia, producer

Awards/Recognition: Honorary Degree, University of Rochester, 1993; Presented the National Medal of Arts by the National Endowment for The Arts, at the White House, October 8, 1993; A plaque and monument commemorating his career was dedicated in Otto Henderberg Square, a small park along Sycamore Street, in Rochester's Swillburg neighborhood, October 1993.

Eulogies/Quotations:

"I had a trombone player; they used to call him Bug... Every time he would get up to play solo, he'd shake. He had the jitters. So I named him 'Jitterbug."

    Cab Calloway
    D&C, Nov 20, 1994

"But I couldn't take it because I was working in night clubs- the Sunset, Dreamland, Grand Terrace. These places were too much, I couldn't study, so I chucked the whole thing and joined the Alabamians... We worked our way to the Savoy Ballroom in New York and we thought we were something, but we bombed all over the place..."

    Cab Calloway
    Times Union, Dec. 11, 1972

"the least intellectual but wisest person I'd ever met."

    Nuffie Calloway (his wife)
    Times Union, July 18, 1978

"I came out all right, I have more now than I had then... I win some and I lose some (about gambling)... I never spent it all but I enjoyed what I spent... It's my whole life to entertain people and make them happy. I just hope to live long enough to do it yet."

    Cab Calloway
    Times Union, September 21, 1976

"He deserves the recognition ... It's very timely, he is the epitome of an entertainer. His whole philosophy was to give everything he had to his audience."

    Camay Calloway Murphy (one of his five daughters)
    Times Union, October 15, 1993

CHANDLER, Florella

Born: Rochester, New York.
Parents: Leroy and Marie Golden.
Family: Divorced, with two children, Pamela McCullough & Stacy Chandler.
Education: Licensed LPN, Rochester School of Practical Nursing; African-American Leadership Development Program, Greater Rochester Area United Way, 1993; Certification, Supervisory Development, Cornell Extension; Certificate, Gerontology, St John Fisher.

Career: *Staff Nurse, Planned Parenthood of Rochester and the Genesee Valley for 27 years*; Previously Nurse, General Hospital.

Professional/Community Involvement: Member, Board of Directors of Threshold Inc., Alternative Youth Services since 1993, Jordan Health Care since 1995, and CONEA since 1981; Member, Rochester Genesee Valley Club of Negro Business & Professional Women since 1980; Listed in the Diversity Resource Directory of Rochester Area Volunteers published by thee Philanthropic Diversity Consortium of the Rochester (NY) Region

Awards/Recognition: Margaret Hays Baum Award, Outstanding Service & Major Achievement; C.O.N.E.A. Dedicated, Outstanding Volunteer Award.

Residence: Greece, New York.

CHAPPELLE, Edward Sr., Dr., 1926-1984

Born: 1926, Washington, D.C.; Moved to Rochester, 1957; died on May 26, 1984, at Howard University Hospital, in Washington D.C.
Family: Survived by a son, Dr. Edward H. Chappelle, Jr., a brother, Stanley Chappelle, his mother, Janie Chappelle; two sisters, Mildred Chappelle and Gladys Freeman; a grandson, Edward H. Chappelle III.
Education: Medicine, Howard University, 1957; Master's Degree, Bacteriology, Rutgers University, 1952; Bachelor's Degree, Lincoln University, 1948; Internship and Residency, Internal Medicine, Rochester General Hospital, 1957-1960; Ffellowship, Renal Ddiseases, Loma Linda University Medical School, Ca, 1961; Post-Doctoral Fellowship, Renal Diseases, National Institutes of Health.

Career: *Instructor of Internal Medicine, Howard University Hospital*; Maintained a private practice in Internal Medicine on Portland Avenue; Was a Kidney Specialist at Rochester General Hospital; Clinical Instructor of Internal Medicine, University of Rochester School of Medicine and Dentistry; Personal Physician of Rochester-born jazz trumpeter Chuck Mangione.

Eulogies/Quotations:

"There are so many people who felt close to him…He was warm and gentle. No one would sit with a patient the way he did."

    Chuck Mangione, Rochester-born jazz trumpeter
    <u>Times Union</u>, May 29, 1984

"He was always optimistic…He always thought something would come through."

    Marla Freeman, Dr. Chappelle's niece
    <u>Times Union</u>, May 29, 1984

"I feel like we just lost our security blanket."

    Nancy Mangione, Chuck Mangione's mother
    <u>D&C</u>, May 29, 1984

CHILDRESS-BROWN, Maxine, The Honorable

Born: Washington, DC, 1944; Moved to Rochester, 1973.
Parents: Thomasina & Herbert Childress
Family: Married to James E. Brown; Three children, Scott, Nikki, and Kimberly.
Education: B.S. Degree, Springfield College; MS Degree, Education, University of Massachusetts, 1973.

Career: *Rochester City Council Member representing South District since 1983;: Presently ice President; Formerly Acting President,*1985-87; Chair, Jobs and Economic Development Committee since 1990; Chaired the Human Services Committee, 1981-85; Member of the Parks, Recreation & Human Services since 1990. Has sponsored the following legislation: Ordinance to declare the City of Rochester's commitment to racial equality and its opposition to apartheid in South Africa and Namibia; Resolution to establish a Minority/Women Business Opportunity Task Force; Ordinance authorizing the establishment of the County of Monroe-City of Rochester Council on Disabled Persons; Resolution, City of Sanctuaries; Ordinance to invest in Youth Services; Resolution establishing a policy regarding the Acquired Immune Deficiency Syndrome and related issues; Amending the Municipal Code with respect to firearms and other dangerous weapons; Resolution establishing an Economic Development Policy. Adjunct Professor, Political Science, St. John Fisher College since 1991; Instructor/Counselor, St John Fisher College, 1989; Associate Executive Director, Health Association of Rochester and Monroe County, 1985-1988; Community Liaison Officer, Department of Recreation and Community Services, City of Rochester, City Hall, directing marketing activities, 1980-1983; Director, People Helping People (PHP), a community-wide information and referral, counseling, and recreation program for disabled persons, 1978-1980; State College of Art & Sciences, Geneseo New York: Assistant Professor, Special Education Department; Director, Learning Disabilities Program, Holcomb Campus; Supervisor; Administrator; 1975-78. Assistant Professor and Coordinator, Advanced Programs, Rochester Institute of Technology, 1973-74. Instructor/Staff Assistant, University of Massachusetts, Media Specialists Program for the Deaf, Amherst, Massachusetts, 1971-73.

Professional/Community Involvement: Ex-Officio member, Monroe County Office of the Aging; Member, Advisory Committee, New York Office of Human Rights; Puerto Rican Youth Development Board of Directors; Advisory Committee, Jefferson Avenue Health Awareness Center since 1985; Vice President, Board of Visitors, State Agricultural and Industrial School at Industry; Chairperson, Arts Reach, Arts for Greater Rochester; Member and President Metropolitan Women's Network, 1980-85; Member, Rochester Area Multiple Sclerosis Board of Directors; Urban League Ad Hoc Committee: Home Economics, Monroe County Cooperative Extension; Association of Personnel Women, 1978-1980. Convener, Nominations Committee, State University of New York College at Geneseo, 1976-77; Member of the Orton Society (Organization for Learning Disabilities), 1975-76; Interpreter for the Hearing Impaired (American Sign Language and Total Communication), Courtroom Trials, Social Functions, and Business Meetings, 1957 to present.

Awards/Recognition: Maxine Childress-Brown Medical Scholarship created by Medical Auxiliary Society to benefit students in two and four-year medical programs; Hispanic Leadership De-velopment Program Volunteer Service Awards, 1986, 1987, & 1988; National Sojourner Meritorian Service Award, 1986; Volunteer Service Award, United Way of Rochester; Metropolitan Women Network's Award; Salute to Black Women, 1986; Urban League Certificate of Outstanding Service, 1986.

Patents/Publications: "A Study Skills Program for the Hearing Impaired Student," *Volta Review, Alexander Graham Bell Journal*, May, 1988; Published seven articles in local newspaper from 1981 to 1984.

Residence: Rochester

CLARK, William G.

Born: Brunswick, GA, 1952; Moved to Rochester, 1974.
Family: Two children, Keisha and Shuna Clark.
Education: MBA, Accounting, Rochester Institute of Technology, 1984; B.S., Management, St. John Fisher College, 1978.

Career: *President and Chief Executive Officer, Urban League of Rochester, inc. since 1994*; Vice President for Finance and Administration, Chief Financial Officer and Chief Program Officer and Personnel Administrator, 1983-94; Manager of Financial and Administrative Services, 1981-1983; Accounting Manager, Genesee Hospital, 1981; Auditor, Blue Cross & Blue Shield, 1978-81.

Professional/Community Involvement: Trustee, Center for Government Research and Zion Hill Missionary Baptist Church; Board Member, LIFESPAN, Boy Scouts of America, Rochester Jobs, Inc.; Advisory Board Member, Rochester Institute of Technology School of Liberal Arts and Chase Manhattan Bank; Commissioner, City of Rochester Planning Commission; Past Member, Rochester/Monroe County Private Industry Council; Past Board Member, Veterans Outreach Center; Past Chairman, St. John Fisher HEOP Advisory Council.

Awards/Recognition: First Church Divine Hall of Fame Inductee, 1996; Monroe Community College Hall of Fame Inductee, 1995.

COLES, Howard W., 1904-1996

Born: Belcoda, New York (Southwest of Rochester) November 12, 1904; Died, December 10, 1996.

Parents: Charles and Grace Coles; Grandfather, Clayton Coles, a former slave, founder of the Mumford Second Baptist Church.

Family: Married twice; A daughter, Joan Coles Howard; A son, Matthew G. Coles; A grandson, Derek S. Lockhart; A granddaughter, Shelaine Peters (Assistant Metro Editor, *Democrat and Chronicle*); Two great-grandchildren.

Education: Graduated from East High School; classes in Sociology, University of Rochester; studied Journalism, Salesmanship and Public Speaking at the YMCA in New York City.

Career: *Publisher and Founder of the Frederick Douglass Voice in 1934*; Before starting the paper: Bell Captain, Coney Island, New York; Waiter, Bethlehem, PA; Messenger and Delivery Man, New York Herald Tribune, 1939; Sold real estate, bought and managed his own properties, and simultaneously sold insurance for various companies, 1948-65; Court Attendant in the City Court, late 1950-1960's; Was a member of the Advertising Production Department of Radio Stations WSAY and WHAM, where he was the first Black Dee-Jay; ran for the Board of Supervisors of Monroe County.

Community/Professional Involvement:
Served as President of the local NAACP; Ran unsuccessfully for several political positions.

Awards/Recognition: Recommended for NAACP Spingarn Medal for Contributions in Social and Civic Work, 1942; Governor's Award for African Americans of Distinction, 1993; Multiple Awards Representative of the County, State, and the Nation; Recipient of the Loftus Carson Award, 1996; The Rochester Association of Black Communicators named their award in his honor, The Annual Howard Coles Award, 1982; Saluted for his work as an activist, historian, publisher and author at a dinner at the Mapledale Party House, July, 1994; Became a resident fellow of the Rochester Museum & Science center, 1988; Honored the week before his death by the Rochester Museum & Science center when Images: *Afro-Rochester*, a book of photographs, was deicated to him.

Patents/Publications: Author, The Cradle of freedom, an historical narrative of Blacks in Western New York and Canada, 1940; *The City Directory of negro Business and Progress, 1939-1940*; Was working on the completion of his second book: *The Negro Family in Rochester*.

Eulogies/Quotations:

"I'm as much a part of it as ever, because when there's been a picket line, if I didn't start it, I joined it."
    Howard Coles,
    D&C, Sept. 10, 1972

"I've run for every office that one could possibly run for, except dog-catcher, when only a miracle could I have won...I kept running because I felt I could plant the seeds of the idea that these sorts of things weren't unattainable even to blacks."
    Howard Coles,
    D&C, Sept. 10, 1972

Howard Coles, 1904-1996
*Reprinted with permission of **about...time** Magazine, Inc.*

"Whatever I've gotten, I had to dig it out of the earth, I've had to scrounge and cling to it like a drowning man clinging to flotsam in the sea."

Howard Coles,
D&C, Sept. 10, 1972

"You rarely saw a black man's name in the daily papers, and never saw his photograph."

Howard Coles, referring to the time he started his newspaper, The Frederick Douglass Voice.
D&C, Feb. 20, 1979

"In those days, if you were black you could shine shoes, polish brass or pick baskets. That was about it. I wanted to do more than that."

Howard Coles, referring to the time he started his newspaper, The Frederick Douglass Voice.
D&C, Feb. 20, 1979

"I'm racing against time to get things done...but I can't race very fast anymore...I'd like to retire, but there's much to do, so much to do."

Howard Coles
D&C, Dec. 4, 1988

"He symbolizes the struggle."

James M. Blount, publisher of about...time Magazine
D&C, Nov. 12, 1983

"Mr. Coles was the first person in Rochester to break the color line in communications."

Marietta G. Avery, president, Rochester Association of Black Communicators
D&C, Nov. 12, 1983

"He laid the groundwork for those of us who came later. If it weren't for him, some of us wouldn't be here."

William Johnson Jr., Rochester's first black mayor, at the tribute dinner at the Mapledale Party House in honor of Coles.
D&C, July 26, 1994

"He was an authentic piece of history, a voice that will be missed in our community.

Minister Franklin Florence, Sr.
Times Union, December 17, 1996

"Howard Coles must be added to the names of those pioneers who had a vision for the future."

William A. Johnson Jr., Mayor, City of Rochester
Times Union, December 17, 1996

"He was unyielding in his quest to make sure Douglass was known in this community... He kept the community aware of what was going on. He was a man of vision."

Dr. Juanita Pitts, program coordinator, Friends of Frederick Douglass, which Mr. Coles co-founded.
D&C, December 11, 1996

COLES, Gregory E., Reverend

Born: Cleveland Ohio, 1960; Moved to Rochester,1985; Has moved to Ohio.
Parents: Robert W. Coles, Jr., and Zelda B. Coles.
Family: Married to Tijuana Howell Coles; Two

children, Vance Robert Coles and G. Eric Coles.

Education: MS, Divinity, Colgate Rochester Divinity School, 1987; BA, Political Science, Rutgers University, 1983; BA, African Studies, Rutgers University, 1983; Certificate, HIV Pre- and Post Test Counseling, New York State AIDS Institute, 1988; Certificate, AIDS Counseling Issues Training, New York State Division of Substance Abuse Services, Narcotic and Drug Research Institute, 1988; Certificate, Seminar in Executive Training for Non-Profit Management, Mandel Center for Nonprofit Organizations, Case Western Reserve University.

Career: *President and Chief Executive Officer of Boys and Girls Club of Rochester Inc., since 1992*; Assistant Pastor of the New Bethel CME Church, since 1992; Deputy Director of New York State Operations, Rural Opportunities, Inc., 1989-92; AIDS Education/Outreach Program Coordinator, Baden Street Settlement, Inc., 1988-89; Pastor-in-Residence, Graves Institutional CME Church, 1988-89; Senior Pastor, Church of the Covenant UCC, Rochester, New York, 1986-88; Assistant Pastor, Union Baptist Church, White Plains, New York, 1984-1985; Evening Manager, Emergency Standby Attendant for Disabled, Peer Academy Advisor, Rutgers College Dean of Students Office, 1980-84.

Professional/Community Involvement: Member, Board of Directors, Rochester Educational Opportunity Center since 1993; Adam Walsh Center, Board of Directors since 1993; Deputy Commissioner, Monroe County Executive's Commission to Analyze Savings and Efficiency, since 1992; Member, Nutrition Consortium of New York State since 1991; Member, New York State Health Department, AIDS Institute Regional Education Committee since 1991; Member, Committee for Farm worker Justice since 1989; Co-Chair, African-American and Latino Committee of Rochester Area Task Force on AIDS (RATFA) since 1988; Member, Board of Directors, Helping People with AIDS, Inc., 1988-91.

Awards/Recognition: Paul Robertson African Prize, Rutgers University, 1983; 1993 United Way/Red Cross Campaign Executive Circle; Certificate of Achievement, Christian Methodist Episcopal Church.

Residence: Rochester, New York

COOPER, Helen

Born: Washington DC, 1929; Moved to Rochester, 1953.
Parents: Gladys and William J. Claytor.
Family: Married to Walter Cooper, Ph.D.; Two sons, Robert and Brian; four grandchildren, Davis, Philip, Kenneth, and Celia.
Education: MS, Analytical Chemistry, Howard University, 1953; B.S. Cum Laude, Chemistry, Howard University, 1951.

Career: *Travel Consultant with Travel Flair, LTD.*; Retired as Director of Professional Recruitment/University Development and Corporate Employee Relations, Eastman Kodak Company; Previously Director of Personal Relations of Manufacturing Resources Division, at the same company.

Professional/Community Involvement: Member, Rochester Women's Network, Career Development Services, Center for Youth Services Board of Directors, Nazareth College of Rochester Board of Trustees; Co-chair of Rochester-Bamako, Mali Sister City Committee.

Awards/Recognition: Nominee for the Firth Annual Athena Award, 1991; Network North Star, Inc. Award (By-laws Committee), 1989;

COOPER, Walter, Ph.D.

GOALS (Graduate Opportunities for Advanced Level Studies) Special Recognition Award for Fund Raising, 1988; Rochester Area Chamber of Commerce International Award, 1982.

Residence: Rochester, New York.

COOPER, Walter, Ph.D.

Born: Clairton, Pennsylvania, 1928; Moved to Rochester, 1952.
Parents: Luda and Alonzo Cooper (deceased).
Family: Married to Helen Claytor; Two children, Robert and Brian; Four grandchildren, Davis, Philip, Kenneth, and Celia
Education: Ph.D., Physical Chemistry, University of Rochester, 1956; BA, Chemistry, Washington and Jefferson College, Washington, PA, 1950.

Career: *Member, Board of Regents, the University of the State of New York 1988-1997*; 30 years at the Eastman Kodak Research Labs: Early retirement, 1986; Manager of the Office of Technical Communications, 1985-86; Administrative Assistant to the Director, 1984-85; Technical Staff Associate to the Director, 1981-84; Research Associate, 1966-1981; Senior Research Chemist, 1961-65; Research Chemist, 1956-60.

Professional/Community Involvement: Presently Board Member, Garth Fagan Dance Theater; Board of Governors, Genesee Hospital; Board of Directors, Genesee Health Service; Chairman, Board of Governors, Genesee Hospital, Rochester, N.Y., 1996-98; Associate Director Anti-Poverty Program of Rochester and Monroe County, 1965; Board of Governors, Genesee Hospital; Chairman, Bamako, Mali-Rochester, New York Sister Cities Committee, 1975-1997; Founding Member, Bamako Children's Committee (an organization designed to improve the medical practices in Bamako), 1985-86; Member, Advisory Board of Agricultural Teams, Inc., 1979-82; Special Consultant to the Administrator, Small Business Administration, Washington, D.C., 1968-69; Past Board Member, Rochester Area Foundation; State Advisory Committee, Federal Civil Rights Commission; Board of Trustees, Washington and Jefferson College; National Advisory Council, Small Business Administration; Social Goals and Policies Committee, United Community Chest; Board of Directors, Finger Lakes Health System Agency; Advisory Committee, Urban/Suburban Pupil Transfer Program; Past Vice President and Founding Member, Urban League of Rochester; Past Chairman, Small Business Administrations' National Advisory Council for Black Business and Economic Development; Member American Association for the Advancement of Science, American Physical Society, and American Chemical Society; Past Chair and Member, Interstate Migrant education Council; Chair, Ralph Bunche Scholarship Committee, 1960-1966.

Awards/Recognition: Engineer of the Year, Rochester Engineer Society, 1997; Masonic Service Bureau's Distinguished Community Service Award; University of Rochester's Hutchinson Medal given to an alumnus of the University in recognition of outstanding achievement and notable service to the community 1992; International Relations Award, Rochester Chamber of Commerce, 1982; Knight of the National Order of Mali, 1984; Charles T. Lunsford Distinguished Community ServiceAward, Rochester Urban League, 1978; Listed in *Who's Who In Community Service*, Vol. II, 1975; *Who's Who* In Black America, 1975; *Who's Who In the East*, 1976; *American Men In Science*, 1976; *International Biography*, 1972; Community Service Award, Rochester Community Involvement Organization, 1975; Achievement Award, International Organization of Eastern Stars; Distinguished Alumni Award, Washington and Jefferson Col-

Walter Cooper, Ph.D., 1993
Photo, Fred Tanksley, Copyright 1993, Norex Publications.

Physical Society, Medical Science Colloquium; holder of three patents, *U.S. Patent 3,532,680, U.S. Patent 3,551,153, GB Patent 1,219,810.*

Residence: Penfield, New York.

Quotations:

"One has to be very careful not to run the risk of institutionalizing themselves in an organization...I've done that with other organizations before, but I didn't want that to happen with something as important as education."

Dr. Walter Cooper, commenting on his leaving the State Board of Regents.
D&C, Feb. 28, 1997

"It's not just that he improves the community...It's how he brings about change in people. He's really a consensus builder."

James Peters, director of community relations and development for Family Service of Rochester Inc., commenting o Dr. Cooper receiving the Family Service of Rochester Inc.'s F. Ritter and Hattie Shumway Award.
D&C, Feb. 28, 1997

lege, 1968; Community Development Award, Chamber of Commerce, 1966; Outstanding Achievement Award of Rochester Club of National Negro Professional and Business Women, Inc., 1966; Leroy E. Snyder Award, Junior Chamber of Commerce, 1966; National Science Foundation, Fellow, 1955-56; Celanese Corporation of America, Fellow, 1952-54; Honorary Sc. D, Washington and Jefferson College, 1987; Honorary D Humane Litt, Nazareth College, 1993; Lions Club, Outstanding Student Award, 1946; Danforth Foundation Award, 1946; Washington and Jefferson Alumni Scholarship, 1946-50.

Patents/Publications: Has published over 30 scientific articles, in *Photographic Science and Engineering, Journal of Physical Chemistry, Chemical Physics Letters, Nature, Journal of The American Chemical Society, Bulletin of the American*

COSBY, Lynnette

Born: Louisville, Kentucky; Moved to Rochester, 1988.
Parents: James and Dorothy Williams.
Family: Married to Garry Cosby, Sr.; One son, Garry II; One granddaughter, Joie.
Education: MBA, General Management, University of Louisville, 1981; Management Certificate, Smith Management Program, Smith College, 1991; B.S. Engineering Management/Industrial Engineering, University of Louisville, 1977.

Career: *Project Manager, Advanced Technical Group, Xerox Corporation*; Responsible for consolidation of the Capital Planning budgets for Manufacturing Support, including domestic and international requirements since 1990; Operations Manager, Business Center II, CMO, Xerox Corporation, 1990; Sr. Manufacturing Supervisor, Wire Harness Area, Xerox Corporation, 1989; Manufacturing Supervisor, Wire Harness Area, Xerox Corp, 1988; Sr. Industrial Engineer, WearEver-Proctorsilex, Chillicothe, Ohio, 1986-88; Engineer II, Mead Corporation, Chillicothe, Ohio, 1980-86; Manufacturing Process Engineer, Ford Motor Company, Louisville, 1978-80.

Professional/Community Involvement: Active member of the United Methodist Church of the Resurrection, participating on theAdministration Board; Financial Secretary, Altar Guild, Choir, United Methodist Women, Sunday School Staff; Member Society of Women Engineers, 1977-1992; University of Louisville Alumni Association, 1977-92.

Awards/Recognition: Freshman Class President for Engineering School; Xerox Team Excellence Award.

COX-COOPER, Rodric

Born: Rochester, NY, 1967.
Parents: Robert and Thelma Cooper.
Family: Married to Jacquelyn Cox-Cooper.

Education: MS, Administration, Central Michigan University, 1993; B.S., University of Dayton, 1990; *African-American Leadership Development Program*, United Way of Greater Rochester Area, 1994.

Career: *Neighborhood Empowerment Team (NET) Administrator, City of Rochester, Mayor's Office since 1997*; Assistant Director, City of Rochester Parking & Municipal Code Violations Bureau, 1995-1997; Budget Analyst, City of Rochester, Bureau of Budget & Efficiency, 1993-1995; Social Worker, Montgomery County (Ohio) Children Services, 1990-93.

Rodric Cox-Cooper, 1998
Photo, Mike F. Molaire. Copyright 1998, Norex Publications.

Professional/Community Involvement: President, Alpha Phi Alpha Fraternity, Inc since 1997; Vice President, Alpha Phi Alpha Fraternity, Inc., 1995-1997; Corresponding Secretary, Rochester Alumni Chapter, Alpha Phi Alpha Fraternity, Inc., 1994-1995; Vice President, Monroe County Young Democrats, 1996; Member, Alumni Association, *African-American Leadership Development Program* since 1994; Chair, AALDP Recruitment & Selection Committee, since 1996; Volunteer, Urban League Black Scholars Mentor Program, 1994-1996; Member, Board of Directors, Planned Parenthood, 1995-1996; Vice Chairman of Program and Project Development, Southwest Area Development Corporation since 1997; Monroe County Democrat Committee since 1997.

Awards/Recognition: Outstanding Young Man of America, 1998; [1]'s (AALDP) Young Adult Role Model Award, 1997; Sigma Iota Epsilon, National Honor Society for Graduate Students in Management and Administration, 1993.

CURRY, Archie C.

Born: Ellenton, Florida, 1940; Moved to Rochester, 1960.
Parents: Archie and Daisy Curry.
Family: Married to Annie B. Curry; Three children, Patrick, T'Hani and Shani.
Education: B.S., Urban Education Planning, Empire State College, 1976; Diploma, Management and Supervision, Rochester Institute of Technology.

Career: *Commissioner, Rochester Board of Education, 1978-1995*; Board Vice President, 1980; Board President, 1987, 1992, 1994, and 1995; Board Vice President, 1993; President, Monroe County School Board Association, 1981-1982; Business Development Consultant, Rochester Minority Business Development Center, 1994-96; Coordinator of Family Life Education for the Urban League and six agencies forming a consortium: YWCA, Catholic Family Learning Center, Puerto Rican Youth Development, Action For a Better Community, Rochester General Hospital, and the Urban League, 1992-94; Equal Opportunity Representative, Monroe County Affirmative Action/Human Relations Department, 1987-92; Urban League of Rochester Inc., 1974-1987: Manager, Community Planning Division, 1981-1987; Assistant Manager, Community Planning Division, 1979; Educational Specialist, 1978-1979; Eastman Kodak Company, 1962-1974: Laboratory Technician, Polymer Synthesis Group, 1971-1974; Leave of Absence to become the Assistant Director for Pro-

grams and Personnel at Wedge, Inc., a social Action For a Better Community, Brown Square Development Corporation; Member, Genesee/Finger Lakes Regional Planning Council, Monroe County School Boards Association, Rochester Area Career Educational Council, Regents Advisory Council of the Genesee Valley Region, Genesee Hospital Institutional Review Board Committee.

Awards/Recognition: Recognition for "Years of Service on the Board of Education and Dedication to the Children of the Rochester City School District," Association of Supervisor and Administrators of Rochester, 1996; Award from the Manatee and Sarasota County Committee, "In Recognition for Years of Dedicated Service to the City of Rochester and Community," 1995; Award from the Staff, Parents, and Participants of the Baden Bulldogs, in Recognition for Outstanding Service to the Youth of the Community, 1995; The Black Educators Award, in recognition of Extensive Service to the Educational Community; Theta Omicron Chapter of Omega Psi Phi Fraternity, Inc. Award for Outstanding Service to the Development of Our Community Youth, 1989; Rochester Business Institute Award, 1988; Rochester Shrine Club's Award, 1987; Monroe County Human Relations Commission Citation, 1982; 1982 Man of The Year Award, Rochester Genesee Valley Club of the National Association of Negro Business and Professional Women's Club; Special Recognition of Outstanding and Dedicated Service to the Minority Community of Rochester, Eureka Lodge No. 36 F & AM (Prince Hall), 1981; Masjid Muhammad Rochester Humanitarian Endeavor's Award, 1979; Title I Award for Outstanding Service to Title #1 Children, District Advisory Council, 1977; Certificate of Appreciation from the 16th Ward Youth Development Program and the Neighborhood Street Academy Student Government, 1976;

Rochester Urban League Executive Director's Award for Outstanding Service, 1975; Neighborhood Street Academy Certificate Award, 1975; Outstanding Community Service Award, RAP and Produce Conference, 1974.

Residence: Rochester, New York.

CUYLER, Johnnie

Born: Mississippi; Moved to Rochester, 1969.
Parents: Ms. Ella Louise Walker, and Mr. Johnny Beauford.
Family: Married to Israel Cuyler; Two sons, Israel, and Jermaine.
Education: Post-Graduate, Alfred State University; Graduate, Dudley's Cosmetology School, Greensboro, N.C., Pivot International School of Beauty, Bruno's International School, Toronto, Canada.

Career: *Owner of Guys and Dolls Phase I and Phase II*; Professional Representative for a major Cosmetics and Hair Products Company in the United States; Revlon Fashion Coordinator.

Professional/Community Involvement: Member, National Cosmetology Association, People To People Delegation, Washington, DC, & the 1992 Delegation to China.

Awards/Recognition: Dudley's Cosmetology, Pivot Point International; Bruno's International, SUNY Brockport's Educational Opportunity Center (EOC).

Residence: Rochester, New York

DAILEY, Herman L.

Born: Yalah, Florida, 1944; Moved to Rochester, 1963.

Parents: George and Rosa Dailey.
Family: Single.
Education: Ordained Elder, Church of God By Faith, 1988; Workshop Certificate from Howard University, Cultural Differences in the Workplace; Summer Workshop Certificate from University of Michigan School of Social Work.

Career: Ordained Minister in the Church of God By Faith; Coordinator of AC Rochester's Employee Assistance Program, which helps workers who have drug and alcohol problems.

Professional/Community Involvement: Unpaid Director and Founder, Outreach Community Center (a non-profit organization that counsels alcoholics and drug addicts); used to be known on Rochester's mean streets as "Slick Red;"Was a pimp and a boozer and a cocaine addict; gave all that to become a minister; Vice President of U.W.A. Local 1097 since 1981; member of the Board of Directors of Volunteers of America; Served in the Board of Directors of Park Ridge Chemical Dependency Inc., 1979-81.

Awards/Recognition: Urban League of Rochester Community Leadership Service Award, 1991; JC Penney Golden Rule Award, 1988, 1990; Veteran of Foreign Wars Plaque for "Service to Country and Community," 1978.

Residence: Rochester, New York.

DANIELS, William James, Ph.D.

Born: Chicago Illinois, 1940; Moved to Rochester, 1988.
Parents: Ethel and William H. McCoy.
Family: Married to Fannie H. Daniels; One daughter, Twanda Delois Daniels.
Education: Ph.D., Public Law and Judicial Behavior, University of Iowa, 1970; MA, Public

Law and Judicial Behavior, University of Iowa, 1964; BA, Political Science, 1962; Institute of Educational Management, Harvard University, Summer 1995; Mediation Training (NYS Certified), Citizens for Law, Order and Justice, Schenectady, NY, 1981-1988; Japanese FALCON (Full-Year Asian Language Concentration) Program, Cornell University, Summer, 1980; National Science Foundation Institute on Mathematical Applications in Political Science, Virginia Polytechnic Institute, Summer, 1968; New York State Seminar of Sub-Sahara Africa and Social Change, Sienna College, 1967-68; General Electric Computer Department, General Electric 400 Basic and Macro Programming, Union College, Summer, 1966.

Career: ***Dean, College of Liberal Arts, Tenured Professor of Political Science, Rochester Institute Technology since 1988***; Associate Dean of Undergraduate Studies, Union College, 1983-1988; Associate Dean for Undergraduate Programs and Minority Affairs, Union College, 1987-88; Associate Dean of Undergraduate Studies, Union College, 1983-87; Administrative Assistant, Office of Administrative Assistant to the Chief Justice of the United States, 1978-79; Budget Officer, Higher Education Unit, New York State Division of the Budget, 1970-71; Professor of Political Science, Union College, 1966-1978, (tenured since 1979); Adjunct Professor of Political Science, Department of Political Science, SUNY, Albany, 1979; Adjunct Professor of Political Science, Department of Afro-American Studies, 1970, Graduate School of Public Affairs 1969, SUNY, Albany.

Professional/Community Involvement: Member, New York State Citizens Utility since 1994; Member, Advisory Committee, Rockefeller Institute, Study of New York State Parks, 1992-1993; Board Member, Urban League of Rochester, Inc. since 1992; Assistant Treasurer, Urban League of Rochester, Inc., 1994-95; 2nd Vice Chairperson, Urban League of Rochester, Inc. since 1995; Chairman of the Board of Directors, Citizens for Law, Order, and Justice, 1986-88; Member, Dispute Mediation Advisory Committee, Citizens for Law, Order and Justice since 1980; Volunteer Mediator, Citizens for Law, Order and Justice, 1981-88; Member, Governing Board, Bill of Rights Education Collaborative, Sponsored by the American Historical Association, American Political Science Association and the Pew Charitable Trusts, 1991-93; Member, Association of American Colleges, since 1988; Board Member, Association of American Colleges, 1992; Member, Executive Committee, Association of American Colleges, 1995; Member, Executive Council, Pi Sigma Alpha, The National Political Science Honor Society, 1989-93; Member, Political Science Oral History Advisory Committee, 1988-91; Consulting Editor, *Perspectives on Political Science*, Heldref Publications, Helen Dwight Reid Educational Foundation, Washington, D.C. since 1991; Member, Editorial Advisory Board, The Civic Arts Review, Arneson Institute for Practical Politics and Public Affairs, Ohio Wesleyan University and Charles F. Kettering Foundation since 1990; Member, American Association of University Professors since 1966; Member, American Political Science Association since 1966; Member, Trust and Development Fund Board of Trustees, American Political Science Association since 1994; Vice President, American Political Science Association, 1990-91; Member, Oral History Project, American Political Science Association, 1987-91; Chairman, Program Section on Public Law and Judicial Politics, American Political Science Association, 1985; Council Member, American Political Science Association, 1981-84; Member, Committee on the Status of Blacks in the Profession, American Political Science Association, 1974-75; Member, Advisory Committee to Develop a Thesaurus for Political Science, American Political Science Association, 1972-73; Member, Committee on Educational Policy and Programs,

DANIELS, William James, Ph.D.

American Political Science Association, 1970-71; Member, Committee on Undergraduate Instruction, American Political Science Association, 1969-73; Member, National Conference of Black Political Scientists, since 1971; President-Elect, National Conference of Black Political Scientists, 1971-72; President, National Conference of Black Political Scientists, 1972-73; Member, Executive Council, National Conference of Black Political Scientists, 1970-71; Member, American Association for Higher Education since 1986; Member, New York Political Science Association, since 1966; Member, Executive Council, New York Political Science Association, 1970-71 & 1979-80; Member, Northeastern Political Conference of Political Scientist, 1961-69; Member, American Academy of Political and Social Science, 1966-69; Member, The Japanese-American Society for Legal Scholars, 1974-85; and Member, Editorial Board, *The American Political Science Review*, 1978-1981.

Awards/Recognition: *Who's Who In American Education*, 1993-1995; *Who's Who In the East*, 1981, 1992: Liberty Bell Award, Schenectady County Bar Association 1988; Distinguished Service Award, Center for Law, Order and Justice, 1988; Certificate of Service, National Conference of Black Political Scientists, 1980, 1984; Judicial Fellowship, Tom C. Clark Award, 1978-79; Fulbright-Hays Fellowship, 1973-74; Honorary Citizen of New Orleans, 1973; Upper Iowa University, Alumni Achievement Award, 1971; Alfred E. Smith Fellowship, 1970-71; Outstanding Young Men of America, 1967; University of Iowa Fellowship, 1970-71; *Who's Who Among Students in American Universities and Colleges*, 1962; Distinguished Service Award, Alpha Phi Omega, National Service Fraternity, 1962; Pullman Educational Foundation Scholarship, 1958-62; Upper Iowa University Scholarship, 1958-62; Bausch and Lomb Honorary Science Medal, 1958.

Patents/Publications: *Governor Rockefeller in New York: The Apex of Pragmatic Liberalism*, co-authored with James Underwood, Greenwood Press, Westport, CT, 1982; "Mr. Justice Marshall and the Race for Equal Justice" in *The Burger Court: Political and Judicial Profiles*, Charles Lamb and Stephen C. Helper, Editors, University of Illinois Press, 1991 pp. 212-237; "Martin Luther King, Jr.," *The Encyclopedia of Democracy, Congressional Quarterly Book*, Washington D.C., April, 1996; "Civil Rights," *The Encyclopedia of Democracy, Congressional Quarterly Book*, Washington, D.C., April 1996; "A Great American: A Tribute to Justice Thurgood Marshall," *about...time*, Special Justice Issue, February 1993, pp.22; "Changing Times at the United States Supreme Court," about...time, June, 1992, pp. 26-28; "The Constitution, The Supreme Court and Racism: Compromises On the Way to Democracy," *National Political Science Review*, 1989, pp. 126-132; "Citizenship, Naturalization, Immigration," *Encyclopedia of the American Judicial System*, Charles Scribners Sons, New York, 1987, pp. 1137-1153; "Policies Toward Crime and Criminal Justice System," in *Rockefeller in Retrospect: The Governor's New York Legacy*, Gerald Benjamin and T. Norman Hurd, eds., *The Nelson A. Rockefeller Institute of Government*, Albany New York, 1984, pp. 250-254; "The American Judiciary," In *Government and Politics in America: Perspectives from Home and Abroad*, B. K. Shrivastava and T. W. Casstevens, eds., Radiant, Meerut, India, 1980 pp. 85-128; "Thurgood Marshall and the Administration of Criminal Justice: An Analysis of Dissenting Opinions," *The Black Law Journal*, special edition, Summer 1980, pp. 1-24; "The Geographic Factor in Appointments to the United States Supreme Court," in *Western Political Quarterly,* June, 1978, pp. 226-237; "Non Occides: Thurgood Marshall and the Death Penalty," *Texas Southern University Law Review*, Summer, 1977, pp. 243-260; "Juridical Formalism: Thurgood Marshall and the Administration of Criminal Justice," *Journal on Political Repression*, Summer, 1977, pp. 40-51; "The Supreme Court and Its Publics," Albany Law Review, June, 1973, pp. 632-661; "Public Opinion and the Supreme Court: Dominant Questions and Tentative Answers," *Politics*, Nay, 1972, pp. 67-73; "Reflections in a Black Eye, *Union College Symposium*, Summer, 1969, pp. 3-8.

Residence: Rochester, New York.

DAVIS, Ernie, 1940-1963

Born: Elmira, New York,1940; Died of leukemia, May 18, 1963; Buried in Woodland Cemetery, where author Mark Twain is buried also.
Education: Attended Elmira Free Academy, Elmira, New York; Syracuse University, 1958-1961.
Career: *A Running Back for the Syracuse Orangemen Football Team, 1958-196*1; Rushed for 2,386 yards in three seasons, Eclipsing the school records of his idol, Jim Brown; the focal point of Syracuse's 1959 national championship football team; Helped Syracuse cap an 11-0 season with a 23-14 victory against Texas in the Cotton Bowl; Art Modell owner of the Cleveland Browns traded All-Pro flanker Bobby Mitchell to the Washington Redskins for the rights to Davis; Diagnosed with leukemia shortly after signing with the Brown; Never played for the Cleveland Browns; Played with the Browns basketball team during the winter of 1962-63.

Awards/Recognition: First Black winner of the Heisman Trophy, an annual award to the nation's top collegiate football player; Earned 11 varsity letters at Elmira Free Academy; All-American honors in football and basketball; 10,000 mourners attended his funeral; A $75,000 life-sized bronze statue was erected in June 1988 on the grounds of the Ernie Davis Junior High School in Elmira; The statue was the work of Bruno Luc-

chesi; A scholarship was established in his name that same year.

Eulogies/Quotations:

"The world was his oyster...He had everything going for him at the time, Looks, Ability, Character, Charm, Youth. Just about anyone would have trade places with him."

> John Brown, Davis' college teammate and closest friend.
> *Times Union*, Jan 19, 1960

"The thing that bothers me is that there probably are a lot of young people who attend Ernie Davis Junior High who don't even know who he was...Maybe this will prompt some of them to learn about his story of courage, Maybe he can be a role model."

> Marty Harrigan, Davis' high school coach, commenting on the statue erected in Davis' honor.
> *Times Union*, Jan 19, 1960

"Whenever he went into the hospital, he would tell me to tell anybody who called for him that he was out of town...He didn't want anybody to feel sorry for him. He kept such an upbeat, positive outlook right to the end."

> John Brown, Davis' college teammate and closest friend.
> *Times Union*, Jan 19, 1960

"He 'd always tell me, 'Don't worry, Mr. Modell, I'm going to shake this thing and play 10 years and lead the Browns to some championships. I'm going to give you your money's worth."

> Ernie Davis, referring to his leukemia.
> *Times Union*, Jan 19, 1960

"We got into the lobby of the theater, and there's this lady there, and she asks Ernie for some money so she can get a meal...Ernie gives her his 50 cents. He convinces me to give up mine, too. We never did see the movie because we were out of money. We wound up going back to the dorm. But that was Ernie. Always generous. Always looking out tor others."

> John Mackey, former All-Pro tight end with the Baltimore Colts, remembering a time during Davis' senior year at Syracuse when the two scrounged up just enough money to take in a movie.
> *Times Union*, Jan 19, 1960

"Imagine that"...The president of the United States wanting to meet me. I got to shake hands with him. That was almost as big a thrill as winning the Heisman."

Ernie Davis, commenting when President John F. Kennedy asked to meet him after the Heisman awards ceremony at the Downtown Athletic Club in Manhattan. <u>Times Union</u>, Jan 19, 1960

"To this day, I regret that he didn't at least get to play one official play in the NFL...I think that would have made him feel that his life was complete."

Art Modell, owner of the Cleveland Browns <u>Times Union</u>, Jan 19, 1960

"All of us are born with grace, few of us die with it."

Marty Harrigan, Davis' high school coach <u>Times Union</u>, Jan 19, 1960

DAVIS, Beverly A., Ph.D.

Born: Townsend, Delaware, 1939; Moved to Rochester, 1961.

Parents: Marion Pettiford and William Andrew Davis.

Family: Two children, Jini Elizabeth and Joshua Eric.

Education: Doctor of Philosophy in Education, Century University, Albuquerque, New Mexico, 1995; Certificate of Advanced Studies in Educational Administration, SUNY Brockport, 1986; Master's Degree, Counseling, University of Rochester, Rochester, New York, 1968; B.S., Science in Elementary Education, Delaware State College, Dover, Delaware.

Career*: Education Consultant and Author since 1996*; Rochester City School District, 1968-1996: Supervising Director, Safe Schools and Community Relations, 1994-96; Coordinating Director, External Relations and Community Planning, 1992-94; Director, Human Resources, 1991-92; Director, Organization Development, 1989-91; Supervisor, Staff Development, 1986-89; Secondary School Guidance Counselor, 1968-86; Elementary Classroom Teacher, 1961-

68; Adjunct Professor, Nazareth College, Rochester, New York, 1992-93.

Professional/Community Involvement: Member and Director of Christian Education, Zion Hill Missionary Baptist Church; Member, Urban League of Rochester; Rochester Urban League Guild; Past Member, Advisory Council of SUNY Brockport Educational Opportunity Center (E.O.C.), Alpha Kappa Alpha Sorority; National Alliance of Black School Educators; Past Member, Advisory Council, SUNY Brockport; Treasurer, Bamako-Rochester Sister Cities Committee; International Medicine Programs, University of Rochester; Board Member, Families & Friends of Murdered Children & Victims of Violence; Past Board Member, The Harley School, and The Center For Dispute Settlement; Board Member, Genesee Region Home Care; Frederick Douglass Museum and Cultural Center and Boys & Girls Club of Rochester.

Awards/Recognition: Co-Teacher of the Year, 1978; Phi Delta Kappa Service Award, 1990; Salute to Local Leaders, "I Dream A World"; Urban League Community Service Award; Dr. Martin Luther King Leadership Conference Award; Chapter 1 Professional Service Award; Community School Council Outstanding Volunteer Service Award; Rochester LINKS Inc., Salute to Black Women, International Trends and Services Award; Black Business Association, Professional Accomplishment Award; Black Educators Association of Rochester, Inc., Contribution to Education Award.

Patents/Publications: *'Bout My People and a Little Bit More* (poetry), B. A. Davis and T. M. Associates, 1995; *Preparing Black Children for School and Life, Pre-Pregnancy to Age Five* (A Guide for Parents and Educators), B. A. Davis and T.M. Associates; "Journey to An Ancestral Homeland" in *The Dogan Universe, Another*

World's Wonder; *'Bout My People* (tape of Children Songs and Poems).

Residence: Rochester, New York.

DELAPERRIERE, Earleen, Ph.D.

Born: Saginau, Michigan; Moved to Rochester, 1989. **Parents**: Mabel Burden and James DeLaPerriere (both deceased).
Family: Single.
Education: Ph.D., American Culture, University of Michigan, 1987; MA, American Culture, University of Michigan, 1976; MA, English Language and Literature, University of Michigan, 1974; BA, English Language and Literature, 1973.

Career: *Assistant Professor of English, SUNY College at Brockport since 1989*; English Teacher, Huron High School, Ann Arbor, Michigan, 1987-88; English Teacher, Pioneer High School, Ann Arbor, Michigan, 1986-87; Program Staff, Training Module for Trainers, School of Education, University of Michigan, 1985-86; Campus Academic Dean, Jordan College-Flint Campus, 1982-83; Teacher Developmental English, Pre-College Seminar, University of Michigan, 1972-83;

Professional/Community Involvement: Humanities Chairwoman, Rochester Chapter of the NAACP's Afro-Academic Cultural and Technological Scientific Olympics Program (ACT-SO), 1992; Member, Dreiser Studies Society, Metropolitan Women's Network, National Congress of Black Faculty, National Council of Teachers of English, Northeast Popular Culture Association; Member, Board of Directors, New York Folklore Society; Book Review Editor, Journal of African and Afro-American Affairs at the Flint Campus, University of Michigan, under the editorship of Dr. Levi Nwachuku; Coordinator, Annual Black History Month Commemoration; Consultant, Judge of Folk Arts Proposals, State of Massachusetts Arts Council, 1991; Judge of Kwanzaa Celebration at Center for African American Culture in Rochester, 1992; Teacher in Camp Liberty Program at SUNY Brockport, 1991; Lecturer on "Great Kings of Africa" for Anheuser-Bush, 1991.

Awards/Recognition: Workshop Presentation Award, Black Family Conference, Rochester New York 1991; Distinguished Service Award, Saginaw County Community Action Council, 1981; Outstanding Faculty Award, University of Michigan, 1977-78, and 1978-79; Community Programmer Award, WFBE-FM Radio (Folklore series), 1980; National Media Woman of The Year, 1980.

Patents/Publications: "Sister Carrie, Sisters in Sable Skin, and Gestures of Exclusions", in *Dreiser Studies*, Vol. 21, No 2, Fall 1990; Author of *Developmental English Handbook*, a textbook, 1980;"Go-Long", published in *American Speech*, Summer 1980; Editor and *Contributing Poet, Nascence of Natural Art*, 1977; Contributing Poet, *Feelings*, an anthology, 1982; over eight Invited Lectures from 1977-1991.

Residence: Brockport, New York

DIGGS, Kathleen Moore

Born: High Point, N.C., March 9, 1922; Moved to Rochester, 1946.
Parents: Elbert E., and Laney Moore.
Family: Married to Cleveland Diggs (deceased); one son, Robert C. Diggs.
Education: GED, Monroe High School; Psychology courses, Monroe Community College; Teacher Training for Rural Disadvantaged Migrant Children, Geneseo University College of Arts & Science.

Career: *Retired Teacher/Guidance Aide for the City School District*; Veteran of World War II- U.S. Army.

Professional/Community Involvement: Has been a major force informing the Rochester Chapter of the Black War Veterans of the United States Inc., which received its charter on October 20 1991; Organization has been since named officially The Black War Veterans of the United States Association, Inc, Crispus Attucks Post # 1 (Crispus Attucks was the First Black Hero to die in America's Fight for Freedom, during the Boston Massacre-Revolutionary War); Founded Black War Vets of the U.S. Association, Inc., March 5, 1993 (Crispus Attucks Day); Member, Congresswoman Louise M. Slaughter's Veteran's Advisory Board; Life Member, American Veterans of World War II Korea and Vietnam (AMVETS Henry Pollard Post # 5, Buffalo, NY); Board Member, Genesee Valley Veterans Housing Council; In the process of establishing the "Upward Bound Veterans Community Center".

Awards/Recognition: Honorable Discharge Certificate from the U.S. Army; World War II Victory Medal; Women Army Corps Service Medal; Honorable Service Lapel Button, 1943; Recognized by the Department of Veterans Affairs, Canandaigua N.Y., 1992-93; Pennington/Moye VFW Post #9251, Rochester New York; American Legion Post #1952; The only known Black Woman Commander of a Veterans Post; American Legion-Florence Nightingale Post #309.

Residence: Rochester, New York.

DIXON, Geraldine L.

Born: East Saint Louis, Illinois, March 16, 1946.
Parents: Both deceased.
Family: Married to Rev. Roosevelt Dixon, Pastor of Grace-Unity Fellowship Church; Two children, Roderick L., and Maija C. Dixon.

Education: Licensed Funeral Director, Simon's School of Mortuary Science, Syracuse New York, 1972; Graduated from California School of Nail Techniques, 1977; Attended Monroe Community College, Medical Technology, 1968-70; Attended Robert Wesleyan College, Human Resource Management, 1988-90.

Career: *Owner and Manager, G. L. Dixon Funeral Home, founded in1989*; Project Advisor, Continuing Education, Rochester School District, 1987; Chief Mortician of Pathology, University of Rochester School of Medicine, 1978-85; Funeral Director/Public Relations/Office Management, Millard E. Latimer & Son Funeral Home, 1977-79; Manager, Buffalo Memorial Chapels, Inc., Buffalo, New York 1972-77; Technical Engineer, WROC-TV, 1969-70.

Awards/Recognition: Frigid Fluid Award for Embalming Excellence,1972; Rochester Gas & Electric Business Award, 1991, 1993.

Residence: Rochester, New York.

DORSEY, Gwendolyn

Born: Pittsburgh, PA, 1950; Moved to Rochester, 1960.
Parents: Elizabeth Dorsey McGee and Charles McGee.
Family: One daughter, Taisei Lens McCullough-Johnson.
Education: ABA Lawyers Assistant/Paralegal Program, Roosevelt University, Chicago Illinois, 1986; Radio Broadcasting Program, Omega School of Communications, Chicago Illinois, 1979.

Career: *President, and Founder of Dorsey P.R. & Media Communications, "Rochester's first African-American owned Full Service Public Relations/Advertising Agency,"* December

1992; Public Relations/Marketing Director for Unique Audio & Video Concepts, 1992; Human Resources Director, WHAM/WVOR Radio, 1986-1992; FMC Corporation, Chicago, Illinois; Paralegal/Legal Assistant, 1980-1986; Office Manager, 1979-80; Supervisor, Purchasing Department, 1972-1980; Public Relations Assistant, Rochester Gas & Electric Company, 1968-1972.

Professional/Community Involvement: Public Relations Committee, Action For a Better Community (ABC), 1991-92; Media Coordinator, Ad Council (Rochester Advertising Council), 1992-93; Board Member and Chairperson of the Public Relations/Communications Committee of Big Brothers/Big Sisters, 1992-93; Member, Black Business Owners Association (BBOA), 1992-93; Freddie Thomas Foundation Board of Directors, 1991-1993; National Association For The Advancement of Colored People (NAACP-Rochester); Rochester Association of Black Communicators (RABC); Rochester Events Network (REN, formerly Rochester Downtown Trust Fund) Board of Directors, 1991-93; Urban League of Rochester's Public Relations Committee; Women's Council (Chamber of Commerce), 1991-93; Grantmakers Forum Board of Directors (Communication Committee Member) 1992-93; Martin Luther King, Jr. Greater Rochester Commission (Chairperson, Public Relations/Communications Committee); Member, United Way Speaker's Bureau, 1992-93; American Red Cross Rochester-Monroe County Chapter Board of Directors, 1993-94; Listed in the Diversity Resource Directory of Rochester Area Volunteers: Published by The Philanthropic Diversity Consortium of the Rochester (NY) Region, 1993-1994.

Awards/Recognition: 1993 Recipient of Rochester Gas & ElectricBusiness Award.

Residence: Brighton, New York

DORWAY, Gordon, 1961-1995

Born: Brooklyn's Bedford-Stuyvesant Neighborhood, 1961; Died, August 16, 1995.
Parents: Edris and David Doorway, from Guyana, South America.
Family: Single.
Education: B.S., Aerospace Engineering, Boston University, 1982;Enrolled in Master's degree Program, Secondary Education, Brooklyn College, 1987.

Career: *Chemistry Teacher, Franklin High School, 1990-1995;* Coordinator of Technology Department (Acting A.P.), New York City Board of Education, 1988; Dean/Mathematics Instructor, New York City Board of Education, 1985; Mathematics/Computer Instructor, New York City Board of Education, 1984; Research Consultant, Gibbs and Cox, Incorporated, New York City, 1984.

Awards/Recognition: Special Series in Democrat & Chronicle Newspaper: "Working in Mr. D's Class, A Year of Discovery," by reporter Linda K. Wertheimer and Photographer Will Yurman, 1992. The Rochester Teachers Association instituted a memorial scholarship in his honor in 1996.

Patents/Publications: Co-Host of *Homework Hotline* (an interactive children's show on Public Broadcasting Station), WXXI-TV 21.

DOUGLAS, Benjamin, The Honorable

Born: Washington, D.C., 1946; Moved to Rochester, 1974.
Family: Married with two children.
Education: MBA, University of Pittsburgh, 1974; B.S., Physics, Fisk University, 1968.

The Honorable Benjamin Douglas
Photo, Mike F. Molaire. Copyright 1998,, Norex Publications.

Career: *City of Rochester Councilman since 1992*; City School Board Member, 1986-1992; President, City School Board, 1988-89; Workplace Program Manager for American Red Cross; Former Manager at Jet Enterprises; former Budget Analyst for Xerox Corporation; former Engineer, PBG Industries;

Professional/Community Involvement: Member, Board of Directors, Genesee Settlement House; Former Member, Junior League of America Advisory Committee and Center For Dispute Settlement Board.

Awards/Recognition: Distinguished Citizen Award, 1992.

Residence: Rochester, New York.

DOUGLASS, Frederick, 1818-1895

Born: Frederick Augustus Bailey, February 1818, Tuckahoe, Talbort County, Maryland; Changed his name at first to Frederick Johnson, then to Frederick Douglass after escaping from slavery in 1838; Lived in Rochester, 1847-1872; Died in Washington, D.C., 1895.
Parents: Mothered by Harriet Bailey; Father reported to be his mother's white master; Grandparents, Betsy and Isaac Bailey.
Family: Married Anna Murray (daughter of Mary and Bambarra Murray and a free slave), 1838, in New York City; Anna Murray Douglass died in 1882 and is buried in Mt Hope Cemetery near the grave of Douglass; Married Helen Pitts, a white woman, 1884 after Annas death; Helen Pitts Douglass is buried also in Mt Hope Cemetery near Douglass' grave.
Children: Rosetta, June 24, 1839, and Lewis Henry, Oct. 9, 1840, New Bedford, Massachusetts; Frederick Douglass, Jr., March 3,1842, Lynn, Massachusetts; Charles Redmon, second son, 1845; Annie, fifth and last child, March 22, 1849 in Rochester, NY.

Career: Worked for Captain Aaron Anthony, 1824; Worked for Hugh Auld, Baltimore, Maryland, 1826; Worked on the Anthony farm for Thomas Auld, 1833; Worked for Edward Covey, 1834; Worked for Williams Freeland, 1835; Attempted to escape and imprisoned, 1836; Met Anna Murray, 1837; Escaped to New York and married Anna Murray, 1838; Spoke at the American Anti-Slavery Society meeting, 1841; Began lecture tour, 1847; Began the North Star newspaper in Rochester, New York, 1847; Attended the first women's rights convention, 1848; Urged women to fight for the vote, 1848; Became involved in the Underground railroad, 1850; Broke with William Garrison, 1851; Began lecture in England, 1859; Met with President Abraham Lincoln, 1863; Met with President Andrew Johnson to discuss Black suffrage, 1866; Declined President Johnson's offer to head Freedman's Bureau, 1867; Appointed Assistant Secretary to the Commission of Inquiry into the possible annexation of Santo Domingo, 1871; Nominated for vice-president by Equal Rights Party on a presidential ticket headed by Victoria Woodhull, 1872; Became president of the Freedman's Saving and Trust Company, 1874; Became U.S. Marshall, 1877; Appointed Recorder of Deeds for Washington, D.C., 1880; Became American Consul-general to Haiti, 1889; Resigned the Haiti post and returned to the U.S.

Awards/Recognition: Nominated for the office of State of New York by the Liberal Party, the first American Negro to be accorded such an honor, August 1855; 19th Century America's most famous Black leader; One of America's greatest citizens in the likes of Lincoln and Jefferson; Honored with a 25-cent postage stamp, 1967; The Frederick Douglass Memorial Monument, the first national monument honoring a Black man was unveiled on June 9, 1899, Rochester, NY,

Patents/Publications: *The North Star Newspaper*, Rochester, NY, began in 1847; *Narrative of The Life of Frederick Douglass, An American Slave* (5000 copies), Frederick Douglass, May 1845; *My Bondage and My Freedom,* Frederick Douglass, May 11, 1855; Editor and owner of the *New National Era* newspaper whose goal was to herald the progress of Blacks throughout the country, 1870-1874; *Life and Times of Frederick Douglass*, Frederick Douglass, 1881; *Escape From Slavery*, Frederick Douglass, edited and illustrated by Michael McCurdy, Alfred A. Knopf; His speeches, letters and newspaper pieces are

compiled in, *The Life and Writings of Frederick Douglass*, a five-volume set, Professor Phillip Foner, editor, International Publishers; *The Frederick Douglass Papers*, Professor John Blassingame, editor, Yale University Press; *The Frederick Douglass Papers*, Professor John W. McKivigan, editor, West Virginia University.

Eulogies/Quotations:

"While it is that Anna never learned to read and write, she was the source and strength of all my success in the formative and as well as the maturing years of my life, a companion who was truly a helpmate."

Frederick Douglass
"A short Frederick Douglass Biography"

"As a speaker, he has few equals...He has wit, arguments, sarcasm, pathos-all that first rate men show in their master effort."

Herald of Freedom newspaper, Concord Massachusetts, praising Douglass at the beginning of his oratory career, 1851.

"This proves I am impartial. My first wife was the color of my mother and the second, the color of my father."

Frederick Douglass, commenting laughingly about his second marriage to Helen (Pitts) Douglass.
<u>Genesee Valley Woman</u>, *1743-1983, pp 96,* Irene A. Beale, Chestnut Hill Press, Geneseo, NY, 1985.

"Love came to me, and I was not afraid to marry the man I loved because of his color."

Helen (Pitts) Douglass
<u>Genesee Valley Woman</u>, *1743-1983, pp 96,* Irene A. Beale, Chestnut Hill Press, Geneseo, NY, 1985.

"There are many colored ladies of my acquaintance who are as good as I and who are a great deal better educated, yet in affairs of this nature, who is to decide the why and the wherefor?"

Frederick Douglass, commenting about his second marriage to Helen (Pitts) Douglass.
<u>Genesee Valley Woman</u>, *1743-1983, pp 98,* Iene A. Beale, Chestnut Hill Press, Geneseo, NY, 1985.

"What to the American slave is your Fourth of July? I answer, a day reveals to him more than all the other

The Talman Building, 25 East Main Street.

Photo, Mike Molaire. Copyright 1998, Norex Publications.

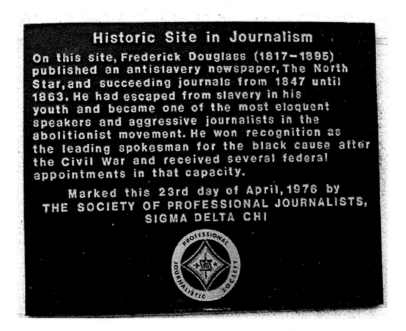

Frederick Douglass, 1818-1895
Photo Courtesy Rundel Rochester Public Library.

days of the year, the gross injustice and cruelty to which he is the constant victim...To him your celebration is a sham...a thin veil to cover up crimes which would disgrace a nation of savages. There is not a nation of the earth guilty of practices more shocking and bloody than are the people of the United States."

Frederick Douglass, speech in Rochester on Independence Day of 1852
Rochester Years
http://www.rochester.edu/douglass/part3.html

"The paper became my meat and drink...My soul was set all on fire."

Frederick Douglass, commenting on the Liberator, William Lloyd Garrison's newspaper.
From Slave to Abolitionist/Editor
http://www.rochester.edu/class/douglass/part2.html

"Power concedes nothing without a demand. It never did, and it never will. Find out just what people will submit to, and you have found out the exact amount of injustice and wrong which will continue till they have resisted with either words or blows, or with both. The limits of tyrants are prescribed by the endurance of those whom they suppress."

Frederick Douglass

"Right is of no sex-Truth is of no color-God is the father of us all, and we are all Brethren."

Motto on North Star masthead
"Rochester Years"

"Rebellion has been subdued, slavery abolished, and peace proclaimed, and yet our work is not done...We are face to face with the same old enemy of liberty and progress...The South today is a field of blood."

Frederick Douglass, commenting on the terrorist tactics of the Klan.

"I shall treat with unmitigated scorn and contempt any paltry imitation of a man who can find no better reason for offering me an insult than that his skin differs in color from mine."

Frederick Douglass
Oct. 11, 1858

"He was born a slave...He was a mere piece of valuable property-simply and only a thing!...And yet, life was as dear to him, and liberty as sweet, as to any of us...

Honorable William A. Sutherland, at Douglass Monument unveiling, June 9, 1899, Rochester NY

"I am proud to do my part in honoring the memory of a man who was worthy of his race, because he was worthy representative of the American nation."

Honorable Theodore Roosevelt, Governor of New York, at Douglass Monument unveiling, June 9, 1899, Rochester NY.

ELY, Michele

Born: Buffalo, New York, 1947; Moved to Rochester, 1964.

Parents: Edith L. Knuckles and James C. Knuckles, Sr.

Family: Married to James S. Ely, Jr.; Six children, Cynthia, Victoria, Maude, James, Michael, Nicole Ely; Eight grandchildren.

Education: BA, English, University of Rochester, 1969; Leadership Rochester, Class of 1996; National Coalition Building Institute, Rochester NY, Train-the-Trainer, 1994.

Career: Consultant, Title I Paraprofessional, Rochester School District since 1991; Corporate Vice President, Photogenesis Camera and Video, LTD., 1972-88; First Female Claims Adjuster, Allstate Insurance Company, 1969-72.

Professional/Community Involvement: Life Member, Metropolitan Women's Network of Rochester; Board Member, Children Awaiting Parents- publisher of The CAP BOOK, Rochester, NY (since 1977);President (1980-83 and 1985-86); Member, Effective Parenting Information for Children (EPIC) Facilitator since 1991; National Coalition Building Institute (NCBI) Trainer since 1994; Co-Organizer, University of Rochester Black Alumni Group, 1988-1993; Rochester Riverside Convention Center Management Corporation, 1986-92; Rochester City Planning Commission, 1984-91; Monroe Marlins Swim Team (YMCA) Parent Volunteer, 1977-91.

Awards/Recognition: White Rose Award for Services to Youth, The Links, Inc., 1997: Finalist, Rave Award, United Way of Greater Rochester, 1988.

EVANS JR., James H., Ph.D.

Born: Detroit, Michigan, 1950; Moved to Rochester, 1979.
Parents: Mrs. Annie B. Evans and Rev. James H. Evans, Sr.
Family: Married to Linda Hickmon Evans; Three children, Jamila, Jumaane, & James III.
Education: Ph.D, Union Theological Seminary, New York, 1979; Masters' Degree, Philosophy, Union Theological Seminary, New York, 1979; Master's Degree, Divinity, Yale University Divinity School, 1975; A. B. Degree, University of Michigan, 1971; Ordained at the Immanuel Baptist Church, New Haven, CT, 1973.

Career: *First Black President of the 174-year old Colgate Rochester Divinity School/Bexley Hall/Crozer Theological Seminary since 1990*; Dean of Black Church Studies, 1989; Visiting Associate Professor of Religious Studies, University of Rochester, New York, 1988; Associate Professor, Martin Luther King, Jr. Memorial Professor of Theology and Black Studies, Colgate Rochester Divinity School, 1984-1988; Adjunct Associate Professor of English, University of Rochester, NY, 1989-90; Visiting Professor of Theology, Princeton Theological Seminary, Princeton NJ, 1984-85; Assistant Professor of Theology and Black Church Studies, Colgate Rochester Divinity School, 1980-84; Adjunct Assistant Professor of English, University of Rochester, 1983; Acting Director of the Program of Black Church Studies and of the Alternate Education Program, Colgate Rochester Divinity School, 1979-1982; Associate Pastor, Chambers Memorial Baptist Church, New York, NY, 1975-1979; Tutor in Systematic Theology, Union Theological Seminary, New York, NY, 1977-78; Faculty Member in the Study Skills Department, Malcolm-King College, New York, NY, 1977; Research Assistant, New Haven Afro-American Historical Society, New Haven, CT, 1975; Student Chaplain, Southern Connecticut State College, New Haven, CT, 1974-75.

Professional/Community Involvement: President of the American Baptist Association of Seminary Administrators since 1995; Member, General Board of the American Baptist Churches, U.S.A. since 1995; Member, George Eastman House Board since 1995; Social Action Network (SAN) Blue Ribbon Committee since 1995; Martin Luther King Greater Rochester Commission since 1995; Chair, Martin Luther King, Jr. Greater Rochester Commission, 1991-94; Board Member, Al Sig'l Center of Rochester, NY since 1993; Marine Midland Bank of Rochester since 1993; United Way of Greater Rochester since 1991; Rochester Jobs, Inc. since 1991; Rochester Area Colleges, Inc.(RAC), since 1990; Member, Greater Rochester Metro Chamber of Commerce CEO Roundtable since 1990; Chair, Higher Education Division, 1991 United Way Campaign, 1991; Member, Editorial Board, *Journal of American Academy of Religion*, 1989; Member, Baptist Theology Project, American Baptist Churches, Division of Education Ministries, 1987; Member, Issues Research Advisory Committee, ATS since 1984; ATS Accreditation Team, 1987; Omega Psi Fraternity, American Academy of Religion, Society for the Study of Black Religion (SSBR), The American Baptist Churches, U.S.A., Eastern Commission on Ministry, International Association of University Presidents (IAUP), Council of Independent Colleges (CIC), Baptist World Congress, American Council on Education (ACE), Industrial Management Council of Rochester (IMC), Greater Rochester Visitors Association, Inc., Greater Rochester Metro Chamber of Commerce, Rochester Rotary Club.

EVANS JR., James H., Ph.D.

Awards/Recognition: Stone Lecturer, Princeton Theological Seminary, 1996; Williams Lecturer, Methodist Theological School in Ohio, 1995; Hoover Lecturer, Disciples House, University of Chicago Divinity School, 1995; Doctor of Letters (Lit.), Honoris Causa, Colgate University; 1991-92 Distinguished Alumnus, Cranbrook Alumni Council, Cranbrook Schools; National TRIO Achievers Award, National Council of Educational Opportunity Associations, 1986; Union Theological Seminary Graduate Fellowship, 1975-77; George Day Fellowship, Yale University Divinity School, 1975; First Black member of the exclusive 90-year-old Oak Hill Country Club.

Patents/Publications: Author, *We Shall All Be Saved: Social Problems and Theological Renewal*, Fortress Press (forthcoming); *We Have Been Believers: An African American Systematic Theology*, Fortress Press, 1992; *Black Theology: A Critical Assessment and Annotated Bibliography*, Greenwood Press, 1987; *Spiritual Empowerment in Afro-American Literature: Frederick Douglass, Booker T. Washington, Rebecca Jackson, Richard Wright, and Toni Morrison*, Edwin Mellen Press, 1987; "Eschatology, White Supremacy, and the Beloved Community," in *Reconstructing Christian Theology*, Fortress Press, 1994; "Literature and Theological Education: Notes on a Resurrected Romance," in *Theological Education, Sacred Imagination: The Arts and Theological Education*, Vol. XXXI, No. 1, Autumn 1994; "What is the Character of the Institutional Resources Needed for the Good Theological School?" in Theological Education, The Good Theological School, Vol. XXX, No 2, Spring 1994; "Black Theology," in *New Handbook of Christian Theology*, Abingdon Press, 1992; "The Graduate Education of Future Theological Faculties," *Theological Education*, Autumn 1991; "A Christian response to the Israeli/Palestinian Conflict, "Minister: A Journal of the American Baptist Ministers Council (Val-

ley Forge, PA), Vol. XII, No 1, Fall 1991; "Women, Men and Black Theology," in *Redefining Sexual Ethics, A Sourcebook of Essays, Stories, and Poems,* The Pilgrim Press, 1991; "African-American Christianity and the Postmodern Condition," *Journal of the American Academy of Religion,* Vol. LVIII, No 2, 1990; "Deconstructing the Tradition: Narrative Strategies in Nascent Black Theology," *Union Seminary Quarterly Review* 44, 1990; "Black Church Studies and the Theological Curriculum," in *African-American Religious Studies: An Interdisciplinary Anthology*, ed. Gayraud S. Wilmore, Duke University Press, 1989; "To Study War No More: Martin Luther King, Jr. and Non-Violent Resistance," *A.M.E. Zion Quarterly Review*, January, 1988; "Prisoner of the Flesh: A Literary Analysis of Augustine's Confessions," The A.M.E. Zion Quarterly Review, January, 1987; "Faith and Praxis in Theology," *Counseling and Values*, October 1986; "Black Theology and Cuban Theology: The Emerging Dialogue," *Christian Century,* October 29, 1986; "Whither the Dream?: Martin Luther King, Jr. and The Black Church," *The American Baptist Quarterly*, April 1986; "The Struggle for Identity: Black People in The Church of England," *Theology and Racism 2*, Fall 1985; " I Rose and Found My Voice: Black Church Studies and Theological Education," *Theological Education*, Spring 1985; "Toward an Afro-American Theology," *The Journal of Religious Thought*, Spring-Summer 1984; "Afro-American Theology and Marxist Thought," *The A.M.E._Zion Quarterly Review*, April 1983; "Liberation Authority and the Cognitive Crisis in the Theology of David Tracy, " *Union Seminary Quarterly Review,* Fall 1983; "Apartheid, as Idolatry," *Christianity and Crisis*, December 14, 1981; "Black Theology and Black Feminism," Journal of Religious Thought, Spring-Summer 1981; Presented over 25 major papers and lectures.

Residence: Pittsford, New York.

EVERETT, John R.

Born: Montezuma, Georgia, 1936; Moved to Rochester, 1969.
Parents: John B. and Rosie L. Everett.
Family: Married to Bernice; Two daughters, Jocelyn, and Jennean.
Education: B.S., Chemistry; JD, Law, St. John University Law School.

Career: *Patent Counsel and Attorney-at-Law, Eastman Kodak Research Labs since 1969*; Chair of the Intellectual Property Section, National Bar Association; Member, International Committee, AIPLA.

Awards/Recognition: Various awards from the Urban League of Rochester, the United Way, and National Bar Association; The first Black to be elected to the Board of Directors of Bankers Trust Company of Rochester in 1975.

Residence: Rochester, New York.

FAGAN, Garth

Born: Kingston, Jamaica; Moved to Rochester, 1970.
Parents: Louise I. Walker and S.W. Fagan
Education: BA Degree, Wayne State University; Studied dance with Ivy Baxter, Pearl Primus, Lavinia Williams, Martha Graham, Jose Limon, Mary Hinkson, and Alvin Ailey.

Career: *Founder, Artistic Director, President and Chief Executive Officer of Garth Fagan Dance;* Began the company in 1970; Distinguished University Professor of Dance at SUNY Brockport; The company has toured throughout the US and abroad with performances throughout Europe, Australia, New Zeland, Brazil, Asia, Africa, The Near East, Jamaica, and Bermuda.

Professional/Community Involvement: Board Member, Dance USA, and the New York Foundation for the Arts; Panelist for the New York State Council on the Arts, and a Consultant for the National Endowment for the Arts.

Awards/Recognition: Tony Award, Best Choreographer for the *Lion King*, Disney's big Broadway hit, June 1998; Outer Critics Circle Award for outstanding choreography, *The Lion King*, 1998; Fred Astaire Award for best choreography, Theatre Development Fund, 1998; Drama Desk Award for Choreography, 1998; Fulbright 5th Aniversary Distinguished Fellow (one of 25 people nationally so designated), 1996; Dance Magazine Award for "Significant Contributions to Dance during a Distinguished Career," 1990; Recommended by the N.Y. Times as the "Critics Choice"; selected by the Los Angeles Times as one of the Faces for the 90's, January, 1990; Recipient of the "Bessie" Award (New York Performance Award, Dance World's equivalent to an Oscar) for Sustained Achievement; Holds several Honorary Doctorates; Recipient of a Guggenheim Fellowship and a National Endowment for the Arts three-year Choreography Fellowship.

Residence: Rochester, New York.

Quotations:

"I feel absolutely honored...The Tony is the big one, and I'am proud that Rochester took it."
    Garth Fagan
    D&C, June 8, 1998

"Rochester often doesn't get behind unless the world does...What Garth accomplished by combining many forms of art in the Lion King is extremely difficult to pull off. He did it wonderfully, and he deserves our congratulations."
    imothy Draper, director of the Rochester City Ballet
    D&C, June 8, 1998

Garth Fagan, receiving a recognition plaque from the City of Rochester for winning the 1998 Tony Award for choreography.

Photo, Mike F. Molaire. Copyright 1998, Norex Publications.

FAGBAYI, Mutiu O.

Born: Lagos, Nigeria, 1953; Moved to Rochester, 1977.

Family: Married to Patricia Fagbayi; Two children, Jumolle, Yinka.

Education: MS, Chemical Engineering, Pennsylvania State University, 1978; B.S., University of Dayton, Ohio, 1976.

Career: *Chief Operating Officer, National Center on Education and the Economy in Rochester, 1992-1995*; Director of Education Programs, Eastman Kodak Company, 1991-92; Also former Manager of the Kodak 21st Century Learning Challenge (a partnership to improve math and science achievement of students); Business Research, 1985; Research Scientist, Research Laboratories, 1978-85.

Professional/Community Involvement: Involved with the Oxford International Roundtable on Education Policy, based in England; Advisory Board Member of Industry and Higher Education, a Quarterly Journal; National Advisory Council of the National Engineering Education Coalition, with aims to increase the number of engineering graduates, particularly among women and minorities; Former President, Rochester Chapter of the National Organization of Black Chemist and Chemical Engineers, (NOBCChE); Co-Founder, NOBCChE Adopt-a-School Program to engage Rochester Inner City Elementary Students in Science and Computer Literacy.

Residence: Penfield, New York.

FAGBAYI, Patricia

Born: Eleuthera, Bahamas, in 1955; Moved to Rochester, 1977
Parents: Rachel Martin and Audley Rusell.
Family: Married to Mutiu Fagbayi; Two children, Jumolle, Yinka.
Education: MS, Chemical Engineering, University of Rochester, 1982; B.S. Engineering, University of Dayton, 1977.

Career: President & Founder of Bliss Unlimited, Inc. since 1993; Bliss Unlimited major areas of focus include Personal & Organizational Transformation, Achieving Full Potential, Unifying Purpose with Action and Getting What We Desire; Founder and President, The Russell Group, 1993-1995; the Russell Group conducted seminars in the area of Empowerment, Diversity, Strategic Management, and Organizational Transformation for corporate clients, educational institutions and professional groups; Eastman Kodak Company, 1982-1993: Supervisor, Making Dept., Emulsion Manufacturing, Black & White Film Manufacturing, Kodak Park, 1992-93; Supervisor, Process Excellence Group, Melt/Coat Manufacturing Unit, Black & White Film Manufacturing, KP, 1992; Senior Engineer, Black & White Film Manufacturing, KP, 1990-91; Product Engineer, Professional Film Manufacturing, Professional Imaging; 1988-89; Total Quality Control Engineer, Professional Film Manufacturing, 1987-88; Applications Engineer, Emulsion Processing Division, Material Research & Engineering Organization, 1986-87; Quality Consultant, Quality Technology Unit, Material Quality Assurance Organization, 1984-86; Product Engineer, Manufacturing Assurance Organization, 1982-84; Process Engineer, Xerox Corporation, 1977-1982.

Professional/Community Involvement: Member, Business Evolution Network, Rochester Chapter, formerly World Business Academy since 1997; President, United Nations Association of Rochester, 1996-97; Vice President, Rochester Association for the United Nations, 1995-96; Board Member, Rochester Association for the United Nations, 1993-97; Black Business Association-Chair, Corporate Development Committee since 1997; Board Member, The Women's Council of the Rochester Chamber of Commerce since 1997; Member, Society of Human Resource Management, 1993-96; Secretary, National Black MBA Association, Western New York Chapter, 1994-95; Member, National Organization of Black Chemists & Chemical Engineers,(NOBCCHE) 1990-95; Board Member, NOBCChE, 1990-1991; Mentor, Minority Achiever's Program, 1996-97.

Awards/Recognition: 1994 Nominee for the nationally recognized Athena Award, an award honoring women in business;

Residence: Penfield, New York.

FARLEY, Ena L., Ph.D.

Born: Jamaica, West Indies; Moved to Rochester, 1966.

Family: Married to Rawle Farley (since 1961), Ph.D., Economics (London), Professor of Economics Emeritus, SUNY Brockport; Mother of four sons, Anthony Paul Farley, JD, Harvard, BA, UVA (with distinction), Assistant Professor of Law, Boston College; Christopher John Farley, AB, Harvard (cum laude), on the staff of Time Magazine; Felipe Jose Farley, JD, Harvard, AB, Harvard (cum laude), Attorney, Atlanta, Georgia, and Jonathan David Farley, AB, Harvard, (summa cum laude), Mathematics; Winner of the Detur Prize, the Wendell Prize, a Marshall Scholar to Oxford University; Ph.D, Mathematics, Oxford University.

Education: Ph.D., American History, University of Wisconsin, Madison,1973; MA, Education, Putney Graduate School of Teacher Education; BA, History (With Honors), University of London, University College of the West Indies.

Career: *Regent, New York State Board of regents, 1997-2002*; Retired in 1995 as Professor and Chairperson, Department of African and Afro-American Studies, SUNY Brockport since 1973; Assistant Professor of American History, SUNY Buffalo, 1967-73.

Professional/Community Involvement: Contributing Editor, *Afro-Americans in New York Life and History* since the inception of the journal, 1977; Elected to Board of Education, Brockport Central School District, 1986-1989; re-elected, 1989-94; Advisory Board, New York State African-American Institute; Member of several Albany and SUNY Brockport committees over the years: Honorary Degree Committees, Excellence in Teaching Committees, Professional Ethics Committees, Faculty Senator, several Search Committees; Served on a two-member Evaluation Team to examine the Black Studies Department of SUNY New Paltz; Served as History Consultant for the Rochester City School District in the Development of an Afro-American History curriculum for fifth grade and in the development of History Video for instructional use; Reviewer, University Awards Program, The Research Foundation of SUNY; Member, SUNY Central Office Teaching Awards; Selection Committee for the Improvement of Undergraduate Instruction; Annual Organizer, Martin Luther King Commemoration and Black History Month Events, SUNY Brockport; Past Member of Program Committee of the Association for the Study of Afro-American Life and History; Appointed to serve on a State-Mandated Educational Opportunity Advisory Board, 1988; Appointed to serve on a Special Education Advisory Committee representing the BOCES of five school districts, 1988 to present; Chair, Sub-Committee on Diversity, Middle States Self Study, 1991; Served on the Urban League of Rochester Committee; Member of Rochester Standing Committee on Blacks in Higher Education, 1980-81; Association for the Study of Afro-American Life and History; Organization of American Historians; American Historical Association; Afro-American History Association of the Niagara Frontier; Historical Society of Western Monroe County.

Awards/Recognition: Urban League Distinguished Volunteer Award,1981; Rockefeller Foundation Humanities Fellowship; State University of New York Faculty Research Fellowship; University of Wisconsin Fellowships and Scholarships; Fulbright Grant; Reader's Digest Award; Jamaica Government Exhibition to the University College of the West Indies; Inducted into the Delta Kappa Gamma Society International, Alpha Alpha Chapter, 1988; Recipient of a Distinguished Alumna Medal from the University of the West Indies, at the 50th anniversary of the founding of the University.

Patents/Publications: Author, *The Underside of Reconstruction New York: The Struggle Over the Issue of Black Equality, Garland* Press, New York, 1993; Has written chapters in the following books, *The African American Presence in New York,* Monroe Fordham, Editor, The African-American Institute, SUNY, 1989; *Black Studies: Theory, Method and Cultural Perspectives*, Talmadge Anderson, Pullman Washington State University Press, 1990; *Black Women in American History: The Twentieth Century*, Darlene Clark Hines, Editor, Carlson Publishing, Inc., 1990; *Black Women in America*, Darlene Clark Hines, et al, Carlson Publishing, Inc. 1993; Author of over thirty articles in *The Western Journal of Black Studies, Afro-Americans in New York Life and History, Wolmer's 250: 1729-1979*, a commemorative magazine, *Review of Black Political Economy, Integrated Education, Journal of Negro History, Revista Interamericana, Civilizations, Journal of American History, American Historical Review, New York Historical Society Quaterly, New York History.*

Residence: Brockport, New York

Cecil D. Felton
Photo, Mike Molaire Copyright 1998, Norex Publications.

FELTON, Cecil D.

Born: Rochester, N.Y., August 1966.
Parents: Emma Felton and Charles Martin.
Family: Married to Kimberly M. Felton formerly Sims.
Education: Bachelor of Arts in Communications with a concentration in Film and Television and a minor in Studio Photography, Adelphi University, NY, 1988.

Career: *Executive Director of Rochester Community Access Cable Channel 15 since 1992*; Video Production Instructor/Coordinator, Tough Changes Program, 1992; ESPN Sport, c/o Wind Fall Productions, 1991; Production Assistant, WXXI TV 21, 1988-1989; Owner/President, CALIBER Productions since 1988.

Awards/Recognition: Urban League of Rochester Black Scholar, 1984; Student recognition/highest grade point average, Center for African-American Studies, Adelphi University, 1988; Sixth Annual Film Festival Recognition Award, Rochester Association of Black Communications, 1989; Community Arts Grant Recipient, Rochester Area Foundation; New Artist of the Year Award, Theta Alpha Zeta Chapter of Zeta Phi Beta Sorority, Inc., 1991; Emerging Artist Award, Pyramid Arts Center, 1991; Lift Grant Recipient, Arts for Greater Rochester, 1991; Diverse Forms Grant, Jerome Foundation/Rockefeller Foundation, 1991; Reynolds Library Video

FIELDS, Karen Elise, Ph.D.

Project Grant Recipient, City of Rochester, 1992; Rochester Brainpower Hall of Fame Inductee, Eastman Kodak Company, 1994; Special Opportunity Stipend Grants, Arts & Cultural Council of Greater Rochester, 1994; Ujima Service Award, Congress of African Unity, 1996; Outstanding Achievement in the area of Community Awareness, The Monroe Council on Teen Pregnancy, 1996.

Patents/Publications: Creator/Producer/Director of *Gospel House*, a weekly music video show; Creator/Director/Associate Producer of *Rhythm & Business,* a weekly music video/talent showcase; Writer/Director/Producer of a 54-minute, anti-drug video movie, *Pipe Dreams*; Writer/Director/Producer of *Girl-Friend*, a 30-minute film that examines the peer pressures that young people endure when faced with the issue of premarital sex; Executive Producer/Technical Director of *Rochester Talks,* a 30-minute, weekly public affairs talk show.

Residence: Rochester, New York.

FIELDS, Karen Elise, Ph.D.

Born: Washington D.C.; Moved to Rochester, 1986.
Parents: Robert Lionel Fields, A.I.A, and Lilian Wheeler Fields, M.D.
Family: Married to Moussa Bagate, Ph.D., Civil Engineering; One daughter, Maimouna Fields Bagate.
Education: Ph.D., Sociology, Brandies University, 1977; MA, Sociology, Brandeis University, 1973; License Es Lettres, Sociology, Sobornne, Paris, France, 1968; BA, Social Studies, Cum Laude, Radcliffe College, 1967.

Career: *Professor of Religion, University of Rochester since 1986*; The first Black Full Professor at the University of Rochester; Founding Director, Frederick Douglass Institute for African and African-American Studies, 1986-92; Tenured Professor, Department of Sociology, Brandeis University, 1983-88; Assistant Professor, Department of Sociology, Brandeis University, 1977-83; Assistant Professor, Instructor, Department of Sociology, Boston University, 1975-77; Swahili Instructor, Department of African and Afro-American Studies, Brandeis University, 1971-73; English Teacher, American Center for Students and Artists, Paris, France, 1968-70; Teacher, Ministry of Education, United Republic of Tanzania, under Volunteer Teachers for Africa, Harvard University, 1965-66; Speaks English, French, Russian, and Swahili; Studying Chinese.

Professional/Community Involvement: Member, Joint Committee on African Studies of the American Council of Learned Societies; Social Science Research Council (SSRC); Chair, Selection Committee for the SSRC's International Doctoral Research Fellowship Program, 1987-92; Member, Free South Africa Movement Boston Steering Committee, 1985; Corresponding Editor, *Theory and Society* since 1979, and Human Studies, 1978-84; Founding Member, Women *a*nd International Development, a Joint Harvard/MIT Group, 1984-85; Member, Advisory Board, Women and International Development, since 1986; Board of Directors, Harvard Square Defense Fund, 1981-84; Board of Directors, Civil Liberties Union of Massachusetts, 1985-86; Member, American Sociological Association since 1982; African Studies Associations: Nomination committee member, 1987-88; Herskovits Selection Committee since 1992; Consulting Editor, Brown Studies In Religion, Brown University; Series Editor, University of Virginia Press; Board of Directors and Advisory Board, The Kokrobitey School at the Milton Academy, Milton, MA (a new Educational initiative to provide a junior semester in Ghana for U.S. High School students and to develop new curricula in art, Social

Studies, and Environmental Science); Vice President and Member of the Board, AHEAD Energy Corporation at the University of Rochester; National Faculty of Humanities, Arts and Sciences.

Awards/Recognition: National Defense Education Act Fellowship (Russian), Indiana University, 1966; Sachar International Fellowship, Brandeis University, 1973-74; Social Science Research Council Foreign Area Fellowship for Post-Doctoral Research on Missions in Africa, 1977; Mary I. Bunting Institute Faculty Fellowship, for study on Charismatic Religion, 1982-83; National Endowment for the Humanities Fellowship for Independent Study, 1983-84; Woodrow Wilson International Center for Scholars, Smithsonian Institution, for a new translation of Emile Durkheims's, *Les Formes Elementaires de la Vie Religieuse.*

Patents/Publications: Co-author, *Lemon Swamp and Others Places: A Carolina Memoir*, New York, The Free Press, 1993; Author, *Revival and Rebellion in Colonial Central Africa,* Princeton, New Jersey, Princeton University Press, 1985; Author, *Les Formes Elementaires De la Vie Religieuse*, new translation of Emile Durkheim's book, The Free Press, forthcoming; Author of over 20 articles and reviews, in *Southern Exposure, Theory and Society, Canadian Journal Of African Studies, Harvard Divinity Bulletin, Literary News, Reviews & Interviews, Oral History, Etnofoor, Democrat & Chronicle Newspaper,* Black Women in America: A Historical Encyclopedia, *Political Dimensions of Religion; United Nations Association Forum, African Studies Review of Books,* 1980 Edition, *Contemporary Sociology, Journal for the Scientific Study of Religion, Sojourner, The Women's Forum, The International Journal Of African Historical Studies;* Has given numerous lectures and Presentations.

Residence: Rochester, New York.

FITZPATRICK, Cynthia, 1864-1983.

Born: December 25, 1864, Pontotoc, Mississippi; Moved to Rochester, 1955; Died in her sleep at home, 164 Reynolds Street, February 24, 1983.
Parents: Born to slave parents.
Family: Married Rice Fitzpatrick (died in 1954); One daughter, Elizabeth L. Miller, One granddaughter, Fannie M. Davis, Two great-granddaughters.

Life: Monroe County's oldest resident; Might have been the oldest person in the world; Abraham Lincoln was still alive at the time of her birth; She had only one year of schooling; Her favorite activities were fishing, gardening, and visiting with children.

Awards/Recognition: Presidents Gerald Ford and Jimmy Carter, and New York Governor Hugh Carey had sent her birthday greetings; was honorary grand marshal of Rochester's Bicentennial parade on July 3, 1976; appeared on ABC-TV's Good Morning America show in 1977; received an honorary diploma from City School District Superintendent John Franco and named an honorary member of the city school board in 1976.

Eulogies/Quotations:

"We didn't have much... but we had food. My parents raised hogs and potatoes."

Cynthia Fizpatrick
D&C, Feb 23, 1983

"She was a kind woman. I had a lot of respect for her and was kind of awestruck because of her age."

Linda Murray, member of Action For a Better Community staff.
Times Union, Feb. 23, 1983

"I asked the Lord to let me live to see my children grow. He let me live to see my children grow, my

Cynthia Fitzpatrick, 1864-1983

Reprinted with permission of **_about...time_** *Magazine, Inc.*

grandchildren grow and my great-grandchildren grow."

Cynthia Fizpatrick
D&C, Dec. 17, 1977

FLAGG, (Bonnie) Sara Lee

Born: Geneseo, NY, 1941; Moved to Rochester, 1974.
Parents: Mildred and Clyde Mathis.
Family: Married to Clarence Flagg; No children.
Education: Business Administration/Retailing, Mohawk Valley Technical Institute, Utica, NY; School of Applied Industrial Studies, Rochester Institute of Technology, Rochester, NY; Fashion Merchandising, Fashion Institute of Technology, New York City, Executive and Leadership Training Program, Sibley's and Gertz Department Stores.

Career: *Urban League of Rochester, Inc. since 1987*:Currently Divisional Manager, Business Development Division; Manager of Housing and Economic Development; Community Planning Specialist; Century 21-Banner LTD., Rochester, NY, Realtor Associate since 1987; Independent Tour Co-coordinator, Rochester, NY since 1986; Buyer/Merchandiser, Just Accessories (Div. Of Handbag Factory Outlet), Rochester, NY, 1984-1986; Buyer, Sibley's Department Store, Rochester, NY, 1974-1984; Executive Trainee, Department Manager, Assistant Buyer, Buyer, B. Gertz Department Store, Jamaica, NY, 1964-1974.

Professional/Community Involvement: Board Member, At Large Executive Committee Member, Program Planning Committee Member, Catholic Family Center, 1991; Board Member, Better Contractors Bureau, 1991; Member, Rochester Real Estate Board since 1987; Program and Dinner Chairperson, Minority Enterprise Development Center, 1990-1991; Chairperson, Minority Enterprise Development Committee, 1988-89; Featured Speaker on Retail Merchandising

Careers at Rochester Institute of Technology, Monroe Community College, and area primary and secondary schools; Speaker for Sibley's Executive Training Program.

Residence: Rochester, New York.

FLUKER, Walter E., Ph.D.

Born: Aug. 26, 1951, in Valden Mississippi.
Parents: Zettie, and the late Clinton Fluker.
Family: Married to Sharon Watson Fluker, a Political Scientist and Assistant Dean, University of Rochester; Two sons, Clinton Rahman, and Hampton Sterling.
Education: Ph.D., Religion, Boston University, 1988; Master of Divinity, Social Ethics, Garrett-Evangelical Theological Seminary, Evanston, Illinois, 1980; BA, Philosophy & Biblical Studies, Trinity College, Deerfield, Ill., 1977; Ordained, Second Baptist Church, Evanston, Ill., 1979; received Ministerial standing in United Church of Christ through New Orleans Association, UCC, 1987; Licensed to Preach by Centennial Missionary Baptist Church, Chicago, 1972.

Career: Dean, Black Church Studies since 1991; Martin Luther King, Jr., Memorial Professor of Theology, Colgate Rochester Divinity School/Bexley Hall/Crozer Theological Seminary, since 1991; Director, National Resource Center for the Development of Ethical leadership from the Black Church Tradition, Colgate Rochester Divinity School/Bexley Hall/Crozer Theological Seminary since 1993; Director/Editor, Howard Thurman Papers Project, Colgate Rochester Divinity School/Bexley Hall/Crozer Theological Seminary; Associate Pastor, Christian Friendship Missionary Baptist Church, Henrietta, New York, since 1992; Evaluator, National Research Center Doctoral Fellowships for Minorities, Ford Foundation, Washington, D.C., 1990, 1996; Consultant, Congressional Black

FLUKER, Walter E., Ph.D.

Caucus Foundation, Inc., "Black Churches in the Delivery of Day Care and Head Start," A National Study, Washington, D.C., 1996; Consultant, Case Western Reserve University, Department of Family Medicine, "Black Church Practices and Health," Cleveland, Ohio, 1996; Consultant, Department of Health and Human Services, center for Substance Abuse Prevention, "Meetings with Faith Communities," San Francisco, California, 1996; Satellite Site Coordinator, American Association for the Advancement of Science, Black Church Health Connection Program, 1996; Consultant, The Pew Charitable Trusts, Pew Evangelical Scholars program, Philadelphia, PA., 1995; Visiting Professor of Afro-American Studies, Harvard University, 1990-91; Assistant Professor of Christian Ethics, Vanderbilt University Graduate Department of Religion and Divinity School, 1987-91; Assistant Pastor, First Baptist Church, Capitol Hill, Nashville, Tennessee, 1987-91; University Chaplain and Assistant Professor of Religion, Dillard University, New Orleans, Louisiana, 1986-87; Pastor, St John's Congregational Church, United Church of Christ, Springfield, Mass., 1981-86; Research Assistant, Multicultural Theological Education Project, Association of Theological Schools, 1985; Assistant Pastor, Second Baptist Church, Evanston, Ill., 1977-1980; Director, Teacher's Aide Services, CERTA Program, School District # 65, Evanston, Illinois, 1978-79; Coordinator, Summer Federal Youth Employment Program, Fort Sheridan, Illinois, 1977-79; Coordinator, Minority Student Affairs, Trinity College, Deerfield, Illinois, 1975-76; Associate Pastor, Gideon Baptist Church, Waukegan, Illinois, 1973-76; Chaplain's Assistant, United States Army, 1971-73.

Professional/Community Involvement: Member, Children's Defense Fund Board, Washington, D.C.; Member, Society for Christian Ethics, Howard Thurman Educational Trust, San Francisco, California; Partners in Ecumenism, New York, New York; National Association for the Advancement of Colored People; United Black Christians/United Church of Christ; Ministers for Racial and Social Justice/United Church of Christ; Arcon, Sigma Pi Phi Fraternity, Gamma Iota Boule (Rochester, New York Chapter); Advisory Board of Penuel Ridge Retreat Center, Ashland City, Tennessee; Chair, Afro-American Religious History Group/American Academy of Religion, November 20, 1988; Chair of America In Search of A Soul/Howard Thurman Convocation, Vanderbilt Divinity School, October 26-28, 1989; Board Member, Trinity Press International; Former Board Member, Urban League of Rochester, New York; Former Board Member, Greater Rochester, New York Martin Luther King, Jr. Commission; Member, African American Initiative Community Advisory Committee, Strong Museum, Rochester, NY; American Academy of Religion, Society for Christian Ethics, Society for the Study of Black Religions, Partners in Ecumenism, New York, New York.

Awards/Recognition: Recipient, Grant for the Study of the Capacity of The Black Church to Provide Services and Support To At-Risk and Gang-Related Youth, The Ford Foundation ($75,000), 1996; Recipient, Grant for Howard Thurman Papers Project, The Pew Charitable Trusts ($150,000), 1994-96; Recipient, Award for Study, Louisville Institute for the Study of Protestantism and American Culture ($39,622), 1994; Recipient, Grant for National Resource Center for the Development of Ethical Leadership from the Black Church Tradition, W.K. Kellogg Foundation ($991,000), 1993-97; Recipient, Grant for the Development of Howard Thurman Papers Project, Lilly Endowment ($800,000), 1992-99; Proclamation of January 18, 1993 as "Walter Earl Fluker Day" by the Mayor of Buffalo, New York; "Do Something for Others" Award, New Hope Missionary Baptist Church, Buffalo New York, 1993; Andrew W. Mellon Faculty Fellowship, Harvard University, 1990-91; Fellow, W.E.B.

Dubois Institute for Afro-American Research, Harvard University, 1990-91; The Younger Scholars Award of the Association of Theological Schools in the United States and Canada, 1990-91; The Johnson Memorial Scholarship, 1982 & 1985; The Whitney M. Young Fellowship at Boston University, 1981-82; The Doctoral Fellowship for the Study of Religion for Black North American, 1980-82; A Fellow of the Howard Thurman Education Trust, San Francisco California, 1979; A Graduate Research Fellow at the Community Renewal Society of Chicago.

Patents/Publications: Author, *The Ground Has Shifted: Visions of National Community From the African-American Christian Tradition* (In Progress); Editor, The Sound of the Genuine: The Papers of Howard Thurman, 3 Volumes, University of South Carolina Press, 2001 (In Progress); Editor, *The Concise Edition of the Papers of Howard Thurman*, University of South Carolina Press, 2001 (In Progress); Editor, *The Stones That The Builders Rejected: Essays on Ethical Leadership From the Black Church Tradition,* Volume I, Trinity Press International, 1997 (Forthcoming); Editor, *Bread Upon the Waters: Essays on Ethical Leadership from the Black Church Tradition*, Volume II, Trinity Press International, 1997 (In Progress); Co-Editor with Catherine Tumber, *The Howard Thurman Reader*, Beacon Press, 1997 (In Progress); "Old Songs and Strong Arms: Remembering Daddy," *In Father Songs: Testimonies by African-American Sons and Daughters*, edited by Gloria Wade-Gayles, Spring 1997 (Forthcoming); "Dear Teddy and Robert and Bay'Broth," *From One Brother to Another*, Judson Press, 1996; "Howard Thurman," *Encyclopedia of African American Culture and History*, McMillan Library References, 1996; "The Politics of Conversion and the Civilization of Friday,", *The Journal of the International Theological Center*, Vol. XXI, Nos. 1 and 2, Fall 1993/Spring 1994; Author, *They Looked for a City, A Comparative Analysis of The Ideal of*

Walter E. Fluker, Ph.D.
Photo, Fred Tanksley. Copyright 1998, Norex Publications.

Community In The Thought of Howard Thurman and Martin Luther King. Jr., University Press of America, 1989; Author, "The Challenge of Contemporary American Evangelism: An African American Perspective," in *Black Evangelicalism Today: Essays in Honor of William Hiram Bentley*, The Center for Urban Theological Studies, edited by A.G. Miller and Ronald Potter, Geneva College, Geneva, PA, 1994; Author, "Howard Thurman," *Encyclopedia of African American Culture and History*, Edited by Charles V. Hamilton and Jack Salzman, McMillan Publishing company (Forthcoming); Author, "A Spirituality of Caring: The Genius and Moral Legacy of Howard Thurman," in *Dynamic African American Pastoral Care and Counseling: Bridging Clinical and Parish Resources*, Edited by Vergel L. Lattimore Completing a manuscript Entitled, *America in Search of a Soul: Visions of National Community from the African-American Christian Tradition*; author of Four articles, in The Journal of Religious Ethics, Encounter, *National Baptist Union Review, The Spire*, and *The Listening Ear; Editor, The Sound of the Genuine: The Works of Howard Thurman,* Documentary Edition in 5 Volumes (The first volume scheduled for Spring 1995); Has made numerous lectures and presentations since 1988.

Residence: Rochester. New York

FRAZIER JR., Charles Wesley

Born: Rochester, New York, 1921.
Parents: Queenie and Charles Frazier.
Family: Presently married to Rosetta; first wife, Catherine Audrey; two children, Charles Frazier, III, and Cariton Frazier.
Education: Attended St John Fisher, Rochester Institute of Technology, the University of Rochester and Nazareth College.

.**Career:** Retired from Eastman Kodak Company after 40 years, the first Black to reach that milestone in Monroe County, 1983; Member of the Memorial A.M.E. Zion Church for 76 years; He received confession in 1940, under reverend Charles Hendersen.

Professional/Community Involvement: Consultant, Rochester Museum, Strong Museum, Landmark Society; Board Member, Landmark, Black Heritage; Historian, Memorial A.M.E. Zion Church; Trustee, Memorial A.M.E. Zion Church, 1989; Deacon, Memorial A.M.E. Zion Church, 1980; Member, Fund Raising Committee for New Memorial A.M.E. Zion Church, 1970.

Awards/Recognition: African-American Leadership Development Program Alumni Elder Award, 1997; City of Rochester, Unsung Hero Award, 1997; Service Award, Rochester's Board of Education, 1995; Man of The Year Award. Me-

Charles Wesley Frazier, Jr.
Photo, Mike F. Molaire.Copyright 1998, Norex Puiblications.

morial A.M.E. Zion Church, 1978; Member of First Black Scout troupe in Rochester, 1928; Service Ward, U.S. Post Office, 1995; 40 years of Service Award, Eastman Kodak Company, 1981.

Patents/Publications: *The Old Ship of Zion, Its History and Its People*, 1995; *The old Ship of Zion, Its History and Its People*, second edition, 1996; *Life and Times of Frederick Douglass*, 1997

FULLWOOD, Emerson

Born: Supply, North Carolina. 1948; Moved to Rochester, 1992.
Parents: Frank S. and Ada Fullwood.
Family: Married to Vernita Fullwood; Two children, Erika, and Elise.
Education: MBA, Marketing, Columbia Univer-

sity, 1970; BA, Economics, North Carolina State University, 1970.

Career: *Vice President and General Manager of Xerox' Worldwide Convenience Copier Business of the Office Document Products Division since May, 1992*; Formerly Vice President and General Manager of Xerox Supplies Marketing and Sales for the United States Customer Operations Division, 1990; Vice President and National Sales Manager, as well as numerous line and staff assignments.

Professional/Community Involvement: Serves on Greater Rochester United Way Committee, "Success by Six"; Has served in numerous community organizations.

Awards/Recognition: Xerox Senior Management Award for Exceptional Contribution/Performance, 1993; Glass Cutter Award, Metropolitan Area Minority Employee Association, 1990; Customer Satisfaction Award, 1992; National Black Achievers in Industry Award from Harlem YMCA and numerous other awards/recognition.

Patents/Publications: Author of several articles in industry journals; has participated in many industrial seminars.

Residence: Pittsford, New York.

GADSON, Jonas Willie

Born: St. Helena Island, South Carolina, Sept. 13, 1953; Moved to Rochester, 1971.
Parents: Joseph and Eliza Gadson.
Education: Liberal Arts Courses, Monroe Community College; Writing Course, Rochester Institute of Technology; Nazareth College, Speech/Communications.

Career: *Coordinator, Diversity Initiatives, Consumer Imaging, HVEM, Eastman Kodak Company since 1996*; Trainer/Facilitator, Diversity Initiatives, Consumer Imaging, HVEM, Eastman Kodak, 1993-96; President & CEO, Jonas Gadson Unlimited since 1990; Previously worked for the Xerox Corporation.

Professional/Community Involvement: Member, Kodak Network North Star, Rochester Chamber of Commerce, Kodak Women's Network, National Speakers Association, Toastmasters International; Past Vice President, Public Relations, Toastmasters International; Taught Evening Adult Education course, Rush Henrietta School District; Tutor, Kodak 21st Century Learning Challenge, Rochester Public School; Helped raise $1,1 million for Rochester's underprivileged in 1993.

Awards/Recognition: Distinguished Area Governor and Distinguished Toastmaster, Toastmasters International.

GANTT, David, The Honorable

Born: Rochester, New York, September 12, 1941.
Parents: Lena M. Gantt (deceased), Community Activist and Public Servant.
Education: Attended Franklin High School, Roberts Wesleyan College and the Rochester Institute of Technology.

Career: *Dean of the Rochester New York State Assembly Delegatio*n; Named Transportation Committee Chairman, One of the assembly's most influential jobs, in November 1993; Representative of the 133rd District; has served nine years in the Monroe County Legislature, representing the 22nd Legislature District (part of Rochester's Group 14621, Marketview Heights, and CONEA neighborhoods; Served as Assistant Majority Leader in the County Legislature, Chairman of the Public Safety Committee, Vice-Chairman of the Finance & Budget Committee and Ranking Minority Member of the Human Resources Committee; Worked as a Youth Counselor for the City of Rochester, as a member of Lithographers & Photoengravers International Union Local 230, and The Anthony Jordan Health Center.

Awards/Recognition: Recognized by the Upstairs Youth Agency, the Mt. Vernon Baptist Church, the Monroe County Public Defender's Office, the Monroe County Board of Elections, and the New York State Association of Counties

Residence: Rochester, New York.

GANTT, Lena Mae, 1928-1982

Born: 1928, Elba, Alabama; Moved to Rochester, 1952; Died of cancer, at Rochester General Hospital, Sept 10, 1982.
Family: Six sons, Honorable David Gantt, Monroe County Legislator, Donald, Columbus, Larry, Freddie and Thomas Gantt; three sisters, Sweetie Carlwell, Pauline Black and Thomas Lillia Buckner; Two brothers, Alvin and George Sims.

Professional/Community Involvement: Was one of the first directors and founders of Action For a Better Community (1965-1982); Helped establish dozens of community organizations including the Northeast District Council, the Rochester Health Network and the Anthony L. Jordan Health Center; Was a member of the Model Cities Neighborhood Council; Board Member, The Anthony Jordan Health Center, and Baden Street Settlement.

Awards/Recognition: The Distinguished Lena M. Gantt Award was established by Action For a Better Community in 1985.

Eulogies/Quotations:

"She just never gave up. Even the very week that her cancer was diagnosed, despite the fact that she wasn't feeling well. Mrs. Gantt brought 20 senior citizens to Action For a Better Community on July 16."

Paulette Watkins, assistant personnel director of ABC.
Times Union, Sept 13, 1982

"She was a great advocate for people in our neighborhood, She established our first tot lot (Play area for children) on Oregon Street."

Maudine Brown, assistant director, Neighborhood Development, Baden Street Settlement.
Times Union, Sept 13, 1982

GAYLE- JONES, Jewelle

Born: Palmetto, Florida, 1938.
Parents: Elmore and Lizzie Mae Gayle.
Family: Divorced; Three adult children, Vickie Jones Bell, Deborah Jones Atkins, Wendy R. Jones; Two grandchildren, Qu'ran Jewelle Bell, Omari Gayle Atkins.
Education: Master's Degree, Education, SUNY College at Brockport, 1979. Bachelor's Degree, Social Welfare, Empire State College, 1974. Attended Skidmore College, Saratoga, New York, 1973; Attended Roberts Wesleyan College, Chili, New York, 1968; A.A.S. Degree, St. Petersburg Community College, 1961; Harvard Graduate School of Education Programs in Professional Education Institute Certificate, 1995.

Career: Elected to the Rochester City School Board as a Democrat, 1992; Retired from Monroe Community College: Professor Emeritus, Human Services, 1996; Visiting Instructor, Counseling, SUNY Brockport, 1982-83; Adjunct Instructor, School of Industrial and Labor Relations, Cornell University, 1980-83; Instructor, Fostering Positive Relationship In Families, Child Development Associate Certificate Program, Western New York Child Care Council, Inc. since 1990; Instructor, Writing Across The

Curriculum Courses, Monroe Community College, since 1989; Instructor, Entry Level and Advanced Skill oriented courses in Human Services Department since 1973; College Supervisor for Human Service students participating in agency field work in the City of Rochester and Surrounding Counties since 1973; Tape Supervisory for Graduate Counseling Students, SUNY College at Brockport, 1982-83; College Supervisor for the Southern Teacher Exchange Program cosponsored by Monroe County Human Relations Commission and Nazareth College, 1978-81.

Professional/Community Involvement: Founding Board Member of Wilson Commencement Park, 1990; Vice Chair, Monroe County Human Relations Commission, 1989; Advisor for the Barbara Merill Scholarship, administered by Rochester Area Foundation and Monroe Community College Foundation since 1980; Mid-Atlantic Consortium of Human Services Educators, 1979-1996; New York State Human Services Educators, 1981-1996; Greater Rochester Women's Fund Advisory Council Rochester Area Foundation, 1990-1993; Chairperson, Advisory Committee, Family and Children Services Division, Urban League of Rochester, 1987-89; Board of Directors, Art for Greater Rochester, Inc, 1986-89; Corporate Board, United Way of Greater Rochester, 1986 87; Member, Delta Sigma Theta Sorority, Rochester Alumnae Chapter; Phi Delta Kappa International Professional Fraternity in Education, Gamma Theta Chapter; Monroe County Teen Pregnancy Coalition, 1984-88; Chairperson, Black and Hispanic Faculty and Staff Committee, Monroe Community College, 1984-86; Chairperson, Section E, Allocation Committee, United Way of Greater Rochester, 1980 89; Executive Board Member, New York State Council for Children, 1980-83; President, Jack and Jill of America, Inc., Rochester Chapter, 1980- 82; Statewide Membership Chairperson, New York State Council for Children, 1980-82; Western Child Care Council Informa-

tion Service Committee, 1980-82; Faculty Senate, Executive Committee, Monroe Community College, 1989-91; Task Force on Minority Women's Issues, New York State, 1986-87; The

cademic Governance Board, Monroe Community College, 1985-87; Monroe Community College Women's Caucus, 1980-1996; Listed in the *Diversity Resource Directory of Rochester Area Volunteers*, published by The Philanthropic Diversity Consortium of the Rochester (NY) Region, 1993-present.

Awards/Recognition: Who's Who of American Women, 1995/1996; Recognition Award, Association of Supervisors and Administrators, Rochester City School Distrcit, 1997; Outstanding Service Award, Monroe Community College, 1996; Community Service Award, Rochester Alumnae Chapter, Delta Sigma Theta Public Service Sorority, Inc., 1993; Certificate of Appreciation for Contributions to Monroe County Human Rrelations, 1991; Distinguished Volunteer Award, Section E, United Way of Greater Rochester Allocation Committee, 1990; Program Service Award, Rochester Alumnae Chapter, Delta Sigma Theta Sorority Inc., 1990; Certificate of Appreciation for Exemplary Volunteer Services to OASIS, Inc., 1990; Certificate of Appreciation, Monroe # 1 Board of Cooperative Services, Fairport, New York, 1991; Distinguished Service Award, The Urban League of Rochester, Inc, 1988; Volunteer Service Award, Martin Luther King, Jr. Greater Rochester Festival Commission, 1986-87; Certificate of Appreciation Award for Support to the Black Student Union, Monroe Community College, 1985: Certificate of Merit, Rochester Chapter, Links, Inc., 1984; Certificate of Appreciation, United Way of Greater Rochester Board of Directors, 1982; Community Volunteerism Award, Black Metropolitan Women's Network, 1981; Certificate of Appreciation, Faculty Advisor to Organization of Human Services Student, Monroe Community

College, 1981; Associate Appreciation Award, Jack and Jill of Rochester, Inc., 1981.

Patents/Publications: Over 25 lectures, papers, and presentations at Local and National Conferences from 1973 to 1996; Has designed, coordinated over 15 conferences and workshops from 1981 to 1997.

Residence: Rochester, New York.

GIFFORD, Bernard, Ph.D.

Born: 1943, Brooklyn, New York; Moved to Rochester 1965; Left in 1971 to study at Harvard; Came back as Vice President of Student Affairs at the University of Rochester; Left to become Dean of Education at Berkeley; Now lived in Palo Alto California.

Family: Married Laura, Gifford; Children, Toni and Butchie.

Education: Ph.D., Biophysics, University of Rochester, 1971; Studied urban affairs on a Kennedy fellowship at Harvard University; Undergraduate work at Long Island University with a full scholarship chemistry major; Graduate of Technical High School with honors in Physics, Chemistry and History.

Career: *Chair, Founder and Chief Instructional Officer, Academic Systems since 1993*; Vice-President of Education, Apple Computer, 1990-1993; Chancellor's Professor and Dean, Graduate School of Education, University of California at Berkeley, 1984-1990; Professor, Division of Mathematics, Science and Technology, University of California at Berkeley since 1984; Kennedy Fellow, John F. Kennedy School of Government, Harvard University, 1971-1972; Vice President and Professor, Political Science and Public Policy, University of Rochester, 1981-1983; Resident Scholar, Russell Sage Foundation, New York City, 1977-1981; Deputy Chancellor and Chief Fiscal Officer, New York City Public Schools, responsible for a $2.5 billion budget for about 100,000 employees, 1973-1977.

Professional/Community Involvement: President, FIGHT, a Black community organization established after the 1964 Rochester riots, 1969-1971; Unseated Franklin D.R. Florence, in a very passionate convention in June 1969; Credited with improvement in job training, housing, education and business opportunities for Rochester Blacks; Member, Trustees Council, the senior alumni advisory body to the University of Rochester Board of Trustees; Former Board Member, FIGHTON, now Eltrex Industries; Former Member, Trustee's Visiting Committee to the University of Rochester library.

Patents/Publications: Community Development Corporation: *New Hope for the Inner City*, Twentieth Century Fund.

Quotations:

"Look at Martin Luther King and the Rev. Jesse Jackson-impeccable middle class backgrounds. When you're black, class distinctions are artificial. People are going to react to you as black, and that's where you have to stand, middle class or slum product..."

> Bernard Gifford
> D & C, June 13, 1971

"I started high school in 1957, the year of the Sputnik. So everyone said, "Be a scientist" So I did. The discipline itself is helpful, the logic, but if I ever use the Ph.D. it will be to get a job on the college level teaching in the social sciences. They don't really care what your doctorate is in."

> Bernard Gifford
> Times Union, Feb 18, 1972

"I am a New Yorker and I'm an educator...If you care about school improvement and you are given the opportunity to be education commissioner of the State of New York, you've got to consider it."

Bernard Gifford
D & C, Dec. 16, 1986

"Day care on the surface is a very good thing...But one of the reasons for it is to free black women for work. In the inner city, right now, there aren't enough jobs for black women...We might wind up destroying more families than relieving turmoil."

    Bernard Gifford
    Times Union, Feb. 18, 1972

"Every time you increase the welfare program, you minimize black economic development..."

    Bernard Gifford
    Times Union, Feb. 18, 1972

"Can we look at a neighborhood and say if it's 30 percent black allis well and if it is 32 percent black, all hell breaks loose? The answer is, we just don't know."

    Bernard Gifford
    Times Union, Feb. 18, 1972

"Every time the minimum wage is increased by 25 cents an hour, it eliminates tens of thousands of jobs for black and Puerto Rican youth...people who are looking around for something, aren't career-oriented and are willing to work for 75 cents or $1 an hour."

    Bernard Gifford
    Times Union, Feb. 18, 1972

"I know I sound like some kind of crazy reactionary or a conservative...but that's because we look at things through a conservative viewpoint. We've got to look at all the forces involved if we want to solve the cities' problems before they become depositories for blacks, Puerto Ricans and elderly whites."

    Bernard Gifford
    Times Union, Feb. 18, 1972

"This is a man who doesn't need any consideration because of race...His qualifications stand on their own, as you can see."

    Judy Brown, University of Rochester director of public relations, commenting on the consideration of Gifford for vice president of student affairs.
    D & C May 2, 1981

"He has just the kind of sure touch, progressive vision, and energetic style that is needed to bring change and improvement to this important area of learning."

    Ira M. Heyman, Chancellor, University of California at Berkeley, announcing the appointment of Gifford as Dean of the School of Education.
    D & C, Dec. 16, 1982

"We realized we probably would be unable to keep him long, because of his experience, background, and ability would clearly place him much in demand by other institutions."

    Robert R. Sproull, president, University of Rochester, commenting on Gifford leaving for a Berkeley post.
    D & C, Dec. 16, 1982

- ***N.B. Dr. Gifford no longer lives in the Rochester area. The above information was completely compiled from public sources. There was no corroboration by Dr. Gifford.***

GILBERT, Moses

Born: Rochester, New York, 1938.
Parents: Horace C. and Pairlee Franklin Gilbert.
Family: Married to Judith S.; Three children, Jeannette, Eric, and Gary.
Education: M.S.W., School of Social Work, Syracuse University 1971; BA, Political Science, Morgan State University, 1962.

Career: *Executive Director of the Montgomery NeighborhoodCenter since 1976;* Community Planning Director, United Way of Greater Rochester, 1973-76; Assistant Professor, Social Work Department, Rochester Institute Technology, 1971-73; Executive Director Economic Development Corporation, Rochester Model Cities, 1971; Project Director, Rochester Rehabilitation Center, Rochester, New York, 1970; Research Coordinator, Rochester Jobs, Inc., 1970; Group Activities Supervisor, Montgomery Neighborhood Center, Rochester, New York, 1965-69; Administrative and Supply Technician, Department of Army Civilian Headquarters, Rochester, New York, 1964-65; Recreation Leader, Bureau of

Recreation, City of Rochester, 1957-61; Administrative Clerk, Gannet News, Inc., Rochester, New York, 1956-57; 12 years of Military Services.

Professional/Community Involvement: Former President of the NAACP Rochester Chapter; Past Treasurer of the Social Workers Club; ForAction For a Better Community; Association of Black Social Workers; Board of Directors, Mental Health Chapter; Rochester Jobs Inc; Board of Directors of Blue Shield; Former Member of the Victor Central School Board of Education.

Awards/Recognition: Ford Foundation Honorific Scholarship (Institute of Political Education); Meritorious Service Award.

Residence: Victor, New York

GOMEZ, Carol, Reverend

Born: Bronx New York, 1950.
Family: Single parent with two sons.
Education: Certificate in Christian Ministry, New York Theological Seminary, 1981; Undergraduate Degree, College of New Rochelle; Master's degree, Divinity, Colgate Rochester Divinity School/Bexley Hall/Crozer Theological Seminary, 1989.

Career: Pastor, West Ave United Methodist Church; The First Black woman ordained in the American Baptist Churches of the Rochester/Genesee Region, 1989; Former Chaplain for Keuka College, Yates County, Upstate New York; Former Protestant Chaplain, University of Rochester.

Awards/Recognition: Recipient of the Black Pastors Award and Scholarship of New York State, 1987; Benjamin E. Mays Fellowship, Fund for Theological Education, 1988; Outstanding Adult Student Award, Rochester Area Colleges, 1989; Certificate of Recognition, Nazareth College as The Celebrated Women of African Descent who have made significant contributions to the Rochester community, March 1992.

Residence: Rochester, New York.

GORDON, Elmer L., 1917-1979

Born: 1917, Portsmouth, VA; Moved to Rochester, 1964; Died of a heart condition at Strong Memorial Hospital, Saturday Sept. 1, 1979.
Family: Married Evelyn Elmer; Two daughters, Beverly and Jeanine; Two sons, Eric and Quentin.
Education: Chemistry degree, Virginia Union University; only one of 100 toxicologists licensed by the American Board of Forensic Toxicology

Career: Member of the first all-Black fighter squadron in the Air Force in World War II; a toxicologist with the Virginia Medical Examiner's office before coming to Rochester; Started with the Monroe County Medical Examiner's Office in 1964; An expert in poisons and their detection; Served two terms as president of the Rush-Henrietta School Board, starting in July 1971; The first Black President of the Henrietta School Boards Association.

Awards/Recognition: A scholarship fund was established in his honor in 1980; The scholarship is awarded to Rush-Henrietta students whose educational interests and future plans reflect the goals advanced by Gordon.

Eulogies and Quotations:

"He was able to do what he did because of his education and he wanted others to be able to do it perhaps a little easier than him."

Elmer L. Gordon, 1917-1979

Reprinted with the permission of <u>about...time</u> Magazine, Inc.

Jann Packard, executive director, Rush-Henrietta School Board Association
<u>D&C</u>*, Sept. 3, 1979*

"He was very active in the community...That was his hobby."

Beverly Gordon, Elmer's daughter
<u>D&C</u>*, Sept. 3, 1979*

"Elmer was dedicated to the idea of education from both the cultural and scholastic point of view...We'll all miss him very much. He was as solid as they come."

John Sebaste, vice president, Rush-Henrietta School Board
<u>D&C</u>*, Sept. 3, 1979*

"There is no margin for error in this work...The life, liberty and happiness of many individuals depends on what we do here."

Elmer L. Gordon, commenting on his work as a toxicologist in a 1975
<u>D&C</u> *interview.*
<u>D&C</u>*, Sept. 3, 1979*

"The only way blacks will be known is through participation in civic activities. The power structure doesn't know blacks and will never know blacks until there is some participation in something where they (the blacks) aren't making money...I hear people say 'give me my rights and opportunities,' but I have yet to hear them say give me the responsibility."

Elmer Gordon
<u>**about...time**</u> ***Magazine, p17, Sept. 1976.***

GROSS, Constance (Connie)

Born: New York, New York, 1937; Moved to Rochester, 1982.
Parents: Samuel and Evelyn Thompson.
Family: Single
Education: BA, Business Administration, Bernard Baruch College, New York; AA, Business Administration, Bronx Community College; Licensed Real Estate Salesperson, 1967-68; Certified Medical Secretary, Eastern School For Physician's Aid, New York, New York; Licensed Notary Public, State of New York.

Career: *Owner/President of ConGro & Associates, Inc. since1985*; Owner/President of Sophisticated Secs, Inc, 1982-89; Teacher of Word Processing/Transcription, English and Business

Skills at Bryant & Stratton Business Institute, 1983-89; Lecturer, Business Management, Rochester Institute of Technology College of Continuing Education.

Professional/Community Involvement: Member, Allocations Committee,United Way of Rochester; Steering Committee, Next Century Leadership Fund, Girl Scouts 80th Anniversary Celebration Committee; Steering Committee, African-American Leadership Development Program; Urban League Guild; Monroe County Minority Advisory Board; Graves Institutional C.M.E. Church and its Neighborhood Action Committee; Frederick Douglas Republican Council; Former Advisor to the Rochester Junior Achieve

ment Program, 1991-92; Chair, Black Business Association, Rochester Chamber of Commerce, 1989-1991; Chair, the Marketing Committee, Private Industry Council, 1986-1989; Co-chair, Rochester Area Women's Political Caucus, Political Action Committee, 1986; Member, Private Industry Council, Executive Committee, 1984-1989; The Tax Assessment Task Force, City of

Rochester, 1986-1987; Mentor, Career Beginnings Program, University of Rochester, 1986-88; Facilitator, Job Service Employers Committee 1986; Co-coordinator, New York State Minority GOP Task Force 1985; Monroe County Republican Party, Secretary, 1985-88; Vice Chair, Rochester Area Women's Political Caucus, 1983-86; Member, Minority Entrepreneur Advisory Council; Secretary and Member, Great Lakes Minority Contractors, Inc.; Member, Concerned Citizen's Council; Listed in the Minority Resource Directory of Rochester Area Volunteers published by The Philanthropic Diversity of the Rochester (NY) Region, 1993-94.

Awards/Recognition: Certificate of Appreciation, Junior Achievement of Rochester, 1992; Certificate of Appreciation, Rochester Area Girl Scouts, 1992; Certificate of Recognition, Monroe County Minority Advisory Board, 1990; Business Award, Rochester Area National Association of Negro Business and Professional Women Club, 1988; Special Recognition, Minority Entrepreneur Development Center, 1988; Member of the Year, Private Industry Council, 1987-1988; Certificate of Appreciation, Rochester Area Women's Political Caucus, 1987.

Residence: Rochester, New York.

HAMM, Bessie, 1894-1974

Born: 1894, in Virginia; Raised in Baltimore; Moved to Rochester, 1925.
Parents: Mr. and Mrs. Richard Howell.
Family: Married James Hamm (Deceased, 1982), 1917.

Career: Employed at the Eastman Kodak Company during Wild War II; Did work on a Navy contract; Retired in 1964, from Bastian Bros after 25 years.

Professional/Community Involvement:
Founded with her husband *the Parents and Students Want to Know Group*, in 1955 to promote an appreciation for Black history and acquaint students with educational opportunities; Founding Chairperson of the local Ralph Bunche Scholarship Fund, late 1950s.

Awards/Recognition: Honored with her husband by the members of the Parents and Students Want to Know group, 1969; Ira Sapozink Memorial Award for her contribution to the youth of the community, 1970; Honored with a party by the Rochester-Monroe County Council of the Campfire Girls, 1970; Special award for her youth work by the Times-Union Women's Club Guide, 1970; Citation from President Richard Nixon for "her outstanding activities" with the scholarship fund and for her "dedication to the young people of our nation, 1971; Received at least twelve awards between 1964 and 1970; Received a birthday card from President Nixon and the first family at her sick bed at Strong Memorial Hospital, July 1, 1974; The Hamm's home (where they operated the Parents and Students Want to Know group) at 301 Adams Street was designated a landmark by the City of Rochester, June 8, 1981; The James and Besie Hamm House Inc. was started, October 1981; The Hamm House is the first Black landmark home in Monroe County,

Eulogies/Quotations:

"I wanted to expose the Black family to professional opportunities and cultural resources. We invaded the museums, great churches, industrial establishments and other institutions of Rochester so that Black mothers and children could see and learn."

Bessie Hamm
D&C, Aug. 26, 1974

"I have had the privilege to serve on her committee and watch her work. Perhaps Mrs. Hamm's most outstanding trait is her great love for young people and her amazing ability to recall names and circum-

stances of each student... Every scholarship is a new individual, not just another grant. She has not been afraid to approach the most important people for contributions, and none have been too insignificant for her to take up their cause."

Mrs. Harper Sibley, prominent matriarch and humanitarian.
D&C, Aug. 26, 1974

"If we live apart, we may not be enemies, but we can never be friends. We've got to live together, go to school together and strive to make the America we have always tried to sell to the people in America and abroad."

Bessie Hamm
D&C, Aug. 26, 1974

HARRIS, Ruth L., Ph.D.

Born: Pittsburgh, PA, 1952; Moved to Rochester, 1990.
Parents: Ernest, and Gussie Harris.
Education: Ph.D., Sociology, Michigan State University, East Lansing, Michigan, 1989; MA, Sociology, Michigan State University, 1980; B.S., American Studies, Simmons College, 1974.

Career: *Assistant Professor, African and Afro-American Studies, and Sociology, SUNY Brockport since 1990*; Instructor, Department, Michigan Sate University, 1989; Instructor, Department of Social Science, Lansing Community College, 1983-89; Instructor, Sociology/James Madison College Overseas Study Program in the Caribbean (Barbados/Guyana), Michigan State University, 1987; Instructor, James Madison College, Michigan State University, 1986; Instructor, Lifelong Education External Courses and Programs, Birmingham, Michigan State University, 1986; Instructor, Department of Sociology and Anthropology, Adrian College, 1985; Teaching Assistant, Department of Sociology, Michigan State University, 1974-78; Research Associate, African Diaspora Research Project, Michigan State University, 1988-90; Research Assistant,

African Diaspora Research Project, Michigan State University, 1978-85.

Professional/Community Involvement: Mentor, Ronald E. McNair Program, SUNY Brockport, 1991-93; Faculty Advisor, National Association for the Advancement of Colored People's Afro-Academic, Cultural, Technological-Scientific Olympics (ACT-SO), Rochester, New York, 1992; Metropolitan Women's Network, Rochester Chapter of The National Council of Negro Women, Inc., Rochester, New York, 1990; State Steering Committee, Michigan Association of Black Social Workers, Michigan Association of Black Social Workers, 1986-1988; Sociology/James Madison College Summer in Barbados Program, Overseas Study Programs Steering Committee, Department of Sociology, Michigan State University, 1984-87; Conflict and Change Area Committee, Department of Sociology, Michigan State University, 1984-86; Steering Committee, Black Woman Writers and the Diaspora Conference, Michigan State University, 1984-85; Presidential Search Committee for the Assistant Graduate School Dean, Michigan State University, 1978; Presidential Minority Advisory Council, Michigan State University, 1977; Council of Graduate Students (COGS) Departmental Representative, Department of Sociology, Michigan State University, 1977; member, National Council of Black Studies, American Sociological Association, Association of Caribbean Studies, Society for International Development, Association of Black Social Workers, Association of Black Sociologists.

Awards/Recognition: New York State/United University Professions New Faculty Development Award, 1991; Martin Luther King-Caesar Chavez-Rosa Parks Visiting Scholars Program, 1988; Martin Luther King-Caesar Chavez-Rosa Parks Dissertation Fellowship, State of Michigan, 1987; Urban Affairs Programs Dissertation Support Award, 1986; Canadian-American Studies Program Travel Grant, 1986; Fulbright-Hays Overseas Study Grant for MA Research in London, 1979.

Patents/Publications: Co-author, "The British Lesser Antilles, Sugar And Banana Monocrop Economies: Fading Remnants of the British Empire in the Eastern Caribbean," *Working Paper* Series, No. 4, Department of Racial and Ethnic Studies and College of Urban Development, Michigan State University, June 1981; Has written a Chapter in Ruth Simms Hamilton, Editor, *Creating a Paradigm and Research Agenda for Comparative Studies of the Worldwide Dispersion Of African Peoples, Monogram No. 1,* African Diaspora Research Project, Michigan State University, East Lansing, 1990; Over 25 talks and conference presentations from 1981-93.

Residence: Brockport, New York

HARRIS, Norflett E.

Born: Barton Florida, 1953; Moved to Rochester, 1996.
Parents: Queen and Phil Harris.
Family: Four children, Evangeline, Norflett, Ivory, and Leronnie.
Education: B.S., Professional Studies, Barry University, Miami Shores, Florida, 1982; Police Management, University of Louisville, 1987.

Career*: Deputy Police Chief, City of Rochester, (1996-1997)*; First Black Deputy Police Chief of Rochester; Administered a $47 million dollar budget; Police Commander, City of Miami Beach, 1996; Captain of Police, City of Miami, 1994-1996; Lieutenant of Police, City of Miami, 1985-1994; Sergeant of Police, City of Miami, 1982-1985.

Professional/Community Involvement: Member Board of Directors, Housing Opportunities

Inc. (1996), Salvation Army (1997), and AIDS-Rochester (1996).

Residence: Rochester, New York.

HARRISON III, Robert W., Ph.D.

Born: Natchez, Mississippi, October 1941; Moved to Rochester, 1993.
Parents: Robert W. Harrison, Jr., DDS (deceased), and Charlotte M. Harrison.
Family: Married W. Gayle Harrison, Ph.D.; two sons, Robert W.Harrison and William S. Harrison.
Education: MD, Northwestern University School of Medicine, 1966; B.S., Chemistry, Tougaloo College, 1961; Intern, Chicago Wesley Memorial Hospital, Chicago, Illinois, 1966-67; Resident-in-Medicine, Chicago Wesley Memorial Hospital, Chicago, Illinois, 1967-68, Hartford Hospital, Hartford, Connecticut, 1970-72; U.S.P.H.S. PostDoctoral Fellow in Clinical Endocrinology and Metabolism, G.W. Liddle, Director; D.O. Toft, Preceptor, Vanderbilt Medical Center, Nashville, Tennessee, 1972-73; Course in Animal Cell Culture, Cold Spring Harbor Laboratories, Claudio Basilico, Director, Cold Spring Harbor, New York, 1974; Course in Molecular Endocrinology and Techniques for Hormone Action, W.T. Schrader and B.W. O'Malley, Directors, Houston, Texas, 1977.

Career: *Chief, Endocrinology/Metabolism Unit, University of Rochester School of Medicine and Dentistry, Strong Memorial Hospital, 1993*; Professor of Physiology, University of Arkansas for Medical Sciences, Little Rock, Arkansas, 1987-93; Professor of Medicine and Director of the Division of Endocrinology/Metabolism, University of Arkansas for Medical Sciences, Little Rock, Arkansas, 1985-present; Associate Dean for Special Projects, University of Arkansas for Medical Sciences, Little Rock, Arkansas, 1985-87; Associate Professor of Medicine, Department of Medicine, Vanderbilt University Medical Center, Nashville, Tennessee, 1981-85; Visiting Assistant Professor of Biochemistry (Sabbatical with Isadore Edelman), Department of Biochemistry, Columbia University College of Physicians and Surgeons, New York, New York, 1980-81; Assistant Professor of Physiology, Department of Physiology, Vanderbilt University School of Medicine Nashville, Tennessee 1978-85; Investigator, Howard Hughes Medical Institute, Vanderbilt University Medical Center, Nashville, Tennessee, 1977-82; Assistant Professor of Medicine, Department of Medicine, Vanderbilt University Medical Center, Nashville, Tennessee, 1974-81; Co-Director of Steroid Receptor Core Laboratory, Center for Population Research and Reproductive Biology, Vanderbilt University Medical Center, Nashville, Tennessee, 1973-74; Instructor in Medicine, Department of Medicine, Department of Medicine, Vanderbilt University Medical Center, Nashville, Tennessee, 1972-74.

Professional/Community Involvement: Member of numerous national professional societies, including the American Association for the Advancement of Science, the Endocrinology Society, and the American Federation for Clinical Research; Member of the Advisory Committees For The Food and Drug Administration, the Roberts Wood Johnson Foundation, and the National Institute of Health.

Patents/Publications: Author or co-author of more than 45 scientific articles, book chapters, and reviews in *Biochem Biophys Res. Communication, Endocrinology, Biochemistry, J. Steroid Biochem, Biochem Biophysics Acta, Journal Biological Chemistry, Journal of Steroid Biochemistry, Mol Cell Endocrinology, Adv Exp Med Biol, Life Science, Steroids, Toxicon, Muscle Nerve, Journal Ster Biochem, Exp Cell Res, Histochemistry, Journal Neuroscience Res, Cell Biology, Clin Res.*

HERRIOTT, Cynthia

Born: Rochester, New York, 1959

Parents: Rosanna Sinkler and Henry Herriott; one daughter, Crystal Sanders.

Education: Colgate Divinity School, working toward a masters eegree; B.S., Organizational Management, Robert Wesleyan College, Rochester, NY, 1994; A.S., Liberal Arts, Empire State College, Rochester, NY, 1993; Courses in Police Science, Monroe Community College, Rochester, NY, 1977-78; Paralegal Degree, National Academy of Paralegals, Rochester, N.Y., 1988; Arbitration/Mediation Certification, Cornell University, 1998.

Career: *Rochester Police Department since 1985; Presently Sergeant*; Patrol Division, Genesee Section since 1997; Commanding Officer, Educational Services Section, responsible for DARE instruction in schools, and Police and Citizens-Together Against Crime (PAC TAC), 1995-97; Sergeant, Patrol Division, Clinton Section, 1994-95; Management Services Division, overseeing the TeleServe Unit, City Booking Division, Security of the Public Safety Building, 1993-94; Assistant to the Deputy Chief of Operations, 1992-93; Juvenile Coordinator, Special Criminal Investigation Section, 1989-92; Crime Prevention Coordinator, 1988-89; Patrol Officer, 1985-88.

Professional/CommunityInvolvement: Board Member, United Way of Greater Rochester since 1998; Co-Chair, United Way Kids on Track Committee ; Board Member, Family Services of Rochester; Alternatives for Battered Women; Vice President, Rochester Women's Network, 1994; Member, Nominating Committee, Rochester Women's Network, 1997-98; Advisory Committee, Downtown Community Forum, 1998; Regional Representative, National Center on Women and Policing, 1998; Member, President Clinton's At The table", 1996; Leadership Amer-

Cynthia Herriott
Photo Courtesy Cynthia Herriott

ica, Class of 1996; Past Board Member, Threshold Center for Youth; Neighborhood Housing Services of Rochester; Monroe County Advisory Committee on Women's Issues (1993 Chair).

Awards/Recognition: Fellow, Colgate Institute for Ethical Leadership, 1998;*Who's Who Among American College & Universitie*s, 1994; United Way Volunteer Recognition, 1997; "Woman First" Award, YWCA, 1994; Jefferson Award Nominee, 1998.

Residence: Rochester, NY

HICKS, Ernest Lewis

Born: Little Rock, Arkansas, 1950; Moved to Rochester, 1986.

Parents: Helen J. Young and Ernest Hicks.

Family: Married to Zell Hicks; Three children, Choya, Kirsten, and Gabrielle.
Education: B. A., Finance, University of Arkansas; Certified Master Practitioner in Neuro-Linguistic Programming, Upstate New York Institute for Neuro-Linguistics; DCHC from the American Institute of Hypnotherapy.

Career: *Diversity Manager, Xerox US Customer Operations since 1997*; Manager, Worldwide Marketing, Xerox Quality Services 1994-1997; Senior Managing Partner, Xerox Quality Solutions for United States Customer Operations, 1992-1994; Manager, Middle Management Training and Quality Consulting, Xerox Corporation, 1990-1992; Program Manager/Consultant, Employee Involvement and Quality Training, Xerox Corporation, 1986-1990; Sales Manager, Major Accounts, Xerox Corporation, 1979-1986; Sales Executive, Major Accounts, 1978-1979; Senior Sales Representative, Major Accounts, Xerox Corporation, 1976-77; Xerox 9200 High Volume Copier Specialist, Xerox Corporation, 1975-1976; Sales Representative, Xerox Corporation, 1974-1975.

Professional/Community Involvement: Member of the Rochester Institute of Technology Adjunct Faculty, teaching three accredited courses, Leadership Skills for Quality, Implementing Total Quality, and Introduction to Quality; Member, Xerox Management Association, Concern Association of Rochester Incorporated (CARI), National Quality Association; Past Co-Chair of the Perinton African American Heritage Committee, the International Association for NLP, the American Society for Training and Development, United Way Disabilities Community Investment Committee; Member, Board of Directors, Vocational Committee, Human Resource Committee, and Organization Committee for the Association for Retarded Citizens.

Awards/Recognition: Black Belt, Martial Arts; Internationally Recognized Orator.

HILL, Jacqueline Elizabeth

Born: Alcoa, Tennessee
Parents: Eldie and Elizabeth Hill.
Family: Single.
Education: MBA, Executive Development Program University of Rochester, 1979; MS, Chemistry, University of Michigan, 1970; B.S., Chemistry, Tennessee State University, 1968.

Career: *Eastman Kodak Company:Division Manager, Roll Coating Estar Divion since 1998;* Director, Film Manufacturing Organization, Kodak de Mexico, Guadalajara, Mexico, 1995-1998; Manager, Materials Manufacturing Printing and Publishing Imaging Division, 1991-1995; Assistant Manager, Materials Manufacturing of the same organization, 1990-1991; Operations Manager, Black & White Film Sensitizing Division, 1989-1990; Production Manager, Chemicals and Recovery Division, 1986-1989; Department Manager, Mixing Department, Chemical Finished Products Division, 1985-1986; Assistant to the Manager, Chemical Manufacturing Organization 1984-1985; Quality Control Supervisor, Electrophotographic Chemistry Division, 1982-1984; Supervisor, Project Development Division, 1980-1982; Market Analyst, Business System Markets Division, 1978-1980; Research Chemist, Chemistry Division Kodak Research Labs, 1971-1978.

Professional/Community Involvement: Board Member, Junior Achievement since 1998; Founding Member of Sisters For A Better Community, 1972-84; Member, Urban League of Rochester, Network North Star (a Kodak Black Employee Network), National Organization for the Advancement of Black Chemists & Chemical Engineers (NOBCChE), the Women's Forum of

Jacqueline Elizabeth Hill

Photo, Fred Tanksley. Copyright 1998,, Norex Publications.

Kodak Employees, The Photographic Society of Science & Engineers; Board Member, United Cerebral Palsy Association of the Rochester Area since 1991; Eastman Kodak Key Executive for Spellman College (since 1998), and for Tennessee State University and Florida A & M University, 1992-1994; Listed in The Diversity Resource Directory of Rochester Area Volunteers Published by The Philanthropic Diversity Consortium of the Rochester (NY) Region, 1993-94.

Awards/Recognition: Beta Kappa Chi Honor Society; *Who's Who in American Universities and Colleges;* 100 of the Best and Brightest Black Women in Corporate America, Ebony Magazine, 1991.

Patents/Publications: Author of two scientific publications, in *Photographic Science and Engineering.*

Residence: Fairport, New York.

HILL, Jr., John R.

Born: Bridgeport, Connecticut, 1961; Moved to Rochester,1982.
Parents: John and Betty Hill.
Family:One daughter, Candace.
Education: B.S., Computer Engineering, Boston University; African-American Leadership Development Program (AALDP), United Way, 1993; Leadership Rochester, 1996.

Career: *Manager, Strategy, Xerox Corporation since 1998;* Systems Engineer, Xerox Corporation since 1982-1998

Professional/Community Involvement: Worshipful Master, Eureka Lodge # 36, Prince Hall Masons since 1996; Past Vice-President Personnel, Xerox Management Association; Chairman Evaluation Committee, African-American Leadership Development Program Executive Committee; Community Partners for Youth; Member, AALDP Alumni Association; Board Member, Big Brothers/Big Sisters; Past Youth Fellowship Advisor; *Who's Who Among Young Men in America*; *Who's Who Among High School Students*; Member, Mount Olivet Baptist Church.

Patents/Publications: Three patents, US 5,038,319, System for Recording and Remotely Accessing Operating Data in a Reproduction Machine, Aug., 1991; US 5,057,866, Remotely Accessible Copier Calculator, Oct., 1991; US 5,155,849, Multilingual Operator Prompting System Which Compares Language Control File Version Numbers in Document and Mass Memory for Changing Language Files, Oct., 1992.

Residence: Henrietta, New York.

HOLLOWAY, Jr., Oscar

Born: Alexandria, Louisiana, 1945; Moved to Rochester, 1980.
Parents: Essie and Oscar Holloway.
Family: Married Cheryl Holloway; One son, Philip Holloway.
Education: JD, Law, University of Akron, 1977; B.S., Accounting, Southern University, 1967.

Career: *Manager, Compliance & Audit, Xerox Corporation since 1989*; Manager, Tax Policy & Programs, Xerox Corporation, 1983-89; Manager, Tax Research & Operation, Xerox Corporation, 1980-83; Staff Tax Accountant, Firestone Tire & Rubber, 1978-80; General Accountant, Firestone Tire & Rubber, 1969-78; Finance Officer, U.S. Army, 1967-69.

Professional/Community Involvement: Secretary, Mt. Vernon Baptist Church Deacon Board since 1982; Treasurer, Urban League of Rochester Board of Directors since 1992; Member, Leadership of Rochester Board of Directors since 1993 (Chair, 1997-1998); Member, Monroe County Industrial Development Corporation; Member, Alpha Phi Alpha Fraternity; Member, American Bar Association Tax Section; Member, Veterans of Foreign Wars, VFW; Member, Ohio State Bar.

HOWARD, G. Jean

Born: Greensboro, North Carolina; Moved to Rochester, 1976.
Parents: Corrine Lee Blair and Ezell Alexander Blair.
Family: Three children, Russell, Randaal and Ingrid.
Education: MS, Education, Indiana University, Bloomington, Indiana; BA, Bennett College, Greensboro, North Carolina; Certificate, Developing Program Evaluation Systems Course,

School of Industrial & Labor Relations, Cornell University.

Career: *Executive Director, Wilson Commencement Park (WCP) since 1990*; Previously held senior management positions with United Cerebral Palsy Association of Rochester; Clinic Coordinator, Substance Abuse, Maternal Infant Care Services, Hutzel Hospital, Detroit Michigan; Project Manager, Well-Being Services for the Aging, Detroit, Michigan; Adult Program Director, YWCA, Springfield, Massachusetts; Case Manager, New York City Mission Society.

Professional/Community Involvement: Trustee, Bennett College, Frontier Corporation Educational Assistance Fund, Mary Cariola Children's Center, WXXI Public Broadcasting, Inc., and Center for Governmental Research; Past Board Member, Housing Council of Rochester, State University of New York, Brockport's Educational Opportunity Center, Rochester School for the Deaf, Coordinated Care Services, Inc., Baden Street Settlement House, and the Martin Luther King Commission; Past Member, Executive Committee, New York State Advisory Council on Mental Retardation and Developmental Disabilities (appointed by former Governor Mario Cuomo).

Residence: Rochester, New York.

HOWARD, Louis

Born: Apopka, Florida, 1943; Moved to Rochester, 1968.
Parents: Maxwell Howard, Sr. and Colanthia Holley (deceased).
Family: Married to Dornell Howard; Seven children, Aubrey, Rochelle, Dionne, Shaka, Kevin, Catherine and Anthony Howard.
Education: B.S., Human Resource Management, Roberts Wesleyan College, 1994; AS, Busi-

HUBBARD, Calvin L.

ness Administration, Monroe Community College, 1990; African--American Leadership Development Program, United Way of Greater Rochester, Class of 1996.

Career: *City of Rochester: Assistant Director, Bureau of Parking and Municipal Code Violations (since 1997)*; Purchaser, Purchasing Bureau, 1993-1997; Sr. Supervising Stock Clerk, Bureau of Municipal Facilities, 1984-93; Assistant Property Clerk/Quartermaster, Police Department,1980-84;, Senior Library Clerk, Public Library, 1979-80; Assistant Bookkeeper/Maintenance Supervisor, TEMPA Services, Rochester NY, 1973-78; United States Air Force, Jet Aircraft Mechanic, 1961--64.

Professional/Community Involvement: Cubmater, Scouts, Pack #37, 1982--87; Assistant Scoutmaster, Troop # 37, 1987--88; Vice President, Parent/Teacher Group, Frederick Douglas Middle School; Member, School--Based Planning Team, Frederick Douglas Middle School; Member, Neighborhood Watch Program; Assistant Teacher, Sunday School, Open Baptist Church; Elder/Teacher, Sunday School, Faith to Faith Fellowship; Chair, Catholic Family Center/Homeless Committee, 1996; Board Member, catholic Family Center since 1998

Awards/Recognition: Graduate with Distinction, Monroe Community College, 1990; Who's Who Among Students in American Junior College, 1989--1990; Phi Theta Kappa, National Honor Fraternity, Two--year College, 1989; Scout Leader Training Award, Boy Scouts of America, 1987; Nominee, Volunteer of The Year Award, Catholic Family Center, 1998.

HUBBARD, Calvin L.

Born: Dallas, Texas, July 23, 1940.
Parents: Ressie and Mildred Hubbard.

Calvin L. Hubbard
Photo, Mike F. Molaire. Copyright 1998, Norex Publications

Family: Married to Evelyn Hubbard; Three children, Katrina, Tyletha, and Yuressa.
Education: Master of Art, Rochester Institute of Technology (R.I.T.), 1971; B.A.E., Contemporary Art, Texas Southern University, Houston, Texas, 1960; Aspen School of Contemporary Art, Aspen Colorado, 1963; Pottery Class, R.I.T., 1996.

Career: *Owner, Turtle Pottery Gallery (594 Brown St., Rochester, NY) since 1987*; Retired from the Rochester City School District, 1970-1996; Summer Workshop for children, Turtle Pottery, 1987-1990; Houston Independent School District, Houston, Texas, 1969-1970; United States Army, 1966-1969.

Major Works : Commission Busts of Frederick Douglass for the Memorial A.M.E. Zion Church, 1998; Commissioned Busts of Mr. & Mrs. Hamm, 1993; Flint Street Recreation Center Mural Project, 1992; Miss Jane Pitman Fountain Project (at the Liberty Pole, Downtown), 1989; Shuttle Memorial Sculpture Project, East High School, 1987; Austin Steward Memorial Bust, (Downtown Holiday Inn), 1986; Sculptured Memorial of Isaac and Amy Post, Hochstein School of Music, 1985; Commissioned to design a bench honoring Mrs. Cynthia Fitzpatrick, Rochester's oldest citizen, 1983; Commissioned the Seasons Symbols, Downtown Rochester, 1981; Mural Painting, Texas Southern University, 1976.

Professional/Community Involvement: Member and Past Master, Eureka Lodge # 36; Deacon, Second Baptist Church, Mumford, New York; Member, National Conference of Artists.

Awards/Recognition:Dewitt Clinton Award, Towpath Lodge # 117, 1998; Mirror Project, Lake Effect Magazine, 1997; Martin Luther King Freedom Ride, Strong Museum, 1992; Artist of The Year, Pyramid Art Gallery; Martin Luther King Jr. Cultural Award, 1984.

Residence: Rochester, New York.

HUMMINGS, Armenta Adams

Born: Cleveland, Ohio, June 27, 1936; Moved to Rochester,1994.
Parents: Albert Adams (deceased) and Estella Adams (deceased).
Family: Divorced; Four sons, Amadi, Gus Jr., Martin and Marcus.
Education: B.S. and MS, Juliard School of Music, New York, New York, 1954-60; Studied with eminent pianist Sascha Gorodnitski at Galleried; One year of study in London, England, 1963-64; Girls' Latin School, Boston, MA, 1947--53; Elementary School CC Perkins, Boston, MA, 1941-47; Piano and Violin, Early Music Training, New England Conservatory, Boston MA, 1941-43.

Career: Distinguished Community Mentor, Eastman School of Music since 1995; Soloist, with the Winston--Salem Piedmont Triad Symphony, 1993; Visiting Professor, North Carolina A&T University, 1987-88; North Carolina Urban Arts Residency, 1985-87; Violin Teacher, Winston--Salem State University, Winston--Salem, NC, 1983-84; Piano Teacher, North Carolina School of Arts, Community Music, Program, Winton--Salem, NC, 1981-83; Piano Teacher, Brunswick Junior College, Brunswick, GA, 1975-76; Piano Class, Henry Street Settlement School, New York, NY, 1973-75; Juliard Preparatory Division, New York, NY, 1968-69; Piano, Piano Class, Theory, Harlem School of the Arts, New York, NY, 1966-69; Piano, Piano Class, Violin String Ensemble; Florida, A&M University, Tallahassee, Fl., 1965-66; Concert Piano, Debut at New York Town Hall, 1960; Appeared in New York Carnegie Hall, Avery Fisher Hal, Alice Tully; International performances sponsored by the US State Dept., Australia; Austria; Belgium, Brazil, Canada, Guyana, Holland, India, Ivory Coast, Liberia, Mali, Malawi; Pakistan, Panama, Paraguay, Sierra Leone, Sweden, Switzerland, Tanzania, and Zambia; Represented the U.S. as Guest Artist at the first International Black Arts Festival, Dakar, Senegal; Solo Performances with the Galleried Orchestra; L'Orchestre de la Suise Romande; Cleveland Orchestra; Greensboro Symphony; Detroit Pops; Miami Pops; Chicago Grant Park; Pierre Monteux Festival Orchestra; Battle Creek Symphony; Symphony of the New World; Premier Performance of All--Black Symphony at Philadelphia Music Academy; Raleigh Symphony, Winston--Salem Piedmont Triad Symphony; Judge Competition, North Carolina Arts Council, Performing Artist Auditions, 1989-91; Wake Forest University, Piano

Armenta Adams Hummings
Photo, Mike Molaire Copyright 1998, Norex Publications.

Competitions, 1988-90; Peabody Conservatory of Music, Piano Competition, 1992; Winston-Salem Symphony, Young Artist Auditions, 1991.

Professional/Community Involvement: Mentors students within their own communities, churches, schools; Her students have appeared at the Eastman School of Music, Jefferson Avenue Seventh Day Adventist Church, the Memorial A.M.E. Zion Church, the Christ Tabernacle Church, St. Bridgett's Church, Mt. Vernon Baptist Church, the Lutheran Church of the Reformation, The New Bethel C.M.E. Church, The Church of Love Faith Center, The Arnett Family YMCA, City Hall, and the Riverside Convention Center; She is the Artistic Director of the Gateways Music Festival which honors African--American musicians and furnishes a network of performance opportunities and role models.

Awards/Recognition: James McCuller Award, Action For a Better Community, Rochester, NY, 1995; White Rose Award for the Arts, The Links Inc., Rochester, NY, 1997; Frida Joewenthal Eising Award; NY Musicians Club First Prize; John Hay Whitney Grant; Martha Baird Rockefeller Grant; Special Prize, Leeds International Piano Competition; Musical America Musicians of the Year Award; International Institute of Education Grant; Full Scholarship, Galleried School of Music; Winner of the John Hay Whitney Competition, the Annual Competition of the National Association of Negro Musicians; Finalist in the Michaels Competition, in Chicago; Special Prize Award, First International Piano Competition, Leeds, England.

Quotations:

"There were many moments of sheer magic...Armenta is a significant talent."

> Joseph Mclellan, Washington Post, commenting on Mrs. Hummings performance as a guest artist at the prestigious International Piano Festival at the University of Maryland.

"A refreshing, well-played concert...Miss Adams has more than technical proficiency. She performs with artistry and complete authority."

> Cleveland Press (after solo with the Cleveland Orchestra

"Her playing was of such inspired intensity, so clear, so brilliant, so authoritative and compelling that it literally quickened his pulse."

> New York Herald Tribune

"Seldom does one find so much physical vitality in a pianist with so much poetic sensibility; nor such clarity of texture in an artist who is not only interested in color but able to achieve it so variedly. And besides being able to play with melting lyricism she can make great chords ring out like a big scale virtuoso."

> The New York Times

"Magic is the unique, the only adequate word."
  Stockholm Tidningen

JACKSON, John "Hank", 1930-1996.

Born: Rochester, May 26, 1930 NY; Died of cancer, on Nov 11, 1996, at Isaiah House, 71 Prince St; Buried in Mumford Rural Cemetery.
Parents: Lincoln and Lula Jackson.
Family: Survived by his former wife, Wilma Sellers; Two daughters, Jackie Jackson and Anita Jackson; A son, L. Bruce Jackson; Two brothers, Edward Jackson and McKinley Jackson; Two sisters, Emma Gibbs and Addie Lu Coleman; Two grandsons; and one great-grand-daughter.
Education: Graduate of Churchville High School, 1949; Attended Rochester Institute of Technology's City Center.

Career: Opened his first business, Royal Art Studio on West Main Street, 1959; Worked in the Commercial Art/Display Department of McCurdy's, early 1960s; Opened an advertising business on Railroad Street, late 1960s; Started publication of *about...time*, early 1970, the first African-American magazine in Rochester; Left *about...time* in 1973; Painted commercial signs in Boston and Philadelphia from 1979-1986.

Professional/Community Involvement
Played in Churchville High School band, sung in the chorus, and held several class offices.

Eulogies/Quotations:

"His dream was a black family magazine. He felt as the title implies it was about time.
  Mary Lou Yawn, a former assistant editor.
  Times Union, Nov 15, 1996

"A multi talented individual. A person with excellent creative abilities."
  James M. Blount, publisher, about...time
  Times Union, Nov 15, 1996

John Henry "Hank" Jackson
*Reprinted with permission of **about...time** Magazine, Inc.*

JACKSON, Marvin

Born: Lakeland, Florida, 1954; Moved to Rochester, 1982
Parents: Emma Lee Moore and J.C. Jackson.
Family: Married to Julien; Six children, Ishmael, Steven, Kelli, Ariel, Jordan, Devin.
Education: B.S., Management of Human Resources, Roberts Wesleyan College, Rochester, NY, 1988; AS, General Studies, Miami-Dade Community College, Miami, Fla, 1975; Public Administration Courses, Biscayne College, Miami, Fla., 1977-82; Community College, Air Force, Maxwell AFB, 1978-82; Financial Planning Masters Training Course, Lifetime Financial Planning Services, Inc, 1994; Managing Winning Proposals, Shipley Associates, Bountiful, Utah, 1993; Writing Winning Proposals, Shipley Associates, Bountiful, Utah, 1992; Advance Performance Management Training, Aubrey Daniels and Associates, Atlanta, Georgia, 1989; Internet/Intranet Publishing Workshop, 1996.

JACKSON, Trenton J.

Career: *Supervisor and Managing Editor, Commercial and Government Systems, Eastman Kodak Company since 1992*; Commissioner of Schools, Rochester Board of Education since 1996; Organizational Consultant, Material Engineering Maintenance Organization (MEMO), Kodak Park, Eastman Kodak Company, 1991-92; Division Safety Coordinator, MEMO, Kodak Park, 1989-91; Assistant Supervisor/Electronic System Development Technician, MEMO Synthetic Chemicals Division, Eastman Kodak, 1982-86; Staff Sergeant, Tactical Air Command, Moody Air Force Base, Georgia. U.S. Air Force, 1978-82.

Professional/Community Involvement: Rochester City School District since 1995: Chair, Budget, Finance and Organizational Development Committee; Vice Chair, Human Resources Committee; Member, Policy Committee; Board Representative, New York State Conference of Big 5 School Districts; Member, National School Boards Association (NSBA); Member, Council of Urban Boards of Education (C.U.B.E.); Member, NSBA Black Caucus, New York State School Boards Association, Monroe County School Boards Association, Title 1 District Advisory Council, Region 2; President, City School District Parent Council, 1991-93; Vice President 1994; Ex-Officio and Consultant since 1994; Charter Member, Kodak 21st Century Learning Challenge Program Council; Member, Urban League's Re-Call to Action Study on School Reform in the City School District, 1991; Franklin High School: Vice President, Parent and Community Association, 1989-91; Parent Representative, Franklin Receivership Team, 1990-91; Representative to the District Parent Council (DPC), 1991; Member, Parent Group; Member, Northeast Middle School Design Committee, Rochester City School District, 1992-93; Member, Transition Team for the Parent Involvement Policy, 1989-91; Member, CIT Panel Subcommittee to Develop Standards and Expectations for Teachers, Home/Parent Involvement, 1991-92; Member, School Selection Appeals Committee, 1990; President, Charlotte Middle School Parents Association, 1990-91; Vice President, 1988-90; Member, School-Based Planning Team, 1988-91.

Residence: Rochester, New York.

JACKSON, Trenton J.

Born: Cordele, Georgia, 1944; Moved to Rochester, 1948.
Parents: Evelyn and James Jackson.
Family: Married Pamela; Four children, Nicole, Yolanda , Heidi, and Trenton, Jr.
Education: MS, SUNY Brockport; B.S., University of Illinois.

Career: First Black Olympian from Rochester; in the summer of 1964, went to Tokyo to compete in the Olympics; Was ready to duel Bob Hayes, the World Fastest Human, in the 100-meter dash, but, he pulled a hamstring in the quarter finals; Played wide receiver In the National Football League: one year for the Philadelphia Eagles, two years for the Washington Redskin; Has taught physical education and coached football, basketball, and track at his alma mater, Franklin High School, the past two decades.

Awards/Recognition: Voted in Track & Field Hall of Fame, Niagara/Rochester, 1998; Voted Section V Basketball Coach of The Year, Class A, 1996; Voted City Catholic Coach of The Year in basketball, 1984, 1986, 1988, 1994, 1994; Amateur Athlete of the Year,Press-Radio Club, 1964; National High School World record, 100-yard 9,4 dash, 1961; Rochester Track Club Hall of Fame; Rochester High School Hall of Fame; All-American Track Team, 1964.; College Sport: five varsity letters for indoor & outdoor track, two for football, and one for baseball, University of Illinois; Drafted by the St. Louis Cardinals

Baseball Team, 1965; N.C.A.A. Track National Record Holder (10.1, 100-meter dash), 1964; Twelve varsity letters in high school for three sports, football, basketball, and track.

Residence: Rochester, New York.

JACOBS, Warren H.

Born: Becket, Mass., Sept. 23, 1921
Education: B.S., Pharmacy, Howard University, 1950.

Career: First Black pharmacy owner in Rochester; Owner of Warren's Pharmacy Inc., at 561 Jefferson Avenue; Served in the U.S. Army Air Force for three years; two years in Italy as part of the 332nd Fighter Bomber Group.

Professional/Community Involvement: Former Member and Delegate, FIGHT, Inc.; Former Member, Omega Psi Phi Fraternity, Inc., Peoples Club, Caribbean Club and Reynolds Street Church of Christ; Advisory Board, Community Savings Bank; Board Member, Better Business Bureau, Blue Cross, Rochester Drug Co-operative, Urban League of Rochester, Monroe County Human Relations Commission, Rochester Consumer Credit Counseling Service, Affirmative Action Advisory Council for the County of Monroe, Rochester Business & Professional League, Advisory Board for the Elderly; Former Trustee, Church of Christ; Former Vice President, Progressive Businessman Association.

Residence: Rochester, New York

JAMES, Thomas, Rev. 1804-1891

Born: Canajoharie, New York, in 1804, as a slave; Moved to Rochester, 1823.

Reverend Thomas James
*Reprinted with permission of **about...time** Magazine, Inc.*

Parents: Third of four children.
Education: Was taught to read by Mr., Freeman at a Sunday school for colored youths; Largely self-educated.

Career: Escaped slavery to the Canadian border, June 1, 1821; Returned to the American side, 1823; Came to Rochester as an employee of the Hudson & Erie Warehouse; Became a member of the African Methodist Episcopal Society, 1823; Started to teach a school for colored children on Favor Street, 1828; Organized the society known as the First African Methodist Church, 1827; Began preaching, 1829; bought the site of the first Zion's church, 1830; Joined the anti-slavery forces, 1830; Ordained minister, May, 1833, by Bishop Rush; Left Rochester to form a colored church in Syracuse, 1835; Moved to Ithaca in 1838; to St. Harbor, Long Island, 1840; Then to New Bedford, Massachusetts; Met Frederick Douglass in New Bedford; Moved then to Boston; Returned to Rochester, 1856 and lead the A.M.E church; Appointed by the American Missionary Society to labor among the colored people of Tennessee and Louisiana, but went to St. Louis instead; Elected general superintendent and missionary agent by the general Conference of the African Methodist Episcopal Connection, June, 1868; Appointed by Bishop Wayman a missionary preacher for the colored churches in Ohio, 1878; Moved back to Rochester, 1829.

JEFFERSON, Jr., Frederick C, Ph.D.

Born: New Orleans, Louisiana.
Family: Married; Three children.
Education: Ed.D., Counseling Education, University of Massachusetts, Amherst, Massachusetts, 1981; MA, Guidance and Counseling, SUNY Hunter College, New York, New York, 1967; MA, Music, SUNY Hunter College, 1959; B.S., Music Education, SUNY Hunter College, 1957.

Career: *University of Rochester: Assistant to the President for University & Community Affairs, Assistant Professor of Education And Chair of Counseling Faculty (Graduate School of Education and Human Development) since 1985*; Associate Dean of Students and Director of Minority Student Affairs, 1985; Director of Special Student Services, 1976-85; Director, Educational Opportunity Program/Program Office for Intercessor's Office, 1973-76; Program Associate, Program in Humanistic Education, SUNY Albany, 1971-73; Director, Educational Opportunity Program, Corning Community College, Corning, New York, 1971; Project Associate, Program in Humanistic Education, SUNY Albany (on leave from Corning Community College),

Frederick C. Jefferson, Jr., Ph.D.
Photo, Fred Tanksley.Copyright 1993, Norex Publications.

1970-71; Director, New Studies Division, Educational Opportunity Program Corning Community College, 1969-70; Director, Educational Opportunity Program, Corning Community College, 1968-69; Director of Financial Aid, Assistant Director of Activities, Assistant Professor of Music, Corning Community College, 1967-68; Director of Financial Aid, Job Placement Director, Assistant Professor of Music, Corning Community College, 1966-67; J.H.S. 136-750 Jennings Street, New York, New York: Teacher Of Mathematics and Music; Chairman of Eighth Grade Mathematics Department, Guidance Counselor, Basketball Coach, 1962-66; Teacher of Orchestral and General Music, 1959-61;

Teacher of Orchestral and General Music, 1958-59; Social Investigator, New York City Department of Welfare, 1958; Recreation Leader, New York City Department of Parks, 1957.

Professional/Community Involvement: Member of African-American Leadership Development Program Advisory Committee; American Red Cross Board of Directors; Austin Steward Professional Society, (Civic Organization of African-American Professionals); Consortium For Youth Outreach; International Museum of Photography at George Eastman House; Martin Luther King, Jr., Greater Rochester Festival Committee; Rochester Child's, Rochester City School District Committee on Multicultural Education; Rochester Philharmonic Orchestra Development Committee; Seneca Zoo Society, Board of Directors; the ABC James McCuller Memorial Golf Outing Committee; The Manhattan Golf Academy for Juniors; United Neighborhood Centers of Greater Rochester Foundation, Board of Directors; United Way of Greater Rochester; Formerly, Chairman of the Board, Action For A Better Community, 1979--86; Branch--Wilbur Fund; Brighton Democratic Club; Chase Lincoln Bank Metropolitan Advisory Board; Community Roundtable on Educational Change; Finger Lakes Health Systems Agency; First Thursday Club of Rochester; Junior League of Rochester, Advisory Board; Primary Mental Health Project; PRIS2M; Rochester's Child Steering Committee; Rochester City School District, Blue Ribbon Committee on Restructuring Secondary School Curriculum; Rochester New Futures Initiative, Board of Directors; Rochester/Monroe County Youth Bureau; Urban League of Rochester; William Warfield Scholarship Fund.

Awards/Recognition: Nathaniel Rochester Community Service Award, Central Trust Bank of New York, 1987; Helen Walker Dunbar Community Service Award, Zeta Phi Beta Sorority, Rochester, New York, 1987; Hannah G. Solomon Humanitarian Award, National Council of Jewish, Rochester, New York, 1989.

Paents/Publications: "Multicultural Education: Diversity in Organizations and Programming", in Valuing Diversity on Campus: AMulticultural Approach, ed. Cynthia Woolbright, Association of College Unions-International 1989; "Training Develops Multicultural Awareness," ACU-I Bulletin, March 1986; over 14 keynotes and conference papers between 1987--89.

Residence: Rochester, New York.

JOHNSON, Loretta Dunville

Born: Indianapolis, Indiana, 1938; Moved to Rochester, 1969.
Parents: Mable L. and Larry C. Dunville.
Family: Married William S. Johnson; one child, Camaron Johnson.
Education: M.A., Counseling and Guidance, Michigan State University, 1967; B.A., Elementary Education, Michigan State University, 1959; Education/Administration courses (36 credits), SUNY Brockport and St. John Fisher.

Career: *Senior Associate, National Center on Education and the Economy since 1996*; Deputy Superintendent, Rochester City School District, 1995-96; Interim Superintendent of Schools, Rochester City School District, Provide leadership and management of a District with more than 5,000 employees, 60 facilities, 36,000 PreK-12 students, and 17,000 adults students, and oversight of a budget of approximately one third of a billion dollars (1994-95); Assistant Superintendent, Community Alliance Schools, RSCD, 1992-94; West and Southwest District Superintendent, RSCD, 1989-92; Deputy Superintendent, Curriculum & Instruction, RSCD, 1984-89; Assistant Superintendent, Student Support Services, RSCD, 1981-84; Acting Supervising

Director of Elementary Education, RSCD, 1979-81; Acting Director of Elementary Intermediate Instruction, RSCD. 1978-79; Elementary Vice-Principal, School No. 37, RSCD, 1977-78; Helping Teacher, RSCD, 1976-79; Reading Teacher, School No. 14, RSCD, 1973-76; Elementary Classroom Teacher, School Nos. 4 & 14, RSCD, 1969-73; Elementary Classroom Teacher, School No. 56, Indianapolis Public Schools, 1959-69; Fulbright Exchange Teacher, Colchester, Essex, England, 1964-65.

Professional/Community Involvement: Board Member, Urban League of Rochester; Member, Rochester Chapter of Links, Inc.; Past Board Member, United Way of Greater Rochester, PRISM, Metro YMCA, Alternatives for Battered Women, Rochester Business Education Alliance; Adjunct Faculty Member, SUNY Geneseo.

Awards/Recognitions: Wall of Fame, National Women's Hall of Fame, 1996; Athena Award Nominee, Women's Council of the Greater Rochester Metro Chamber of Commerce, 1996; Rochester's Outstanding Women's Leadership Award, New Life Fellowship, 1995; Appreciation Award, National Alliance for Restructuring Education, 1995; Recognition Awards, Rochester Board of Education, 1995, 1996; Leadership Award, Phi Delta Kappa, 1989; Certificate of Distinguished Service, Urban League of Rochester, 1984; Certificate of Appreciation, Rochester Sesquicentennial, Inc., 1984; Who's Who in the East, 1983-84; Volunteer Service Award, United Way of Greater Rochester; Fulbright Grant, Exchange teacher, 1964-65.

Patents/Publications: Co-Author, of the first written Mohawk Language Curriculum, 1978; several Op--Ed articles in the Democrat & Chronicle, and Times Union.

Residence: Rochester, New York.

JOHNSON, Mildred, 1911-1992

Born: Aug 30, 1911, Brighton, NY; Died Aug 2, 1992, at Strong Memorial Hospital.
Parents: Virginia Wilson.
Family: Predeceased by husband, Thomas Johnson; Survived by a son, Phillip E. Johnson, a daughter-in-law, Patricia A. Johnson, five grandchildren, and goddaughter, Luriesa R, Padgett.
Education: Attended School 17 and the old West High School; Took courses at Howard University, in Washington DC.

Career: Worked in clerical jobs in Washington DC; Returned to Rochester, 1953; Worked for Action For a Better Community, and FIGHT, in the 1960s; Served as liaison between city officials and residents during the 1964 race riots; Ran unsuccessfully for City Council on the Liberal Party Ticket.

Professional/Community Involvement: Sang in the Mount Olivet Baptist Church senior choir; Was active in the NAACP; Founded the Negro Information Center in her home to help people find jobs, 1960; Renamed the center, the Virginia Wilson Interracial Information and Helping Hand Center Inc., in honor of her mother; Working with defense lawyers, was instrumental in getting Monroe County to establish the Public Defender's Office; Wrote a column for The Frederick Douglass Voice.

Awards/Recognition: Linda Balkum wrote her biography, *Millie the Hell raiser*, 1980; Cited in *Newsweek Magazine* among "100 Unsung Heroes" in the nation, 1985; Received the Lotus C. Carson Human Rights Award for fighting discrimination, 1991; Greater Rochester Metro Chamber of Commerce Social Services Award, 1990; the 36th annual Rochester Rotary Award.

Eulogies/Quotations:

Mildred Johnson, 1911-1992
Reprinted with permission of __about...time__ Magazine, Inc.

"I'm Mildred Johnson. I don't wait for anyone."

> Mildred Johnson, as recalled by Esther Manhertz, a secretary at the Urban League.
> __Times Union__, Aug. 4, 1992

"I never met a more dedicated or committed community activist... Mildred had the concerns of all citizens, regardless of race, creed or color, at heart... Her home became a sanctuary for many people who came to the community and had no place to live. She was the original pioneer in helping the homeless. I had nothing but admiration, respect and love for her."

> Constance M. Mitchell, the first black woman elected to public office in Monroe County.
> __Times Union__, Aug. 4, 1992

"We've lost a dedicated, hard-working person who was concerned about all people, but specially those in the inner city... Mildred was marvelous."

> Ronald J. Goode, former 7th Ward supervisor, city councilman and County legislator.
> __Times Union__, Aug. 4, 1992

"People called her an activist. I called her a humanitarian... When she came on the scene, everyone smiled."

> Kathryn Terrell, a longtime friend.
> __D&C__, Aug. 7, 1992

"Mildred moved mountains and molehills alike. She insisted on proper treatment for everyone."

Thomas Mees, past president of the Rochester Rotary
D&C, Aug. 7, 1992

"Whether you saw her in the courtroom or the supermarket, she'd say, all God's children are created equal. They all deserve the same rights.'... She wouldn't say, 'We'll try to get help.' She'd say, 'We're going to get help, and right now.'"

Daisy Holmes, a longtime friend
D&C, Aug. 7, 1992

"She said, 'In (America), we're always looked upon as a minority. When I went to Africa, it was the first time I was part of a majority.'"

Howard Coles, publisher of the black-oriented newspaper,
The Frederick Douglass Voice.

"She's been a mother to hundreds, a grandmother to thousands and a friend to everyone."

Ronald Good
D&C, Aug. 7, 1992

"All I stand for, by and large comes as a result of Mildred Johnson. Mildred was the one who said no matter how rocky the road, you stand up straight, you stand up firm."

City Councilwoman Maxine Childress-Brown
Times Union, Aug. 7, 1992

"She didn't leave the community ever... She really admonished us to do things to make the community better, She believed in the strength and spirit of one person. When nobody would do things, she'd do it herself. You know that God has smiled on you when you have a Mildred Johnson."

Ruth Scott
Times Union, Aug. 4, 1992

JOHNSON, Teresa D., The Honorable

Born: Akron, Ohio, December 31, 1953; Moved to Rochester, 1983.
Parents: Mrs. Dorothy Taylor, and Paul Taylor (deceased).
Family: Married to Allen K. Williams; Two sons, Allen K. Williams II. and Elliot A. Williams.
Education: BA Degree with honors, Yale University, 1975; JD, University of California at Ber-

keley, 1978; Member of Bar of California, Washington D.C., and New York.

Career: J*udge Rochester City Court since 1990*; First Deputy County Attorney, Monroe County, New York, 1988-90; Trial Attorney, Harter, Secret & Emery, Rochester, New York, 1983-88; Trial Attorney, U.S. Department of Justice, Civil Rights Division, Washington, D.C., 1978-83.

Residence: Rochester, New York.

JOHNSON, Jr., William A., The Honorable

Born: Lynchburg, Virginia, 1942; Moved to Rochester, 1972.
Parents: William A. Johnson, Sr. and Roberta Davis Johnson.
Family: Married to Sylvia Andrews McCoy Johnson, Esq.; Four daughters, Kelley M. Johnson, Kristin Johnson-Maring, Wynde Johnson and Sylvia A. McCoy; Two grandsons and two granddaughters..
Education: MA, Political Science, Howard University, 1967; BA, Political Science, Howard University, 1965; Harvard University Human Services Management Executive Program United Way of America, 1986 and 1987; Aspen Institute for Humanistic Studies; Executive Development Seminar, Aspen, Colorado (May 1985); Completed Training program offered by New York State Public Employment Relations Board (PERB) to become a mediator and fact-finder, March 1984-June 1985; University of Pittsburgh, Graduate School of Planning and International Affairs (September-December, 1980; Case Western Reserve University, Cleveland, Ohio, 35-Hour Seminar in Management Information Systems; Large Agency Executives Seminar, six monthly seminar series conducted for 15 Human Service Agency Executives in Rochester by College of Business, Rochester Institute of Technology (1976-1978); Mediator and Fact

Finder, Certified by New York State Public Employment, 1985.

Career: *Reelected as Mayor of Rochester, Nov. 1997*; First African American elected to four-year term as Mayor of the City of Rochester, beginning January 1, 1994; Winner of the Democratic Primary for Mayor of the City of Rochester, September 1993; Appointed Rochester Institute of Technology's Frederick H. Minett Professor for the 1993-94 academic year in RIT's College of Continuing Education; President and CEO of the Urban League of Rochester, 1972-1993; President and Director, Urban League of Rochester Economic Development Corporation, 1985-1993; Consultant, National Urban League Community Mobilization for Education Project, 1990-92; Deputy Executive Director, Urban League of Flint, Michigan, 1971-72; Director of the National Urban League's Voter Registration Project in Flint, 1972; Instructor of Political Science, Genesee Community College, Flint Michigan, 1967-71; Legislative Analyst, National Highway Users Conference, Washington, D.C., 1966-67; Student Assistant, Office of The Reporter of Decisions, U.S. Supreme Court, Washington, D.C., 1966; U.S. Park Ranger, Grand Teton National Park, Wyoming, 1964-65, Gettysburg National Military Park, Pennsylvania, 1966; Licensed Apprentice Funeral Director, Washington, D.C., 1966-67.

Professional/Community Involvement: Chairman, Rochester New Futures Initiative, Inc., 1992-93; Vice Chairperson, Rochester New Futures Initiative, Inc., 1989-91; Member, New York State Board of Social Work, 1988-92; Co-Chairman, Sigma Pi Phi Fraternity Youth Mentoring Project at School # 9, 1990-1994; Commissioner, Rochester Civil Service Commission, 1980-90; Trustee, Monroe Community College, 1976-82; Chair, New York State Employment and Training Council, 1979-83; Chairman, National Urban League Education Initiative Task Force, 1987-89; Board Member: Eltrex Industries, Inc., 1975-1994; Center for Educational Development, 1984-91; Hochstein School of Music, 1988-92; Main West Attorneys, Inc., 1988-90; WRI, Inc., Albany, New York, 1987-1997; Member of the National Urban League Education Initiative Task Force, 1985-1992; Co-chairman, Citizens Advisory Committee, Rochester Fights Back (anti-drug coalition), 1989-91; Mentor, Urban League of Rochester's Black Scholars Program, 1989-1994; Co-Founder and member, African-American Education Oversight Commission since 1984; Member, Greater Rochester Focus Steering Committee, 1987-1989; Member, Finger Lakes Regional Economic Development Council, 1985-89; Concerned Citizens Committee of Rochester, 1983-1992; William Warfield Scholarship Committee, 1985-1989; Member, Transition Team to advise newly elected County Executive Thomas R. Frey, 1987-88; Appointed Trustee, Monroe Community College by Gov. Hugh L. Carey (1976-82); Member, Advisory Panel to the Statewide Study of Nonprofit Organizations, Rockefeller Institute of Government, 1988-89, Task Force on Children & Youth at Risk, New York State Dept. of Education, 1988-89; Appointed to the New York State Job Training Partnership Council by Governor Mario Cuomo, 1983-1988; Member Mayoral Transition Task Force, 1984-85; Committee on Liberal Arts Education & Career Preparation, St. John Fisher College, 1988; New York State Council of Urban Leagues, President, 1975-79, Vice President, 1973-75; Annual Eastern Regional Council; Convener, Howard University Alumni Association, Rochester Area, 1975-78; New York State Developmental Disabilities Council, 1984-88; Executive Committee and Issues Committee, Rochester/Monroe County Private Industry Council, 1983-88; Honorary Chairperson, Black Seeds Scholarship Committee, 1982-84; Standing Committee on Blacks in Higher Education, 1980-86; Governor's Task Force on Adolescent Pregnancy, 1984-88; Board of Directors, Rochester Jobs, Inc., 1973-84; Citizens Alliance to Prevent Drug Abuse, 1982-84; United Way of Greater Rochester Planning, Evaluation and Allocation Committee, 1981-83; Chairman, Employment Task Force, Statewide Emergency Network for Social and Economic Security, 1980-81; Citizens Task Force on City School District Finances, 1977-78; Civil Service Study Commission, 1979; Monroe County Affirmative Action Advisory Council, 1974-79; Secretary and Director, The Urbanium, Inc., 1978-80; Downtown Development Corporation, 1978-84; New York State Community Services Block Grant Advisory Council, 1988; Albany Jefferson Awards Selection Committee, WROC-TV, 1983-88; Give 5 For Rochester Awards Selection Committee, 1989; Genesee County Economic Development Commission, Flint, Michigan, 1971-72; Board of Directors, Michigan ACLU, 1970-71; Board of Directors, Flint and Genesee Valley ACLU, 1968-71; Vice President, AFT Local at Genesee Community College, 1968-69; Flint Michigan NAACP, 1968-72; American Political Science Association, 1968-73; American Society of Public Administration, 1974-80; Rochester Rotary Club, 1974-81.

Awards/Recognition: Doctor of Humane Letters (L.H.D.), Honoris Causa, Keuka College, Keuka Park, New York, 1990; Vernon E. Jordan, Jr. Fellowship, 1986; Executive of the Year, United Community Chest of Greater Rochester, 1979; Commencement Speaker, Graduate School of Education and Human Development, University of Rochester, 1987; Jefferson Award for Outstanding Public Service Benefitting a Local Community, 1986; Swore in Mayor Thomas P. Ryan, Jr. the first Elected Rochester mayor in 56 years, 1986; Community Networking and Education Award, Delta Sigma Theta Sorority, Rochester Alumnae Chapter, 1987; Rochester Chamber of Commerce Civic Award for Education, 1986; Rochester Chamber of Commerce Civic Award for Social Services, 1982; Leadership in Education Award, Department of Minority Student Affairs, University of Rochester, 1989; Community Service Award, Rochester Community Hospitality Club, Inc., 1990; Outstanding Lay Person Award, Phi Delta Kappa, Rochester Chapter, 1987; Distinguished Service Award, Monroe County Schools Board Association, 1987; Man of The Year, Rochester Genesee Valley Club, Negro Business and Professional Women Clubs, 1978; Citizen of the Year, Omega Psi Phi Fraternity, 1977; Listed in *Who's Who In Black America*, 1st, 2nd, 3rd editions; Recipient of more thand 20 other awards and citations.

Patents/Publications: Contributing Columnist for the *Rochester Democrat & Chronicle, Times Union, about...time Magazine,* and *CITY Newspaper* since 1975; Author of more than 25 essays.

Residence: Rochester, New York

Quotations:

"I am mindful of the awesome task that awaits me...These are bleak times financially and tragic times socially...We will not fail."

> Mayor William A. Johnson, Jr.,Iinauguration Day,
> Saturday January 1, 1994
> <u>D&C.</u>, January 2, 1994

"I am prepared to be your mayor...to lead this city to great opportunities...I have the faith, the determined belief, that Rochester can become a totally revitalized city...I stand here to tell you. I do not intend to be the African-American mayor of a dying city. I do not expect to preside over Rochester's demise-but over its revitalization."

> Mayor William A. Johnson, Jr., Inauguration Day,
> Saturday January 1, 1994
> <u>D&C.</u>, January 2, 1994

"This advocate is now going to be working from the inside of the system. And I'm not going to accept any excuses."

Mayor William A. Johnson, Jr.
Taking the oath of office in 1994.
Photo, Mike F. Molaire. Copyright 1998, Norex Publications.

Mayor William A. Johnson, Jr.,Iinauguration Day,
Saturday January 1, 1994
D&C., January 2, 1994

"We have achieved this great victory, but there also is
the sobering reality of the challenge that are
ahead...We, not me."
Mayor William A. Johnson, Jr., at the Mapledale Party
House on election night, November 2, 1993.
D&C, Nov. 3, 1993.

"It's always reassuring to talk things over. We gain
perspective, a better understanding of the community, and expanded sense of possibility when we discuss important issues."
Mayor William A. Johnson, Jr.
What's your vision of Rochester?
Speaking Out, D&C, April 21, 1998

"The proposed comprehensive plan will suggest ways
to strengthen Rochester's position as a cultural, in-
stitutional and financial hub for the benefit of the en-
tire region
Mayor William A. Johnson,, Jr.
Commenting on the Vision 2000 Plan
What's your vision of Rochester?
Speaking Out, D&C, April 21, 1998

JONES, Marsha Regina

Born: Brooklyn, NY, 1962; Moved to Rochester,
1967.
Parents: Iona and Eudolphin Jones.
Family: Married to Donald Collins; One daugh-
ter, Hollis Danielle Collins.
Education: BA, Journalism/Spanish, Purdue
University, 1984; AP Spanish classes, Nazareth
College, Rochester, New York.

Career: *Marketing & Communications Manager, Planned Parenthood of Rochester & The
Genesee Valley since 1997;* Director of Communications, Camp Good Days & Special Times,
1995-1996; Public Relations Coordinator, Hillside Children's Center, 1993-1995; Marketing
Communications Manager, SUNY Brockport,
1989-1993; Assistant editor, *about...time Magazine*, 1984-1989; Freelance Writer and Colum-

nist, *The Challenger Newspaper*, about...time
Magazine since 1989; *Rochester Business Magazine*, 1988-1993; *Scene Entertainment Weekly*,
1995-1996; *Rochester Museum & Science Center News*, 1992.

Professional/Community Involvement: Co-
Chair, 1999 Women Fest Committee; Board
Member, Boys & Girls Club of Rochester (co-
chair Public Relations & Marketing committee
and bowl-a-thon committee member) since
1994; Co-chair, Art Diversity Project, Hillside
Children's Center, 1994-1995; Member,
Guyanese-American Association, 1992; Action
For a Better Community's 20th Anniversary Gala,
1985; Mentor, Boy Scouts of America, 1985; Co-
Chair, Rochester Association of Black Communi-
cations (RABC), 7,8,9,10th Annual Ethnogenre
Film Festival, 1991-1995; President, RABC,
1992; Secretary, RABC, 1992; Volunteer, Shar-
ing and Caring Sibling Support Group of Camp
Good Days, 1995-96; Chair SUNY Brockport's
Admissions Search Committee, 1992; SUNY
Brockport's African & Afro-American Studies
Dept 20th Anniversary Gala Committee, 1991;
President's Campus Safety Committee, SUNY
Brockport, 1991; Public Relations Chair, Center
of African-American Culture's Fund-Raising
Gala, 1994; Mentor, East High School's Ebony
Culture Club, 1986-1988; Volunteer, Gannett
Rochester Newspaper's Lend-A-Hand Charity,
1990-1991; Publicity Chair, Bill Klein's Acad-
emy Awards Party since 1994; Publicity Chair, R.
Nelson Mandela Scholarship Fund, 1989-1993;
Vice President, Montgomery Neighborhood Cen-
ter Youth Advisory Board, 1990-93; Member,
Purdue University Alumni Association since
1991; Member, Purdue University Black Alumni
Organization since 1984; Hillside's Working To-
gether Team, 1993-1995; Member, National As-
sociation of Black Journalists since 1989; City
Newspaper Advisory Board; American Red
Cross Minority Screening Committee; SUNY
Brockport Faculty Senate's Appropriations, Ap-

Marsha Regina Jones
Photo, Mike Molaire. Copyright 1998, Norex Publications.

Patents/Publications: "My Father's Child, My Mother's Daughter", *Visions & Viewpoints: Voices of The Genesee Valley,* (1993); "Friendship 1337", *Visions & Viewpoints: Voices of The Genesee Valley,* (1994); "She Was Right", *The healing Power of Friends,* published by COMPEER; Copy Editor, *Shadow of Dreams* by Mike Molaire, Norex Publications, 1996, Rochester New York; Copy Editor, *African-American Who's Who, Past & Present, Greater Rochester Area,* by Mike Molaire, Norex Publications, 1998; Author of several Op-Ed pieces, *Democrat & Chronicle.*

Residence: Rochester, New York.

JONES, Portia

Born: Rochester, New York.
Parents: Theresa and Ronald Jones.
Education: Enrolled in a MS, Management program, Nazareth College; B.S., Human Resource Management, SUNY Fredonia, 1991; *African-American Leadership Development Program, 1996.*

pointments and Tenure Committee, 1990-1991; Member, 1995 Women Fest Committee; Member, Womwn In Communications; Member, Public Relations Society of Americas; Member, Monroe Council on Teenage Pregnancy.

Awards/Recognition: Howard G. McCall Award, Purdue University, 1984; Capital Award, National Leadership Council, 1991; *Who's Who Among Black Americans,* 1986-present; *The World's Who's Who of Women,* 1989; Urban League Black Scholar Award, 1980; President's Award, United University Photographers Association of America, 1991; *Who's Who Among American Women,* 1997.

Career: *Human Resources Director, Lifetime Assistance, Inc. since 1996*; Human Resource Assistant, 1992-93, and Employment Specialist, 1993-1996, Hillside Children's Center; Credit Analyst, Marine Midland Bank, 1991-92.

Professional/Community Involvement: Vice President, Boys & Club Advisory Board, 1994-1996; Co-Chair, Recruitment & Selection Committee, African-American Leadership Development Program since 1996; Ralph Bunche Scholarship Committee, Interview Committee, since 1991; Board Member, Rochester-Monroe County Youth Bureau (since 1995)-Co-Chair, Communications Committee; Society for Human Resource Management since 1995 (Member of the JOBS Committee); Black Human Resources Network since 1997.

JONES, Theresa

Born: Rochester, New York
Parents: Claude (deceased), and Sarah Copeland
Family: Married to Ronald Jones; Three children, Portia, Ryan, and Clayton.
Education: MS, Social Work, Syracuse University, Syracuse, NY, 1995; B.S., Social Work, Nazareth College, 1993; African American Leadership Development Program, Greater Rochester Area United Way, 1992.

Career: Rochester City School District, Society for the Protection & Care of Children since 1996; Social Worker, Hillside Children's Center, 1994-95; Teen-age Parent Support System (TAPSS) Site Supervisor, 1993; Internship at Hillside Children's Center, Family Preservation/Crisis Intervention, Spring 1993; Strong Memorial Hospital, Day Treatment Program, Spring, 1992; TAPSS, Social Work, Fall 1991; Faith Community Health Awareness Center, Human Services (Spring, 1991), School # 19, Pre-1st Grade, Spring 1991; Bethany House, Residence for Battered Women, Social Work, Fall 1990; General Railway Signal Co., Administrative Secretary to The Treasurer & Assistant Secretary, 1970-1990.

Professional/Community Involvement: Volunteer Work, Center For Educational Development, 1993 and Faith Community Health Awareness Center, 1991; Member, N.Y. State Social Work Education Association, National Association of Social Workers (NASW), NAACP, Urban League of Rochester, Rochester Area Children's Collaborative, African-American Leadership Development Program Alumni Association, Aenon Baptist Church, Pastor Aide Committee, Usher Board, N.Y.S. Notary Public Association.

Awards/Recognition: *Who's who Among Students In American Colleges & Universities*, 1993.

Residence: Rochester, New York.

JORDAN, Anthony L., Dr., 1896-1971

Born: British Guyana, South America, 1896; Died of cancer, Dec. 19, 1971, at Columbia Presbyterian Hospital, New York City.
Family: Married to Ruth Jordan; Survived by a son, Dr. Herman Jordan; Three daughters, Dr. Winefred Simmons, a psychiatrist, Mrs. Mildred Arrington, and Mrs. Katherine (Jordan) Harris (deceased), and 14 grandchildren.
Education: Howard University Medical School, 1926.

Career: Practiced medicine in High Point, N.C., and Newburgh; Came to Rochester and practiced at 136 Adams Street for 39 years.

Awards/Recognition: The Rochester Neighborhood Health Center was renamed the Anthony L. Jordan Center, 1973.

Eulogies/Quotations:

"He did a tremendous job among the poor people... He was their friend."Dr. Charles T. Lunsford, Dr. Jordan's classmate at Howard University.
    D&C, Dec 20, 1971.

"He was never known to turn anybody away."
    Rev. E. L. Long, head of the Baptist Ministers Alliance. D&C, Dec, 20, 1971

Dr. Anthony L. Jordan, 1896-1971
*Reprinted with permission of **about...time** Magazine, Inc.*

JORDAN, Sr., Isaac L. (Ike) 1934-1994

Born: Fernandina Beach, Florida, 1934; Moved to Rochester, 1962; Died, Feb. 19, 1994 in his Pittsford home of complications from a long illness.
Parents: Sam and Marian Jordan.
Family: Married; Two adult children.
Education: MS, Education; Master of Divinity, Theology. B.S. Degree.

Career: Chairman of Rochester Institute of Technology's (RIT) new Commission on Cultural Diversity, 1990-1994; Assistant Professor, School's College of Continuing Education, 1988; Former Eastman Kodak Employee, 1968-90; Pastor, Faith

United Methodist Church; Former Pastor, Bluff Point United Methodist Church.

Professional/Community Involvement: Board Member, Genesee Neighborhood Settlement; Founder/President, Dads Only, Inc.; Listed in the Diversity Resource Directory of Rochester Area Volunteers, published by The Philanthropic Diversity Consortium of the Rochester (NY) Region, 1993-1994.

Awards/Recognition: Family of the Year 1982; The Isaac L. Jordan Sr. Fund was established by RIT in 1997; Two scholarships will be awarded yearly to a upcoming first-year student based on a writing contest on a diversity topic and to a returning student who has demonstrated an understanding of the concept of diversity through overt contributions in this area; also faculty and staff who have made significant contributions to enhance pluralism a RIT will be recognized.

Patents/Publications: "Affirmative Action and the Black Manager,"1982, *Personnel Journal*; "The Corporate Visit", *Mobility Magazine,And Relocation Communication Magazine*, 1989.

Eulogies/Quoations:

"He truly exhibited the characteristics of a person that had an inclusive attitude"

Sarah Reynolds, acting chairwoman, RIT Commission for Promoting Pluralism chairwoman
Times Union, Feb. 28, 1994

"I consider him a mentor"

Andrew Turner, member, Dads Only Inc., a group founded by Mr. Jordan.
Times Union, Feb. 28, 1994.

"Community means connectedness. One of the challenges of higher education is to connect the two domains of intellectual life and everyday life. As long as we pretend the two can be handled separately, we cannot help students break down the tendency toward territorial behavior and separation...If we choose to celebrate our diversity-a mark of our human creativity-rather than reject it, we can build on our commonality to enhance our unity."

JORDAN, Katherine "Kay", 1927-1996

"I have seen my role as a father and black man changing in my generation. It began for me a long time ago before it was popular for men to help with the laundry and change the diapers."

Isaac I. Jordan, Sr. **about...time** Magazine, p19, Dec. 1988

Isaac L. (Ike) Jordan, Sr., 1934-1994
*Reprinted with permission of **about...time** Magazine, Inc.*

"A man needs someone to listen to him. He needs something or someone to bounce off his concerns rather than going to a bar and drinking. There are support groups with psychologists...but on a broader level, I was more concerned about black men. I felt that we needed a forum or an environment in which we could come together and express ourselves in terms of problems we encounter and perhaps share solutions which have been found to work in our lives."

Isaac Jordan, Sr., commenting on Dads Only, Inc., an organization he founded.
about...time Magazine, p19, Dec. 1988

JORDAN, Katherine "Kay", 1927-1996

Born: Oct 30, 1927, High Point, N.C.; Grew up in Rochester; Died in her 19th Ward home, Saturday March 23, 1996.
Parents: Ruth and Dr. Anthony L. Jordan
Family: Two daughters, Lydia Micheaux Marshall, and Dr. Anne Micheaux Akwari; Two sisters, Mildred Reynolds and Dr. Winifred Simmons; A brother, Dr. Herman C. Jordan; Four grandchildren.
Education: Studied at Howard University and Morgan State College.

Career: Social worker, Monroe County Department of Social Services for 25 years.

Professional/CommunityInvolvement: Worked to eliminate discrimination; Participated in a class action lawsuit against the Monroe County Department of Social Services, charging discriminatory and promotional practices against Black & Hispanic persons; Worked with Metro-Act to eliminate restrictive ordinances; Board Member, Judicial Process Commission; Worked with the National Alliance Against Racism and Political Repression, the Committee for Peace in the Middle East; Established the South African Refugee Project; Supported the Cuban and Nicaraguan revolutions; Member, African-American History Initiative Task Force during the planning and development of the Strong Museum *Between Two Worlds* exhibit; Worked to get landmark designation of her father's home, on Adams street, in October 1992; was instrumental in the formation of the Jordan African-American Heritage Committee; Action For a Better Community, 1977-79; Member, Board of Directors, Community Child Care Center, 1985-87; Member, Rochester/Bamako Mali Sister Cities Committee, 1978; Lead Attorney, Defense Team, Operation Rescue, Monroe County Chapter, 1988; Member, Board of Directors, Monroe County Legal Assistance Corp., 1970-73; Member, Board of Directors, Orleans County Legal Aid Bureau, Inc., and Oak Orchard Legal Services, 1971-75;

Residence: Rochester, New York.

Katherine "Kay" Jordan, 1927-1996
Reprinted with permission of about...time Magazine, Inc.

Member, Merit Selection Panel for Position of Monroe County Public Defender, 1977; Member and

Legal Counsel, DADS Only, Inc. Interdenominational Christian Support Group, 1984-90; Volunteer Attorney, Sawyer Road Action Coalition, Carlton Manor, Kent, NY, 1971-75; Board Member, Montgomery Neighborhood Center, 1966-75; Vice-President, (1971-73)-President, 1973-74.

Awards/Recognition: Charles F. Crimi Award for Providing Outstanding Legal Service to the Poor and the Disadvantaged, Monroe County Bar Association, 1995; The Fozzie and Steven McClary Award, Seneca District No. 293, Boy Scouts of America, 1997; West Indian and American Community Award, 1984; Community Service Award, Troop # 293, Boys Scout of America, 1978; United Memorial Gospel Association Community Award, 1977; Monroe County District Attorney Certificate of Merit, 1977; Black Communication Award, 1971; Bahamian Scholarship Fund Certificate of Achievement, 1966.

LAIRD, Robert

Born: Patterson, New Jersey, June 14, 1948.
Parents: Rober, and Elise Laird.
Family: Married to Zodiwa E. Laird; Three children, Dumisani, Nyamekye, and Kholiswa.
Education: BA, Sociology/Psychology, St John Fisher College, 1970.

Career: Deputy Director, Community Services, Action For a Better Community, Inc. since 1987; Rochester Product Division of General Motors, Rochester New York; Industrial Engineer/Planning Analyst, 1984-86; Industrial Engineer/Value Engineer, 1983-84; Divisional Coordinator, Personnel Department, 1982-83; Suggestion Coordinator/Personnel Department, 1981-82; Administrator, Department of Microbiology, University of Rochester, 1977-81; Associate Director, Catholic Youth Organization, 1975-77; Director, Inter City

Outreach Program, 1973-75; Director, Project Upward Bound, Rochester Institute of Technology, 1970-71.

Professional/Community Involvement: Presently Member, St John Fisher College Trustee's Council; Board Member, Monroe County Health Department; Vice President, Metro Act, 1992; Citizen Advisory Committee, Department of Social Services; Chairperson, Income Maintenance Sub-Committee, Department of Social Services; New York State Community Action Agencies Director's Association; Rochester Area Children's Collaborative; Board of Directors, Diocesan Office of Black Catholic Ministries; Genesee/Finger Lakes Regional Planning Council; Past Member, American Management Association; Genesee Grants Board of Directors, Office of Human Development; Genesee Valley Personal and Guidance Association; Board of Directors, Catholic Charities of the Diocese of Rochester; Chairperson, Medical Center Administration Group; Chairperson, Volunteer Board, Orleans Correctional Facility; Early Childhood Advisory Board; Rochester/Monroe County Early Childhood Education Steering Committee.

Patents/Publications: Has made dozens of presentations at churches, prisons, colleges, and local and state hearings on various issues of concern to Action For a Better Community, and the Rochester Community-at-Large; Appeared frequently on radio, electronic, and the print media in the Rochester area.

Residence: Rochester, New York.

LANGSTON, Andrew

Family: Married to Gloria M. Langston; One son, Andre Marcel Langston.
Education: MBA, New York University; attended Morris Brown, and Morehouse Colleges, Atlanta, Georgia; Graduate of the American Institute of Finance and Banking, New York City; attended Radio and Television Techniques, Inc. School in New York City.

Career: *Owner of WDKX 104-FM Radio since 1974*; Founder of Monroe County Broadcasting Co. LTD., Rochester, New York, Licensee for WDKX 104-FM-Radio; Principal Stockholder, Chairman of The Board, General and Sales Manager; Owner of Andrew Langston Insurance Agency; Life and Qualifying Member of the Million Dollar Round Table, the highest achievement in the Insurance Industry.

Professional/Community Involvement: Board Member, Otetiana Council of the Boys Scouts of America; The American Heart Association Genesee Valley Chapter; The Martin Luther King, Jr., Greater Rochester Commission; The Salvation Army; The Health Association of Rochester and Monroe County, New York State Broadcasters Association; National Association of Black-Owned Broadcasters; Founder, National Association of Black-Owned Broadcasters.

Awards/Recognition: President's Club and Citation Awards, Prudential Insurance Company of America; Many awards and honors from many Rochester and New York groups (too numerous to mention); Man of the Year Award from the Genesee Valley Club of the National Association of Negro Business and Professional Women's Club, 1996.

Residence: Rochester, New York

LATIMER, Sr., Millard Earl, 1898-1980

Born: Anderson, S.C., June 17, 1898; Moved to Rochester, 1917; Died at St. Mary's Hospital, June 18, 1980.
Parents: Luther and Mahalia Latimer.
Family: Survived by his wife of 57 years, the former Lydia Mae Butler (Died in 1996 at the age of 100); A son, Millard E. Latimer Jr.; Two daughters, Frances Montgomery and Betty Coles; Two brothers, Raymond and Albert Latimer; Eight grandchildren; One great-grandchild.
Education: Attended grade school and high school in Atlanta; The first Black graduate of Simmons School of Embalming, Syracuse, 1922.

Career: Worked at the Powers Hotel as a porter; promoted to supervisor of service; The first black to open a funeral home in Rochester as a partner with Walter R. Myers (688 Bay St.), 1922; Worked part time for other funeral directors and at the New York Central Station as a chauffeur; dissolved the partnership and opened a funeral home at 133 Adams St., on the property of Mt Olivet Church, 1926; Moved the business to 179 Clarissa St., where it remained for 31 years, 1929; Fought to gain zoning approval to move the business to 983 S. Plymouth Ave, 1959; Retired as vice president of the funeral home, 1979.

Eulogies/Quotations:

"Times were hard in those days…There were very few blacks in Rochester, so he had to supplement his income to help send his children through college."

Millard E. Latimer Jr.
D & C, Jun 19, 1980

"In those days, you went to New York City…There were very few black morticians in Western New York."

Millard E. Latimer Jr.
D & C, Jun 19, 1980

LATTIMORE, Terry

Born: 1947; Moved to Rochester, 1969.
Parents: James Lattimore and Eddie Lee Lattimore. **Family**: Married to Bettie S. Lattimore; One daughter, Terri; Three sons, Anthony, Demetrice, and Todd.
Education: Business Management Certificate, LaSalle University, Chicago, Illinois, 1980; Liberal Arts, Florida A & M University, Tallahassee, Florida, 1965-66, 1968-69; High School Diploma, Marshall High School, Plant City, Florida, 1965; Certified Human Relations Program Instructor in the following areas: Customer Relations for Electric Utilities, You Are Not Alone, Creating Satisfied Customers' Selling Naturally, Everybody Has a Customer; Resolving Conflict and Restoring Harmony; *African-American Leadership Development Program*, Greater Rochester Area United Way, 1992; Leadership Rochester.

Career: *Rochester Gas & Electric Corporation: Customer Relations Representative since 1986*; Senior Customer Service Representative, 1977-1986; Customer Service Representative, 1976-77; Gas Appliance Service, 1975-76; Utility II, 1971-75; Eastman Kodak Company: Shipping Assistant, 1969-71; United States Army: Infantryman and Military Policeman, 1966-68 (Honorably Discharged in 1968).

Professional/Community Involvement: Board Member, Greater Rochester Area United Way, 1993; Chairman (first appointed chairman), African-American Leadership Development Program Alumni Committee, 1993-1995; Corn Hill Association since 1987; Manhattan Golf Club Scholarship Committee since 1983; Urban League of Rochester, since 1983; Action For a Better Community, 1985.

Residence: Rochester, New York.

LAWRENCE, James F.

Born: Orlando, Florida, 1949; Moved to Rochester, 1992
Parents: James and Ethel Lawrence.
Family: Married to Betty, with three children, Terrance, Jamil, and Ebony.
Education: Graduate of Howard University.

Career: *Editor/Editorial Pages, Democrat and Chronicle since 1992*; Associate Editorial Page Editor, Gannett Suburban Newspapers, in White Plains, New York, 1987-1992; Editorial Writer, The Orlando Sentinel, 1985-1987; Reporter and Editor, United Press International, Denver, 1973-1985; Cleveland Call & Post, Reporter, 1972-1973.

Professional/Community Involvement: Alpha Phi Alpha Community Outreach, 1988-1992; Listed in the Diversity Resource Directory of Rochester Area Volunteers, published by The Philanthropic Diversity Consortium of the Rochester (NY) Region, 1993-1994; Leadership Rochester Graduate, 1994; Member, National Conference of Editorial Writers and the National Association of Black Journalists; Senior Steward, Baber A.M.E Church.

Awards/Recognition: Mighty Pen-Best Commentary-Gannett, 1991; Second place, Best of Gannett Editorial Writing, 1997..

Residence: Chili, New York

LEE, Odell

Born: May 2, 1949.
Parents: Odell Lee Sr. and Sara Louise Wool Fork Lee.
Family: Married to Peggy Lee; Three daughters, Lashonm, Latoya, and Arlana Lee.
Education: MBA, Rutgers Graduate School of Business; BA, Iowa Wesleyan College, Mount Pleasant Iowa.

Career: *Manager, Operations Control, Xerox Corporation.*

Professional/Community Involvement: Member, Perinton African-American Heritage Committee; Zoning Board, Town of Perinton, New York; Regional Council on Aging Board of Directors, Western New York, 1989-92; Dollars for Scholars Board of Directors, Fairport, New York, 1992; United Negro College Fund, Board of Directors, 1987-91; Rochester New York; United Church of Christ Board of Trustee since 1990; Member, Alumni Chapter, Kappa Alpha Psi Fraternity, Inc., Toastmaster, Rochester, New York; listed in the First edition of the Diversity Resource Directory of Rochester Area Volunteers, published by The Philanthropic Diversity Consortium of the Rochester (NY) Region, 1993-94.

Awards/Recognition: Xerox Corporation President's Award.

Residence: Fairport, New York.

LEE, Jr., William E., Ph.D.

Born: Louisville, KY, 1928; Moved to Rochester, 1959.
Family: Married, two adult children, Brian and Jay Lee.
Education: Ph.D., Physical Organic Chemistry, Ohio State University, Ohio, 1959; MS, Chemistry, Ohio State University, Ohio, 1956; B.S., Chemistry, Hampton Institute, Virginia, 1949.

Career: *Consultant and Partner in B&L Associates since 1986; Retired Scientist from Eastman Kodak Company, 1986; Eastman Kodak Company*: Technical Associate, Image Stability Technical Center, Photographic Technology Division, 1980-86; Supervisor, Photographic Chemistry Development Section, Paper Service Division, Paper Manufacturing Organization, 1976-80; Head, Photographic Chemistry Laboratory, Photographic Laboratories, 1972-76; Head, Photographic Mechanisms Laboratory, Photographic Research Division, Research Laboratories, 1968-72; Research Associate, Research Laboratories, 1964-68; Senior Research Chemist, Research Laboratories, 1959-64; Fellow, Standard Oil Company of Ohio at the Ohio State University, Columbus, Ohio, 1956-59; Research Assistant, American Petroleum Institute Project, The Ohio State University Research Foundation, 1955-56; Chemist, Ozalid Division, General Aniline & Film Corp., Binghamton, New York, 1952-54; Spectrophotographic Laboratory, Army Environmental Health Laboratory, Army Chemical Center, Maryland, 1950-52; Former Visiting Lecturer, School of Photographic Science, Rochester Institute of Technology, Rochester, New York, 1976-78.

Professional/Community Involvement: Member, American Chemical Society and Society of Photographic Science and Engineering; past Member, Monroe Community Hospital Board of Directors, 1969-75; Vice Chairman, U.S. Selective Service Board No. 73, Rochester, New York, 1963-68; Member, Editorial Review Board, *Photographic Science & Engineering*, 1962-80; Abstractor, Abstract of *Photographic Science & Engineering*, 1962-76; Chairman, Papers Committee, 1970 *Colloquium on Image Amplification*, 1968; Editorial Review Board, *Image Technol-*

ogy 1968-70; Chairman, Papers Committee, 1973 Seminar on Photographic Processing, Society of Photographic Scientists and Engineers (SPSE) 1972; Chairman, 1980 SPSE International Conference on Photographic Papers, Hot Springs, Virginia, 1980; Chairman, 2nd International Conference on Photographic Papers, July, 1984, Vancouver, British Columbia, Canada; Chairman, American National Standards Institute (ANSI) Subcommittee PH4-2, Photographic Processing Procedures, 1978-86; Member, Association for Information and Image Management (AIIM) Subcommittee C-7, Color Microfiche Standard, 1984-86.

Awards/Recognition: Standard Oil Company of Ohio Fellowship,1956-59; Fellow, American Association For The Advancement of Science, 1963; Alumni Award, Hampton Institute, 1969; Elected to Senior Member, Society of Photographic Scientists and Engineers, 1977.

Patents/Publications: Over 10 scientific publications in refereed Scientific journals such as the *Journal of t he American ChemicalSociety, Photographic Science & Engineering, Journal of Organic Chemistry, Journal of Imaging Technology*; has contributed three chapters in the 3rd Edition of *Theory of the Photographic Process*, Editor, T.H. James, The MacMillan Company, New York, 1966; and one Chapter in the 4th Edition of the same publication (1977); Holder of three U.S. patents.

Residence: Rochester, New York, 1959-1997; Moved to Newport News VA, April 1997.

LEVIAS, Clifford Lee

Born: Kirbyville, Texas, 1959; Moved to Rochester, 1992.
Parents: Martha and George Levias.
Family: Married to Veda Beasley-Levias, a reporter for WORK TV 13.
Education: B.B.A., General Business, University of Texas, 1985; Master's Program in Health Services Management, The New School for Social Research, Rochester, NY, 1995; Graduated from Lutcher Stark High School, Orange, Texas; African-American Leadership Development Program.

Career: *Clinic Coordinator, The Arc of Monroe County, Rochester, NY since 1995*; Service Coordinator, The Arc of Monroe County, 1994-95; Residential Counselor, St. Joseph's Villa, Rochester, NY, 1993-94; Program Manager, Communities-in-Schools, Inc., Beaumont, TX, 1992-93; Marketing Specialist/Client Management Specialist, 1991-1992; Case Manager III, Life Resource of Southeast Texas, Beaumont, TX, 1988-1991.

Professional/Community Involvement: Member, Advisory Board, Boys & Girls Club, 1994-97; Member, Greece Democratic Committee since 1996; Vice Chair, PR Committee, *African-American Leadership Development Program* Alumni Association; Board Member, Pre-Trial Services Corp. since 1997; Vice President, Association of Black Social Workers (ABSW), 1991-92; Member, ABSW Regional Planning Committee, 1991-92; Democratic State Convention Delegate, Houston, Texas, 1992; Member, Clean Community Commission, Beaumont, Texas, 1991-93; Member, Youth Challenge Task Force, 1991-1993; Worked to elect Ann Richards Governor of Texas; Worked as a consultant for the 1994 William Johnson Jr. Mayoral Campaign.

Awards/Recognition: *Outstanding Young Men of America*, 1992.

Residence: Rochester, New York.

LEVY, Van Tuly, Dr., 1901-1996

Born: Brooklyn, New York, 1901; Moved to Rochester, 1922; Died, April 17, 1996, at Park Ridge Hospital; Buried at Pittsford Cemetery.
Family: Twice widowed; Survived by his nephew, Dr. Chauncey Levy; A niece, Agnes Ruth.
Education: Bachelor's and Dental Degrees, Columbia University.

Career: Rochester's first Black Dentist; Was the only Black member of the track team at Columbia University; Raced in the Penn Relays; Rode show horses at Madison Square Garden.

Professional/Community Involvement: Very active in community affairs; Did many things behind the scenes; Charter Member, Ontario Golf Club, Ontario, Wayne County; Eta Rho Lambda Chapter, Alpha Phi Alpha Fraternity; Leks Club.

Awards/Recognition: Urban League of Rochester Community Leadership Award, 1988; Many medals as a rider in local equestrian competitions.

Eulogies/Quotations:

"He and Dr. (Charles) Lunsford opened a lot of doors. They were pioneers, trailblazers."

> Alice Young, Dr. Levy's friend
> D &C, Apr 21, 1996

"He was instrumental in getting me into Howard University...He was very positive...a great sportsman."

> James "Buddy" Young
> D &C Apr 21, 1996

"He was a man who wouldn't take no for an answer when it came to helping others realize their dreams... He was very active in community affairs and did a lot of things behind the scenes."

> Charles Price, Dr. Levy's friend
> D &C, Apr 21, 1996

LIKELY, Phyllis Frye

Born: Caledonia, New York, 1942; Moved to Rochester, 1966.
Parents: Charles T. Parker and Mary Parker.
Education: MS, Education, SUNY Brockport, 1984; C.A.S., Educational Administration, SUNY Brockport, 1984; B.S., Education, Geneseo State University, 1966.

Career: *Assistant Principal, French Road Elementary School since November 1991*; Associate Director of PREP Summer Program, Rochester Institute of Technology since 1989; Assistant Director, Rochester Institute of Technology PREP (since 1991), Coordinator (1990), Teacher Advisor (1989); Teacher on Special Assignment, Council Rock Primary School, Brighton, New York School District, 1988-89, 1990-91; Elementary Principal, Caledonia-Mumford Central School, 1989-90; Teacher, Grade Three and Grade Four, Brighton Central School District, 1974-88; Teacher, Grade Three, Four, Five, and Six, Rochester City School District, 1966-74.

Professional/Community Involvement: Assessment Consortium Team Leader, 1996-97; Team Member, New York State Education School Review, 1995; Chairperson, Brighton, New York School District Censorship Committee, 1990; Chairperson, K-5 Language Arts, Brighton, New York School District, 1990-92; Co-President, Teacher's Investment Club, Brighton, New York School District since 1990; Chairperson, Brighton Elementary School Report Card Committee, 1986-88; Teacher in Charge, Brookside School-French Road, 1977-88.

Residence: Rochester, New York

LINDSAY, Samuel Dr., 1896-1980

Born: Augusta, Georgia, 1896; Moved to Rochester, 1918; Died of cancer at Park Ridge Hospital, Sept 3, 1980.
Family: Married Margaret N. Lindsay.
Education: BA, Lincoln University, Pennsylvania; Graduated from the Dentistry School of Howard University.

Career: The second Black dentist in Rochester; World War I Veteran; U.S. Army, 1918-1919; Discharged as a sergeant; Bellman for several summers at former Powers Hotel, Rochester, New York, 1918-1925; Opened his first dental practice, November, 1925; Retired in 1975.

Professional/community Involvement: Life Member of the NAACP; Member, Baha'i Spiritual Assembly of Rochester; Life Member, American Dental Association; One of the Founders and Former President, Howard University Alumni Association's Rochester Chapter; Board Member, Negro Branch of the YMCA; Member, Elks, Masonic Lodge and Shriners; Charter Member of the Rochester Graduate Chapter of Omega Psi Phi Fraternity; One of the organizers of the First Local Spiritual Assembly of the Baha'i Faith in Rochester.

Eulogies/Quotations:

"He was one of the finest gentlemen I've known...He was very amiable and a very good technician...We started from scratch and there were no carpets laid out for anyone in those days."

Dr. Tuly Van Levy, Rochester's first Black dentist
D&C, Sept 4, 1980

"He was a marvelous dentist...You could almost go to sleep while he was working on you. He had a marvelous touch and all his patients-white or colored-swore by him...Money was secondary to him, service was the main thing. I don't remember him turning down anyone."

Dr. Charles T. Lunsford, Rochester's first Black physician.
D&C, Sept 4, 1980

"He always tried to treat people right, whether they had money or not...People owed him thousands of dollars. But in 50 years, he never once used a bill collector."

Mrs. Margaret Lindsay, Dr. Lindsay's wife
Times Union, Sept. 4, 1980

LOFTON, Josh M., 1927-1986

Born: Mississippi, 1927; Moved to Rochester, 1956; Died at Genesee Hospital, as a result of heart decease and diabetes, Oct. 25, 1986.
Family: Married to Althea Lofton; Sister, Minnie Williams; Two brothers, J. V. Lofton and John Lofton
Education: MS, Guidance & Counseling, SUNY Brockport; B.S., General Sciences & Biology, Boston University, 1954.

Career: *Science Teacher, Jefferson High School, 1956*; Counselor, Madison High School, 1965; Director of Operation Young Adult (evolved into Center Junior High School), 1970; Supervising Director of Student Equity and Placement; worked for desegregation in the Urban-Suburban Transfer Program; Retired from the district in 1982; After retirement worked as a Science/Math Coordinator for the Program for Rochester to Interest Students in Science and Math (PRIS^{2}M).

Professional/Community Involvement: Member, Advisory Board, WHEC-TV10; The Board of Governors of Bethume-Cookman College, Datona, Florida; Founder and Mediator at the Center For Dispute Settlement.

Eulogies/Quotations:

"He was a humanitarian ... with helping all people understand each other."

LONG, Tracey

Josh Lofton, 1927-1986
*Reprinted with permission of **about...time** Magazine, Inc.*

Benjamin Richardson, retired district administrator.
Times Union, Oct. 27, 1986.

"He helped ease some of the tension in the early 70's... It was his demeanor and his honest approach. He was a very sincere person and very respected."
   Johnny Wilson, Center High School Principal
   Times Union, Oct. 27, 1986.

"He was concerned for the education of al children ... He said children were being warped- they were either isolated in the city or isolated in the suburbs."
   Rabbi Judea Miller, who worked with Mr. Lofton
   Times Union, Oct. 27, 1986.

LOMAX, Janet

Born: Louisville, Kentucky; Moved to Rochester, 1980.

Parents: James and Sedalia Lomax.
Family: Married to Charles Smith; Two children, Erica and Charles.
Education: B.S., Radio-TV Production, and Journalism, Murray StateUniversity, Murray Kentucky, 1976.

Career*: News Anchor at TV Channel 10, WHEC since 1981*; Anchor for the 5, 6 and 11p.m. News, since 1982; Previously worked at WAVE -TV, Louisville Kentucky, for four and half years, as a reporter, producer, photographer, and talk show host.

Professional/Community Involvement: Served on a number of Community Boards; Mentor for high school journalism students; Has spent more than nine years raising funds for Children's Hospital at Strong; Founding President of the Rochester Association of Black Communicators; Member of the National Association of Black Journalists, Delta Sigma Theta Sorority and Jack & Jill of America.

Awards/Recognition: 1993 Urban League Outstanding Volunteer Award; Communicator of the Year, New Bethel CME Church, Delta Sigma Theta Communication Award; Outstanding Woman, Nazareth College; F.C.D. Hall of Fame Inductee.

Residence: Rochester, New York.

LONG, Tracey

Born: Rochester, New York, 1961.
Parents: Earl and Etherine Cleveland.
Family: Married to Bob Long, President ,y Long & Associates, Inc.; One stepson, Ro long and one stepdaughter, Drina Long.
Education: B.S., Business Finance, California State University-Dominguez Hills in Carson, California, 1986; Leadership Through Quality,

and Total Quality Management training, Xerox Corporation, 1985-1988; Currently enrolled in a Master of Public Administration Program, SUNY Albany.

Career: *Director, New York Sate department of Transportation's Office of Equal Opportunity Development and Compliance (OEODC) since 1995*; Executive Director/Job Placement Manager, 1989-1995; Host and Producer of Life Views on Greater Rochester Cablevision Channel 9; Former Producer & Host of the local talk show "Shades of Grey", 1988-92; Asset Control Analyst, Xerox Corporation, 1987-89; Worked for Cable-Access programs in Los Angeles, 1987; Financial Analyst Xerox Corporation, El Segundo, CA, 1983-87; Founder of Solong Productions, an Independent Video Production Company; Leader of the Target Excel Program (providing job training for at-risk youth and adults); Ran unsuccessfully for the New York State Senate as a Republican in 1992.

Professional/Community Involvement: Currently Board Member, Monroe County Sports Development Former Member, Lupus Foundation (1991-1993), East House, and United Way; Chairwoman, Monroe County African-American Republican Committee, 1995-1996; Member, Freddie Thomas Foundation, 1987-90; Member, Rochester Association of Black Communicators, Mt. Olivet Baptist Church, Rochester Women's Network, COMIDA, and EPIC; Deputy Commissioner of the Commission to Analyze Savings & Efficiency (CASE), 1992.

Awards/Recognition: Rochester Chamber Associates Key Leader Award, 1988.

Residence: Webster, New York.

LUCAS, Margaret O., Ph.D.

Education: D.Ed., Art Education, Pennsylvania State University; MA, Art Education, Virginia Commonwealth University; B.S., Art Education, Hampton University; Executive Communication Program, Communication Excellence Institute, San Dimas, CA, 1990; Management Development Program, Harvard University, 1989; American Council on Education Fellowship in Academic Administration, 1983-84; Faculty/Administration Fellowship for Minorities, Southern Fellowship Fund, 1981-82;

Career: *Dean of College of Imaging Arts & Sciences, Rochester Institute of Technology, 1992-1997*; Dean of the College of Creative Arts at West Virginia University, 1986-92; Chair of the Department of Art, University of Texas, Denton, Texas, 1983-86; Assistant Dean, College of Art and Sciences, University of Texas, Denton, Texas, 1982; Director of Graduate Studies in Art, Department of Art, University of North Texas, Denton, Texas, 1976-81; Tenured Professor, College of Imaging Arts and Sciences, Rochester Institute of Technology since 1992; Tenured Professor, Division of Art, College of Creative Arts, West Virginia University, West Virginia, 1986-92; Tenured Associate Professor, Department of Art, University of North Texas, Denton, Texas, 1975-86; Assistant Professor, Department of Art Education, The Florida State University, Tallahassee, Florida, 1972-75; Teacher, George Wythe High School and Albert Hill Middle School, Department of Art, Richmond Public Schools, Richmond, Virginia, 1971-72; Course Coordinator, Department of Art Education, The Pennsylvania State University, University Park, Pennsylvania, 1970-71; Graduate Assistant, Department of Art Education, The Pennsylvania State University, University Park, Pennsylvania, 1969-70; Coordinator/Instructor, Summer Arts Program, Richmond Public Schools, Richmond, Virginia, 1969; Teacher, Armstrong High

School, Department of Art, Richmond Public Schools, Richmond, Virginia, 1964-69; Instructor, Summer Humanities Program, Department of Communications, Hampton University, Virginia, 1964.

Professional/Community Involvement: Board Member, The International Council of Fine Art Deans since 1989; Graphic Arts Technical Foundation, since 1993; West Virginia Women's Alliance, 1987-92; Texas Association of Schools of Art, 1984-86; David Hochstein Music School since 1995; New York State Systematic Initiative, Urban Network Project for Math, Science & Technology since 1995; Garth Fagan Dance Company Trustees, Rochester, New York since 1993; Montage '93, Rochester, New York, 1992-94; Make-A-Wish Foundation, Morgantown, West Virginia, 1991-92; Monongalia County Red Cross, Morgantown, West Virginia, West Virginia, 1987-90; Denton County Friends of the Family, Denton, Texas, 1984-86; Tallahassee Literacy Council, Tallahassee, Florida, 1975; Cultural Arts Center, Tallahassee, Florida, 1973-75; Secretary-Treasurer, International Council of Fine Arts Deans since 1993; Member of the National Association of State Universities and Land Grant Colleges Commission on the Arts, 1988-92; Treasurer, National Council of Art Administrators, 1988-90; Executive Committee, Council of Fellows, American Council on Education, 1988-90; Nominating Committee, National Council of Art Administrators, 1986-87; Consultant-Evaluator for the Commission on Institutions of Higher Education of the North Central Association; President of the National Council of Art Administrators, 1991-92; Member of the Council for Policy Studies in Art Education; participated in the Harvard University Management Development Program, 1989; Faculty Member, ACE Center for Leadership Development and Academic Administration; Member of the ACE Council of Fellows Executive Committee; Editor, *American Council on Education Fellows Newsletter*, 1988-92; Review Board, *Journal of Multi-Cultural and Cross-cultural Research in Art Education*, 1988-92; Critical Review, Chapter 38, "Art*," Handbook of Research on Teacher Education*, Association of Teacher Educators and Macmillan Publishing Company, 1987-88; Editorial Advisory Board, *Studies in Art Education*, National Art Education Association *Journal of Issues and Research*, 1979-83; Associate Editor, *Trends*, Texas Art Education Association Journal, 1978-82; Member, League of Women Voters, Tallahassee, Florida, 1973-75; League of Women Voters, Denton, Texas, 1976-86; National Association for the Advancement of Colored People, 1964-92; First Presbyterian Church, Morgantown, West Virginia since 1985; Professional Women's Council, Morgantown, West Virginia, 1987-92; Rochester Women's Network since 1993.

Awards/Recognition: Recipient of the Hampton University Alumnus-at-Large Award, 1993; Profiled in the 4th edition of Penn State's Symbols of Our Best, 1989; Listed in *Outstanding Young Women of America*, 1975; named a Penn State Alumni Fellow, 1982; An American Council of Education Fellow, 1983-84; Recipient of a Southern Fellowship Fund Faculty Fellowship, 1981-82; Delta Kappa Gamma International Honor Society for Women, 1976; NDEA Fellowship, The Pennsylvania State University, 1970-71.

Patents/Publications: Lucas, M. O, "A Little Talk About Where You're headed," *Her Say, Chicago Tribune*, January 9, 1994; Lucas, M. O., "Multifaceted Pre-student teaching Experiences in Diverse Community Agencies", *Florida Art Education Association Journal*, 8, 14-15 (1975).

Residence: Rochester, New York.

LUNSFORD, Charles T., MD, 1892-1985

Born: Macon, Ga., 1892; The oldest of nine children; Moved to Rochester, July 10, 1921; Died at Strong Memorial Hospital of complications from pneumonia, Feb 22, 1985.

Parents: Son of a cotton sampler; His grandfather was white and a direct descendant of the Earl of Lunsford in England.

Family: Survived by wife Nan Lunsford and a brother, Marion Lunsford.

Education: Graduate with Honors, College of Arts and Sciences, Howard University, 1913; graduated at the top of his class, Howard University Medical School, 1920.

Career: Internship at Freedmen's Hospital, Washington, DC, 1921; Opened a private practice at 574 Clarissa St., Rochester, New York, becoming the first Black doctor in the city, 1921; Later moved the practice to 718 S. Plymouth Ave; Appointed to the staffs of Rochester General Hospital and St. Mary's Hospital; The State Board of Regents accused Dr. Lunsford of keeping inadequate record and prescribing diet pills without cause in 1978; He surrendered his medical license that year, denying any wrongdoing.

Professional/Community Involvement:
Active in the NAACP for decades; Became president of the civil right organization in 1941; He witnessed and participated in a series of landmark struggles for racial equality between 1920 and 1940; He confronted Dr. George Hoyt Whipple, Dean of the University of Rochester Medical School, for the integration of school, ending 20 years of non-admission of Black students; He challenged Harper Sibley of the YMCA over the refusal to accommodate a well-known Black singer at the downtown YMCA; He charged the University of Rochester, Eastman Kodak Company, Bausch & Lomb with discriminatory hiring and admissions, 1938; He embarrassed the Red Cross over the practice of turning away Black donors, 1944.

Awards/Recognition: Cited by then-Governor W. Averell Harriman on his work "against discrimination in public accommodation, jobs & housing," 1958; Cited for more than 35 years of service to the NAACP at a dinner in New York City, 1959; Awarded the Rochester Museum and Science Center's Civic Medal for Community Service, 1974; The Rochester Board of Education named the new school # 19 on Seward Street, the Charles T. Lunsford School, 1973; A five-hour testimonial dinner was held at the Mapledale Party House on Dr. Charles T. Lunsford Day, 1978; The Urban League of Rochester established the Charles T. Lunsford Distinguished Community Service Award, 1978; Was the local NAACP's Man of The Year; Rochester City Council renamed Plymouth Park, Lunsford Park, 1986.

Eulogies/Quotations:

"There's been a revolution in Rochester, and I'm proud to be a part of it."

> Dr. Charles T. Lunsford, Mapledale Party House Speech on Dr. Charles T. Lunsford Day, June 18, 1978.

"He would go anywhere, any time when anybody needed him... Some doctors treat you like they're above you.... That just wasn't Dr. Lunsford's way... he never looked down on anybody. And his patients were the poorest, the most down and out... He helped everybody."

> Kathryn Terrrel
> *Times Union, Feb 22, 1985*

"He was one of the great pioneers of this community...When he came here, he could have taken the comfortable way out. Black professionals were among the elite and he could have made a lot of money and gotten a lot of fame... But he saw things and decided to challenge them...He was a great man... This community owes him a tremendous debt"

Dr. Charles T. Lunsford, 1892-1985
Reprinted with permission of about...time Magazine

William Johnson Jr., president the Urban League of Rochester.
Times Union, Feb 22, 1985

"He put everything into what he believed in...I marveled at him-a legend of his time-to have institutions named for him while he was still living...He didn't go around blowing his own horn even though he was making extraordinary achievements in the community... He was a fearless man in speaking his convictions."

Rev. Andrew N. Gibson, pastor, Memorial A.M.E. Zion Church.
Times Union, Feb 22, 1985

"He's a very important person in the history of Rochester, a fighter of his times...When you write the history of Blacks in Rochester, he stands out...He was the militant of his time. You have to understand he's an integrationist, an assimilationist, really. He fought just as hard to get Italians into medical school, for example, as he did for Blacks. That's the kind of world he wants to build."

Bernard R, Gifford, the young Black biophysicist who turned theBlack community's FIGHT organization into a progressive force in the City.
D &C, Feb 27, 1972

"When I got here (Rochester), I was met by this slogan, by my own people, by the colored people: No nigger physician will ever cross my footstep."

Dr. Charles T. Lunsford, edited transcript of a 1984 WXXI television interview by William Pearce
D &C, Feb, 6, 1994

"I never saw a person's color-never will see any. If you studied medicine, you wouldn't see anybody's color. We're all the same on the inside...When you see a person's color and make that paramount, you're talking about the insignificant things in life...That's why I never use the word black. I don't follow anyone who teaches hate. The Muslims and Black Panthers started that and spent all their history teaching hate...I teach love. You reap what you sow in this world."

Dr. Charles T. Lunsford
about...time Magazine, p 9, June 1978.

"Eastman sent a message that if I didn't keep my big mouth shut, he'd run me out of this town...I told the messenger to go back and say I'll be here long after he's long forgotten."

Dr. Charles T. Lunsford, after George Eastman's reaction to Lunsford's testimony during the Federal Employment Practices Commission Hearings held in Rochester in 1938. Lunsford told the commission that Jews, Blacks, an d Italians were denied employment at Kodak and other local factories.
about...time Magazine, p 9, June 1978.

MACON, Fred M., Ph.D.

Born: New York City; Moved to Rochester 1973.
Family: Divorced; Two sons, Drew, and Lance.
Education: MS, Management of Technology, Massachusetts Institute of Technology Sloan School of Management, 1991; Ph.D., Physical Organic Chemistry, University of Delaware, 1973; MS, Physical Organic Chemistry, Adelphi University; B.S. Chemistry, Central State University.

Career: Eastman Kodak Company: Technical Leader, Research Management Staff, Imaging Research Laboratories since 1991; Kodak Sponsored Study, Management of Technology Executive Program, MIT Sloan School of Management, 1990-91; Technical Assistant to the Chief Technical Officer/Senior Vice President & Director of Research, Corporate Research Laboratories, 1989-90; Research Associate/Senior Research Scientist, Black & White Technology Laboratories, Professional & Photofinishing Technology Division, 1986-89; Senior Research Scientist, Emulsion Design Laboratories, Photographic Materials Division, 1984-86; Emulsion Research Division, Senior Research Scientist, Phototheory Laboratories, 1980-84; Senior Research Scientist, Silver Halide Mechanism Laboratories, 1977-79; Research Scientist, Sensitizing Dye Synthesis Laboratories, 1973-77.

Professional/Community Involvement: Former Member of Rochester Boys & Girls Club Board of Directors.

Patents/Publications: Holder of three U.S. patents related to Photographic Technology: *US Patent 5,210,014*, "Mid-green sensitizing dyes for potographic materials," May 11, 1993; *US Patent 5,196, 299*, "Tabular grain emulsion containing radiographic elements exhibiting reduced dye stain," March 23, 1993; *US Patent 4,578,348*, "Hydrolyzed azolium speed enhancing/fog-inhibiting agents for silver halide photography," March 25, 1986.

Residence: Penfield, New York.

MASSEY III, Bruce

Born: Bayminette, Alabama, 1958; Moved to Rochester, 1991.
Parents: Louise Massey and Mack Massey Jr.
Family: Single.
Education: Graduated from high school, 1976; Some college courses, 1977.

Career: U.S. Armed Forces, 1977-1981; Inventory Control Specialist, Department Stores, Monticello, NY, 1981-1983; Treatment Team Specialist, Middletown Psychiatric Center, New York State, 1983-86; Youth Counselor, 1986-89; Special Olympics Coach and Recreational Specialist, New Hope Agency, Sullivan County, 1989-91; Residential Supervisor, Salvation Army Homeless Shelter, Rochester, NY, 1991-94; Teacher Assistant, Rochester City School District, 1991-95; Community Activist and Historical Educator since 1995.

Professional/Community Involvement: Co-organizer, Local Million Man March since 1994; Member, Rochester Kwanzaa Coalition since 1994; Co-founder and Member of Concerned African-American Parents and Supporters since 1995; Member, National Coalition Building Institute since 1996; Rochester Community TV Production since 1996; Center For Dispute Settle-

ment Mediation since 1996; Gift Center Ministry since 1996; Eastside Community Center Mediation since 1997; Rite of Passage Institute since 1997; Fatherhood Collaborative/Urban League Fatherhood Project since 1997.

Awards/Recognition: U.S. Army Top Secret Clearance School, U.S. Armed Forces, 1978; Army Commendation Medal, 1978; Good Conduct Medal, 1979; Communication Specialist, 1979.

Patents/Publications: "Black Men Unite," *Frederick Douglass Voice* (3-part series), 1995, 1996, 1997; "Sophisticated Racism," *Challenger Newspaper*, 1996.

Residence: Rochester, New York.

McCULLER, James, "Mamba" 1940-1992

Born: Arkansas, 1940; Moved to Rochester, 1961; Died at St. Mary's Hospital, April 7, 1992, of an undisclosed illness.
Family: Survived by two daughters, Stacy D, Williams and Valerie McCuller; Two sons, James C. McCuller Jr., and Daryl McCuller; Daughter, Alecia, was fatally shot by police in 1983.
Education: Bachelor Degree, Pre-Law, Central State University, Ohio; One semester of graduate work, New York University.

Career: First job was bagging groceries; Group worker, Baden Street Settlement; Interviewer, State Employment Service; Director of the Neighborhood Youth Corps; Joined Action For a Better Community (ABC), a multimillion-dollar human service agency, 1965; Director ABC, 1968-1992.

Professional/Community Involvement: Co-Founder, Teen Pregnancy Coalition; Co-Founder, Project Redirect; Led the fight to in-

James "Mamba" McCuller, 1940-1992
*Reprinted with permission of **about...time Magazine***

crease the representation of African Americans at every level of politics; Founder, Organization of Men of African-American Descent, 1986; Helped found the National Black Media Coalition; Board Member, Rochester Health Network; Member, Black Political Caucus.

Eulogies/Quotations:

"He declined the opportunity to be ordinary."

County Executive Bob King
D & C April 19, 1992

"Anyone who ever met him knew what Jim McCuller was all about and that was change... He did not change the answers, but change the questions. It was not always comfortable to be on the receiving end of Jim McCuller's questions."

Mayor Thomas P. Ryan Jr.
D & C April 12, 1992

"He's like a son to me. We're very close... We all love him so much and had so much respect for him... He has certainly been an eloquent voice for his constituents and spoken so well on behalf of poverty-stricken people in Monroe County, despite race and color."

Constance M. Mitchell, Monroe County first elected Black Official.
Times Union, April, 1992

"He said you've got to be willing to spill blood and guts to the curb...Jim would say when faced with eating an elephant, the first thing one must do is take the first bite... Jim was great. He was a great leader. Jim McCuller may be dead, but the spirit of Jim McCuller lives."

Avery Blackman of BY/BLACK
Times Union, April, 1992

"He certainly has made an outstanding contribution to the community. He will be missed because of his unique style of leadership. He was a very bright, very keen fellow. He had a very keen grasp of history, especially African-American history. When you think of ABC, you think of Jim. He had to fight some really strenuous battles with people who were out to destroy ABC,.He was able to protect it and enable it to survive."

Rev. Raymond L. Graves
Times Union, Feb, 1992

"The community will be at a great loss without him. His name stands high. He was a man who led by example. No one person can fill his shoes. It must be a community effort."

Kathryn Terrell, community activist
Times Union, Feb, 1992

"There's definitely a very serious void created with his passing. He was strong in his advocacy for the community...he was a visionary."

Carolyne Blount, editor, about...times Magazine.
Times Union, Feb., 1992

"Ask not what we can do for you, ask what you can do for yourself...we have to teach people they are the heart and soul of the community.

James McCuller
1990 *Times Union* interview

McKEE, James W. 1940-1992

Born: Michigan, 1940; Died of a heart attack, January 1992.
Family: Married for 31 years to Dr. Barbara McKee; Two daughters, Deborah Johnson, Kristin McKee; Two sons, J. Scott, and Derrick.
Education: Bachelor's and Master's Degrees, Michigan State University; Ph.D., Education, Indiana University.

Career: Associate Professor of Education at SUNY Cortland; Former Adviser to Cortland's Black Student Union; Founded the Black Studies Department at Cortland, 1971.

Professional/Community Involvement: Co-Founder with William Faucette Sr. of the Perinton African-American Heritage Committee; He was active with the Fairport School District Committee on Cultural Diversity; Coached the Fairport Little League Baseball.

Awards/Recognition: Honored by Cortland College's Gospel Choir for his work with the school's Black Student Union; Member of Kappa Alpha Psi Fraternity.

Eulogies/Quotations:

"He was a person who always reached out to others, across racial and class lines."

Rev. Joel Tolliver of Church of the Convenant
D&C, Jan 12, 1993

"He was a man of his word...a gentleman and a scholar."

William Faucette Sr.
D&C, Jan 12, 1993

MOLAIRE, Michel (Mike) Frantz

Born: St Marc, Haiti, July 8, 1950; Came to Brooklyn, New York, 1971; Moved to Rochester, 1974.
Parents: Marie Therese Cherubin and Marcel Molaire (deceased).
Family: Married Tulienne Roche Molaire; Two daughters, Alexandra Michele Molaire & Melissa Marcelle Molaire.

Education: MBA, Executive Development Proram, Simon School of Business, University of Rochester, 1986; Master of Science, Chemical Engineering/Polymer Science, University of Rochester, 1982; Bachelor of Science, Chemistry, University of Rochester, 1977; Associate Applied Science Degree, Chemical Technology, New York Technical College (formerly New York City Community College), Brooklyn, New York, 1974; Diploma, Professional Photography, School of Modern Photography, New Jersey, 1974; *African-American Leadership Development Program*, United Way of Rochester, 1993; Leadership Rochester, 1996; Trained in Decision and Risk Analysis, Quality Engineering Using Robust Design and Taguchi Methods.

Career: *Research Associate Chemist, Organic Photoconductor and Chemistry Laboratories, Office Imaging, Eastman Kodak Company since 1990; Project Manager, OEM Photoconductor Chemicals since 1997;* Senior Research Scientist, Organic Photoconductor Laboratories, Research and Technology Development, Copy Product Division of Eastman Kodak Company, 1988-90; Technical Staff Assistant to the Director, Chemistry Division, Research Laboratories, Eastman Kodak Company, 1986-1988; Senior Research Scientist, Photochemistry Laboratories, Research Laboratories, Eastman Kodak Company, 1985-1986; Research Scientist, Photochemistry Laboratories, Chemistry Division, Research Laboratories, Eastman Kodak Company, 1977-1985; Chemical Technician, Photographic & Adjuvant Laboratories, Chemistry Division, Eastman Kodak Company, 1974.

Professional/Community Involvement: Member, Program Committee, Leadership Rochester since 1998; Member, Kids On Track Committee, United Way of Greater Rochester since 1997; Chairman, Minority Affairs Committee, American Chemical Society Local Section, 1997; Founding Editor/Publisher of the *African-American Who's Who™ Greater Rochester Area*, 1993; Founding Editor/Publisher of the *African-American Shopper™ Magazine*, 1991-92; Founder of the African-American Shoppers Club™, 1991-92; Member, Eastman Kodak Research Scientific Council, 1994-1996; First Elected President of the United Way's African-American Leadership Development Program (AALDP) Alumni Association, 1995-1997; Member, AALDP Steering Committee, 1995-1997; Chairman, By-Laws Committee, AALDP Alumni Association, 1994; Chairman, AALDP Alumni Association's 1996 Community Kwanzaa Celebration; Board Member, Threshold For Alternative Youth Services, Inc., 1993-1996; Member, Revenue Development and Long-Range Planning Committees of Threshold, 1993-1996; Corporate Member,

MOLAIRE, Michel (Mike) Frantz

Hillside Children's Center since 1995; Member, American Chemical Society, Imaging Science & Technology Society; Former Member of American Management Association; American Association for the Advancement of Science, 1984-86; Rochester West Indian Festival Organization; Rochester Kwanzaa Coalition; National Organization for the Advancement of Black Chemists and Chemical Engineers, 1979-85; The New York Academy of Sciences, 1985-86; Former Editor, *Sheffield Square Gazette*, newsletter of the Sheffield Square Homeowners' Association, Penfield New York; First Elected President of the Rochester Chapter of the National Organization for the Professional Advancement of Black Chemists and Chemical Engineers, 1981-82; Chairman of the Ad Hoc Committee, NOBCChE Rochester Local Chapter, 1979; Secretary of the Rochester American Chemical Society Technician Affiliate, 1975; Editor-in-Chief of the Rochester ACS Technician Affiliate Newsletter, *Tech Talk*, 1975-77; Staff Photographer for New York City Community College Yearbook, 1973; Secretary of Haitian Club of New York City Community College, 1972-74; Co-Founder and Co-Editor, *En Troisieme Vitesse*, a high school newsletter, Petit Seminaire College St. Martial, Ecole Secondaire, Port-Au-Prince, Haiti, 1967-69; Listed in *Diversity Resource Directory of Greater Rochester Area, published by* The Philanthropic Diversity Consortium of the Rochester (NY) Region, 1993-94.

Awards/Recognition: Recognized as a "Modern Black Inventor" in Ebony Magazine, October, 1998; Nominated for inclusion in MARQUIS Who's Who in Science and Engineering, 5th Edition, and *International WHO's WHO of Professinals*™, 1998; Inducted to Eastman Kodak Distinguished Inventors Gallery, for reaching the milestone of over twenty (20) US-issued patents, 1993; Recognized on the cover of R&R News, a magazine for the Remanufacturing & Recycling Industry, July 1995; Minority Achiever's Award, YMCA Minority Achievers Program, 1996; Master Invention Award for reaching the milestone of more than 10 US issued patents, Office Imaging Division, Eastman Kodak Company, 1992; C.E.K. Mees Award, the most prestigious recognition of Scientific Research Excellence at Eastman Kodak Research Laboratories, 1983; Elected to Beta Gamma Sigma Management Honor Society, University of Rochester Graduate School of Management, 1986; Dean's Lists, University of Rochester, Graduate School of Management, 1985-86; Dean's List, New York City Community College, Brooklyn, New York, 1973.

Patents/Publications: Holder of 28 US and more than 61 foreign patents, in the area of Polymeric Materials, Photoresists, Optical Storage, Organic Monomeric Glasses, Toner and Photoconductor materials for Electrophotographic applications: *US Patent 4,322,490*, "Photopolymerizable Compositions Featuring Improved Monomers," March. 30, 1982; *US Patent 4,416,965*, "Electrostagraphic Developers Comprising Toners Containing a Polyester Having p-Hydroxybenzoic Recurring Units," Nov. 22, 1983; *US Patent 4,446,302*, "Electrostagraphic Developers Comprising Toners Containing A Polyester Having p-Hydroxybenzoic Recurring Units," May 1, 1983; *US Patent 4,499,165*, "Amorphous Compositions of Dyes and Binder-Mixtures in Optical Recording Elements and Information Recording Elements," 1985; *US Patent 4,473,626*, "Electrohardenable Materials for Photoelectrophoretic Imaging," Sept. 25, 1984; *US Patent 4,485,161*, "Electrophotographic Elements Having Barrier Layers of Crosslinked Polymers of Aliphatic or Aromatic Monomers Containing Alpha., Beta,-ethylenically Unsaturated Carbonyl-Containing Substituents, Nov. 27, 1984; *U.S. Patent 4,419,434*, "Image Transfer Film Unit with Modified Surface Layer Containing Capillaries," Dec. 6, 1983; *U.S. Patent 4,619,890*, "Optical Recording Element Having

Michel (Mike) Frantz Molaire at the Kodak Research Laboratories on Lake Ave., July 1995.

Reprinted with permission of the Eastman Kodak Company

A Polymerized Crosslinked Homopolymer Smoothing Layer," Oct. 28, 1986; *U.S. Patent 4,626,361*, Binder-Mixtures For Optical Recording Layers and Elements, *Dec. 2, 1986; U.S. Patent 4,499,165*, "Amorphous Compositions of Dyes and Binder-Mixtures In Optical Recording Elements and Information Recorded Elements," Feb. 12, 1986; U.S. Patent *4,650,734*, "Color Filter Elements," March 17, 1986; *U.S. Patent 4,661,429*, "Photoelectrophotographic Elements and Imaging Method," Apr. 28,1987; U.S. Patent *4,767,883*, "Polymerizable Cyclohexyleneoxalkyl Acrylates," Aug. 30,1988; U.S. Patent 4,792,517, "Laminate For The Formation of Beam Leads For IC Chip Bonding," Dec. 20,1988; *U.S. Patent 4,902,605*, Photoresist Composition Comprising Cyclohexyleneoxyalkyl Acrylate," Feb. 20, 1990; *U.S. Patent 5,176,977*, "Nonpolymeric Amorphous Developer Compositions and Developing Processes," Jan. 5, 1993; *U.S. Patent 5,204,198,* "Photoelectrographic Elements Utilizing Nonionic Sulfonic Acid Photogenerators," Apr. 20, 1993; *U.S. Patent 5,232,804*, Electrophotographic Element and Method of Making Same," Aug. 3, 1993; *U.S. Patent 5,238,764*, "Electrophotographic Elements Containing a Titanyl Fluorophthalocyanine Pigment," Aug. 24, 1993; *U.S. Patent 5,238,766*, "Coating Compositions Containing A Titanyl Fluorophthalocyanine Pigment," Aug. 24,1993; U.S. Patent 5,240,802, "Aggregate Photoconductive Element and Method of Making Same," Aug, 31, 1993; *U.S. Patent 5,288,691*, "Stabilizers for Dye-Donor Element Used in Thermal Dye Transfer," Feb. 22, 1993; *U.S. Patent 5,523,189*, "Electrophotographic Recording Elements and Preparation Method," June 4, 1996; *U.S. Patent 5,614,342*, "Methods For Preparing Cocrystals of Titanyl Fluorophthalocyanines and Unsubstituted Titanyl Phthalocyanine, Electrophotographic Elements, and Titanyl Phthalocyanine Compositions," March 25, 1997; *U.S. Patent 5,629,418*, "Preparation of Titanyl Fluorophthalocyanine," March 13, 1997; U.S.

Patent 5,733,695, March 31, 1998, "Electrophotographic Elements Containing Polyesterionomer," 1997; US Patent 5,773,181, "Non-Uniformly Substituted Phthalocyanine Compositions Preparation Methods, And Electrophotographic Elements," 1998; US Patent 5,766,810, "Methods for Preparing Cocrystals of Titanyl Fluorophthalocyanines And Unsubstituted Titanyl Phthalocyanine, Electrophotographic Elements, And Titanyl Phthalocyanine Compositions," 1998.

Author of several scientific articles: M. F. Molaire, "A Free-Volume Model for Photopolymerizable/Crosslinkable Dry-Film Systems," *J. Polymer Science*, Vol. 20, 847-861 (1982); J.L. R. Williams, M. F. Molaire, "Photoreactive Polymers," *Kirk-Othmer: Encyclopedia of Chemical Technology*, Vol. 17, 3rd Edition, 680-708, (1982); J. L. R. Williams, M. F. Molaire, "Photoreactive Polymers," *Encyclopedia of Semiconductor Technology, Encyclopedia Reprint Series*, Martin Grayson, Series Editor; M. F. Molaire, "Influence of Melt Viscosity on the Writing Sensitivity of Organic Dye-Binder Optical-Disk Recording Media," *Applied Optics*, Vol. 27, pp 743-746, (1988); M. F. Molaire, Roger Johnson, "Organic Monomeric Glasses, A Novel Class of Materials," *J. Polymer Science,* Vol. 27, pp 2569-2592 (1989); M. F. Molaire, J. T. Henry, T. Zubil, J. E. Keading, "Cocrystalline Mixtures of Titanyl Fluorophthalocyanine and Unsubstituted Titanyl Phthalocyanine," *IS&T 1997*, Seattle, Washington; M. F. Molaire, E, Magin, P. Borsenberger, "Photogeneration In Dual-Layer Organic Photoconductors," SPIE 1997, San Diego, California; M.F. Molaire, "Free-Volume Trapping In Dual-Layer Photoconductors", *IS&T 1998 Proceedings*, Toronto, Canada; Published two books of poetry in French, *La Vie Des Oiseaux Morts* (The Life of The Dead Birds), Port-Au-Prince, Haiti, 1967, and *Plus Pres* (Nearer), Port-Au-Prince, Haiti, 1968; Published several articles and interviews in the two editions of the *African-American Shopper™ Magazine*, 1992; Mike F. Molaire, *Shadow of Dreams*, Norex Publications, 1995, Rochester, NY; Mike F. Molaire*, African-American Who's Who™, Greater Rochester Are*a, Norex Publications, 1994, Rochester, NY; Mike F. Molaire,.*African-American Who's Who™ Past & Present Greater Rochester Area, The NeWMillenium Edition*, 1998, Norex Publications, Rochester, NY.

Residence: Penfield, New York.

MORGAN, Clyde Alafiju

Born: Cincinnati, Ohio, 1940; Moved to Rochester, 1987.
Parents: Harriette and Lee Morgan.
Family: Married to Maria Lais, a Brazilian native and Former Director of the Federal University of Bahia's Dance Department; Three children, Clyde G., Dyana G. and Lee Young G. Morgan.
Education: BA, English-History, Cleveland State University, 1963; Dance, Pennington College, 1965; N.A., Dance, Cleveland Karamu House Training Program, Theater & Dance, 1960-63.

Clyde Morgan
Photo, Mike F. Molaire. Copyright 1998, Norex Publications.

Career: *Associate Professor of Dance, SUNY Brockport;* Choreographer & Artistic Director of Sankofa African Dance & Drum Ensemble, SUNY Brockport; Director of Alafia Axe Afro-Brazilian Dance Ensemble; Director of "Africa Alive", Afro-Brazilian Dance Unit performed by Clyde Morgan, Sr. and Jr. for: Young Audiences, Inc. and Rochester Public Schools Project U.N.I.Q.U.E. since 1987; President, Alafia Associates, a Family Business, promoting Investments and international Cultural Exchange between Brazil and the United States since 1979; Fulbright Professor, Federal University of Bahia, Salvador, Bahia, Brazil, 1985-86; Choreographer & Artistic Director of "The Banda Ilu Dance & Music Ensemble of Bahia, Brazil, 1986; Professor of Dance, University of Wisconsin Madison and Milwaukee, 1979-85; "Melrose and Morgan in Concert," Touring Modern Dance Team featuring Claudia Melrose and Clyde Alafiju Morgan; Professor of Dance and Director of The Contemporary Dance Group at the Federal University of Bahia Salvador, Bahia, Brazil, 1971-79; Principal Dancer, Jose Limon Dance Company, New York, NY, 1965-1970.

Professional/Community Involvement: Board Member, School of The Arts, 1995-97.

MURPH, Irving Gray

Clyde Morgan at the 1997 Second Annual African-American Leadership Development Program Alumni (AALDP) Association Community Kwanzaa Celebration, Midtown Plaza

Photo, Mike F. Molaire, Copyright 1998, Norex Publications

Patents/Publications: *Alafia Axe Music of Africa And The Diaspora*, Compact Disc and Cas*about...time Magazine*, p10, Feb. 1988

"It became clear to me that part of our oral tradition--part of the African tradition--was most maintained in music and dancing and to find out what we are and who we are, I felt dancing was more appropriate. And it was clear that black dancing was unlike any other dancing in the world and it did have its African connection."

> Clyde Morgan
> *about...time* Magazine, p11, Feb. 1988

MURPH, Irving Gray

Born: Utica, New York, 1952; Moved to Rochester, 1961.
Parents: Walter Murph, and Loistine Murph.
Family: Married to Linda Murph; Three children, Alexandria, Arielle and Ephraim Murph.
Education: B.S., Mechanical Engineering, Rochester Institute of Technology, 1975; Graduate, Monroe High School, 1970; Graduate, School No. 15, 1964.

Career: *Construction Specialist, MWBE Officer and Code Inspector, County of Monroe Engineering Department since 1989*; Owner/Partner, Rochester Innovators of Capital Holdings, Inc. since 1989; Mail Handler, U.S. Post Office, 1987-95; Bid Estimator/Loan Processor, Urban League of Rochester, 1988-89; Construction Analyst, Neighborhood Housing Service of Rochester, Inc., 1988; Real Estate Professional: Northnagle Realtors since 1996; J.I. Lloyd Realty, 1986-89; Century 21 Foxall Properties, 1985-86; A.C. Rochester Division of General Motors Corporation, Senior Manufacturing Engineer, 1973-1986; Senior Plant Engineer, 1983-85; Material Handling Engineer, 1982-83; Industrial Engineer, 1982; Maintenance Engineer, 1975-76.

Professional/Community Involvement: Member, United Methodist Church of the Resurrection; Co-Founder and Organizer, International Skill Trades Guild; Member, Genesee River Alliance; Actor, Director, Production Manager, Westside Theater Collective; Member, Coalition for Downtown, Goals for Greater Rochester (Community Design Issues and Housing Issues Committees), Kappa Alpha Psi Fraternity, Inc., and Rochester Alumni Chapter of Kappa Alpha Psi Fraternity; Ran unsuccessfully for Monroe County Legislature to represent the County's 27th Legislature in 1991 & 1992.

Residence: Rochester, New York.

NELSON, Eulah Mae, Reverend

Born: Andrews, South Carolina, 1934
Parents: Alice Jackson
Family: Married I.V. Nelson; Three daughters, Joyce Nelson, Carmelitta Nelson, Mi'Chelle Nelson-Robinson.
Education: Doctor of Theology, Aenon Bible College, Indianapolis, Indiana; Religious Education, Michigan Bible & Art Seminary, Detroit, Michigan; Bachelor of Bible Theology, Moody Bible Institute, Chicago, Illinois; Business Administration, Carver Vocational School, Baltimore, Maryland.

Career: *Pastor, Founder and Overseer, Bibleway Healing Assembly of Rochester, New York since 1966.*

Professional/Community Involvement: Member, Rochester Interfaith Jail Ministry, Rochester Community School Advisory Council; President, Bibleway Bible Institute; Board Member, Aenon Bible College, Indianapolis, Indiana; Executive Board Member, New York State & Ontario District Council.

Awards/Recognition: Outstanding Community Award, Mayor's Office, 1993; Pastor of the Year, 1994; *Cambridge World's Who's Who of Women*, 1993; *Marquis Who's Who In Religion*, 1992; IMCWA Award, Meritorious Service, 1988; Outstanding Woman Pastor, 1988; Humanitarian Award, Channel 10, 1986; Woman of Faith Recognition, Brighton Post, 1984; Hands that Heals award, Channel 13, 1981; Honorary Doctorate of Theology, Florida Beacon Bible College.

Patents/Publications: Hour of Deliverance Radio & Television Broadcast, Channel 15 and WDKX Radio; Leap of Faith Television Broadcast, Channel 15; Publisher of *The Deliverance A flame*, a quarterly magazine.

Residence: Pittsford, New York.

NORMAN, James H.

Born: 1948, Augusta, Georgia, 1948; Moved to Rochester in 1992.
Family: Married Lois Williams Norman; Three children, Brandon, Howie, and Alex.
Education: MS, Social Work (Planning and Administration), Western Michigan University, 1972; Post graduate work in Public Administration, Western Michigan University; BA, Psychology, Mercer University, 1970.

Career: *Executive Director, Action For a Better Community since 1992*; Former Deputy Director, Michigan Department of Labor (1987-1992); Worked nine years heading the Department's Bureau of Community Services; Managed the Community Department Division of the Oakland-Livingston Human Service Agency in Pontiac Michigan; Previous employment includes: Parent Involvement Coordinator with the Kalamazoo Public Schools; Manager of Job Development and Placement for the Douglass Community Association (Kalamazoo, Michigan);

Resident-Advisor, Project Upward Bound, at Western Michigan University; Co-Director of a Junior League Sponsored Summer Youth Employment Program in Macon, Georgia.

Professional/Community Involvement: Former Chairperson, National Association of State Community Services Programs; Life Member of the NAACP and the Western Michigan University Alumni Association.

Awards/Recognition: Honored by Western Michigan University (WMU) in 1980, by having his photo displayed on the "WMU Wall of Distinction;" Member, Phi Mu Alpha National Music and Omega Psi Phi Fraternity; listed in several editions of *Outstanding Young Men of America, and Who's Who Among Black Americans.*

Residence: Webster, N.Y.

NOWLIN, Gloria

Born: Delaware, 1940; Moved to Rochester, 1961. **Parents**: Dr. and Mrs. Alfred J. Waters.
Family: Married to William Nowlin, with two children.
Education: MS, Educational Administration, SUNY Brockport, 1977; B.S., Business Education, Delaware State College, Dover, DE, 1961.

Career: *Principal, Franklin High School, 1991-1997*; West House Administrator, Franklin High School Administrative Vice Principal, East High School, Rochester City School District, 1987-91; Dean of Students, John Marshall High School, Rochester City School District, 1976-82; Summer Teacher, Bryant & Stratton Business School, 1976; Teacher, Business Education, Madison and John Marshall High School, 1974-76; Office Manager, Anthony L. Jordan Health Center, 1972-74; Head Secretary, University of Rochester Medical School, Brain Research Center, 1970-71; Teacher,

Business Education, Benjamin Franklin High School, 1961-69.

Professional/Community Involvement: City-wide Chairperson, Children's Memorial Scholarship Fund Drive; Association of Supervisors and Administrators of Rochester, Representative for Vice Principals; Rochester City School District Representative on the Urban League Task Force for Violent and Disruptive Behavior; Chairperson and Treasurer, Vice Principal's Council; Member, City-wide Standardized test Committee; Member, City-wide Student Course Election Committee; Member of City Wide Report Card Users Group; Member, Steering Committee for Reorganization; Member of Pupil Personnel Service Restructuring Committee, and Facilitator, Administrative Staff Development Training

Awards/Recognition: Eye on Education Award, 1993; National Association of Negro Business & Professional Women's Clubs Award, 1990; Nazareth College Award Recognition, African American Women, 1992.

Residence: Moved to Chicago, 1997.

NOWLIN, William, Ph.D.

Born: Rochester, New York, 1950.
Parents: Mary Nowlin
Family: Married to Gloria Nowlin, with two children.
Education: Ph.D. University of Buffalo, 1986; MPA, SUNY Brockport, 1981; B.S., Business Administration, SUNY Empire College, 1978.

Career: *Dean, College of Business and Public Administration, Governors State University, University Park, Ill. since 1997*; Associate Dean, College of Business, Rochester Institute of Technology (RIT), 1992-1997; Chairman, Management and Marketing Department, RIT, 1991; Operations Executive, McCurdy and Company, Inc., 1969 81; Member, Faculty, College of Business, Rochester Institute of Technology, since 1981; promoted Full Professor, in 1991.

Professional/Community Involvement:RIT: Chair, Curriculum Committee, College of Business, 1990, 1991; Member, Academy Policy and Curriculum Committee, 1987, 1989; Member, Enrollment Management Committee, 1986; Member, Technology Committee, 1986; Chair, Undergraduate Admissions Committee, 1985, 88, 89; Co-Chair, President's Task Force of Sexual Harassment, 1993; Member, Policy Council, 1990-91; Vice Chair, Institute Task Force on Retirement Options, 1990; Member, Provost's Committee on Productivity, 1987 1990; Vice Chair, Faculty Council, 1988 89; Chair, Faculty Council's Rights and Governance Committee, 1988 89; Member, Faculty Council Ombudsman Committee, 1987; Chair, Provost's Committee on Minority Faculty, 1986; Member, Institute Library Committee, 1986; Chair, Eisenhart Outstanding Teacher Committee, Group II, 1983; Institute-wide, 1985; President, Cooperative Extension Association, 1978; President, Center For Dispute Settlement, 1979-81; Monroe County Commissioner of Human relations, 1981-84; Director Better Business Bureau, 1983-85; Director, Hudson Avenue Group Homes, 1981; Director, Brighton Chamber of Commerce, 1977-79; Member, Cooperative Extension Board Nominating Committee, 1988; Member, United Way of Greater Rochester Evaluation Committee, 1981; Member, National Association of Academic Affairs Administrators, World Future Society, Industrial Relations Research Association, Beta Gamma Sigma, and Phi Kappa Phi.

Awards/Recognitions: Awarded Research Grants in 1988, 89, and 1990; Granted Awards for Community Service in 1977, 1978, 1979, and 1982; Graduate of the Provost's Seminar on Academic Leadership.

Patents/Publications: Over 34 articles published in *Labor Law Journal, Industrial Management, International Journal of Continuing Engineering Education, College and University Personnel Journal, Spirit, Anglo American Law Review; The Arbitration Journal; Supervision; Nevada Review of Business and Economics, Business Insights, Business and Society Review, Public Employee Bargaining, Journal of Collective Negotiations in the Public Sector, Labor Law Journal, Rochester Business Magazine, Journal of Long Term Care Administration, Business Society Review, Public Personnel Management, Management World, Educational Technology, Computers in Healthcare, Supervisory Management;* has lectured in the following countries: Czech Republic, Germany, Switzerland, Austria, Hungary, Slovakia, Honk Kong, Mexico, Canada, Antigua, and Bahamas.

Residence: Moved to Chicago, 1997

NSAA, J. K.

Born: Rochester, NY, 1955.
Parents: Alma Kelso Coles Greene and T/Sgt. Henry E. Greene, Sr.
Family: Separated.
Education: BA, Summa Cum Laude, Liberal Studies, SUNY Brockport, 1996; A.A.S., Liberal Arts, Monroe Community College, 1992; Labor Studies Program Certificate, NYSSILR Cornell University, 1989; Leadership Rochester, Class of 1997.

Career: *Manager of the Ford-funded Diversity Initiative, Rochester Area Foundation since 1995*; Legislative Officer for City Councilman, City of Rochester since 1996; President, Words & More, an intellectual strategies, research, public relations, and design firm since 1986; Has provided expertise in fund development and computer technology fo Bruce Nennett Photography,

J.K. Nsaa

Photo, Mike F. Molaire. Copyright 1998, Norex Publications.

Inc., Eastman Dental Center, AIDS Rochester, Inc., and Mason Tilman Associates, LTD.; Has provided computer technology oversight and problem-solving for Robert and Company, 1981-1991; Consultant to All Day Sunday and Elaine Parker Associates, 1981-1989; Retail Industry Experience at All Day Sunday and UHURU, 1970-1990.

Professional/Community Involvement: Member, Board of Advisors, African-American Leadership Development Program (AALDP) Alumni, and University of Rochester Medical Center Strong Behavioral Health; Member, Rochester Kwanzaa Coalition; Commissioner, Martin Luther King, Jr. Commission of Rochester;Board Member and President , YWCA of Rochester and Monroe County; Former Liaison, City of Rochester Enterprise Community Zone, and Honoring Diversity Consortium.

Awards/Recognition: Listed in the 1972 Edition of *Who's Who Among High School Students*.

Patents/Publications: Published in ***about...time*** Magazine, *The Frederick Douglass Voice*, and *The Rochesterian*.

Residence: Rochester, New York.

O'CONNOR, Rodney, D.M.D.

Born: June 25, 1950, in Sharon Pennsylvania; Moved to Rochester, 1968.
Parents: Mrs. Helena O'Connor (deceased, 1995) and Dr. L. E. O'Connor.
Family: Married Andrea O'Connor (1997); One daughter, Elena O'Connor.
Education: D.M.D., University of Kentucky College of Dentistry, 1975; General Dentistry Residence, Eastman Dental Center; Internships: Genesee Hospital, Periodontics; Westside Health Service Milbank, 1975-76; Fellowship, Strong Memorial Hospital Dental Research, 1972; Kentucky State University, 1968-71.

Career: ***Dentist, Private Practice, 503 Arnett Boulevard, Rochester since 1976***; Part-time Dentist, Anthony L. Jordan Health Center, 1983-88; Rushville Clinic, Rushville, New York, 1976-77; Part-time Performing Guitarist/Singer, Lunar Circus (1985), Chaos Matrix (1992); Artist: pencil, paintings, and assemblage.

Awards/Recognition: *Who's Who In America*, 1993; *Who's Who Among Black Americans*, 1993; ASDA, 1972-1975; NSDA, Health Interprofessional Council; ASDC, 1978-83; ADA, AGD.

Residence: Rochester, New York.

OLUBODUN, William Olugbemi

Born: Abedkuta, Nigeria Ogun, 1955; Moved to Rochester, 1994.
Parents: Felicia and Joseph Olubodun
Family: Three children, Olukemi, Adewale, Elijah.
Education: MS, Special Education Technology, Gallaudet University, 1988; MS, Administration & Management, Hood College, 1988; BA, Business Administration/Economics, Gallaudet University, 1983; Certificate, Paralegal Studies, North Essex Community College, 1993; African-American Leadership Development Program, United Way of Rochester, 1996; A.D.A Mediation Training, Cromwell, CT, 1993; Grant Writing Seminar, Independent Living Research Utilization, Houston Texas, 1993.

Career: *Coordinator, Multicultural Student Programs and Assistant Professor, Rochester Institute of Technology, NY since 1994*; Assistant Director, Northeast Independent Living Program, Inc., Lawrence MA, 1992-1994; Program Director, Service to Deaf/HH Community Northeast Independent Living Program, Inc, Lawrence, MA, 1990-92; Residential Program Director, On Our Way, Inc., Quincy, MA, 1988-89; Research Assistant, Gallaudet University, Office of Institutional Research, Planning & Evacuation, Washington, DC. 1984-88; Public Service Intern, Office of Management & Budget, Montgomery County Government, Rockville, MD, 1983-84; Business Manager, Gallaudet College Ratskeller/Abbey, Washington, DC, 1981-83.

Professional/Community Involvement: Lights On-Deaf Theatre since 1996; Chair, Public Policy Committee and Councilor, New York State Independent Living Council since 1995; Governing Board Member, National Council on Independent Living-Chair, Multicultural Committee 1991-95; Chair, Marketing Committee, 1995; Advisory Committee Member, Interpreter Training Program, Northern Essex Community College, Haverhill, MA, 1991-94; Vice Chair, Statewide Independent Living Council, MA, 1992-94.

Awards/Recognition: Outstanding Leadership Award, Access Now Coalition, Boston, MA, 1993; Graduate Students Writing/Research Award, Gallaudet University, Washington, DC, 1988; Kappa Gamma Fraternity Foxx Award for Leadership & Academic Proficiency, Gallaudet University, 1983.

Patents/Publications: *Process of Bridging Global Multiculturalism Communication and Disability*, in Press, Proseer and Litaram, 1997.

OSBORNE, Clayton H.

Born: 1945; Moved to Rochester, 1972.
Parents: Hida Rogers (deceased) and Clayton F. Osborne.
Family: Married to Dorelis; Two sons, Clayton C., and Sheldon A.
Education: Doctoral Candidate (ABD) University of Massachusetts at Amherst, School of Education, 1981; MS, Social Welfare, Nelson Rockefeller College of Public Affairs and Policy, 1972; Bachelors of Arts, SUNY Albany, 1968; Ohio Northern University, 1964-65; N.Y. State Education Department Certification, Social Work; National Association of Group Psychotherapists full Member Certification; New York State Notary Public.

Career: *Corporate Director, Diversity & Work Environment, Bausch & Lomb Inc.*; Monroe County Director of Operations, under the Frey County Administration (responsible for a budget of more than $600 million and more than 3,000 employees), 1988-91; Regional Director of the New York State Division for Youth in Rochester, (responsible for a budget of more than $400 million and more than 1,000 employees), 1979-1988.

Professional/Community Involvement: Chair, African-American Leadership Development Program, United Way since 1997; Chairman, Community Mobilization Against Violence Task Force; Former Member of the following Boards of Directors: Family Services of Rochester, N.Y. State Disability Prevention Council, N.Y. State Association of Counties, Chairman, Drug Abuse Task Force, Monroe County Industrial Development Corp., University of Rochester Management Studies Corporate Advisory Board, Monroe County Board of Ethics, Urban League Economic Development Corp., Monroe County Employees Credit Union, YMCA of Greater Rochester, Rochester Area Foundation, Camp Fire Girls, John Branch Foundation, Judicial Process Commission, IBERO-American Action League, Rochester Voluntary Action, Inc., Statewide Youth Advocacy, Webster Avenue Family Resource Center; Board Member, Urban League of Rochester, Career Development Services, Initiatives for Battered Women, and Eltrex Industries; Honorary Chairman, Planned Parenthood's Steppin' Out Gala, 1997.

Residence: Pittsford, New York

PALMER, Florence Vasciannie

Born:British Columbia
Education: MS, Social Work, Syracuse University, 1984; Internship, Outpatient Clinic of Rochester Mental Health, 1982-83, and Western Monroe Mental Health Center, 1983-84; MS, Education, State University College at Brockport, New York, 1976; BA, Behavioral Science, Andrews University, 1972; LPN License, Rochester School of Practical Nursing, 1968.

Career: Private Practice Therapist since 1987; With special emphasis in working with Black males, intimacy and relationship issues as well as parenting; Outpatient Psychotherapist and Family Therapist at Park Ridge Mental Health Center, 1984-87; Family Therapist at Family Service of Rochester, 1979-84; Counselor Therapist at Paddy Hill School; Director of Counseling, Baird Road School, 1976-78; New York State Certified in Education, 1976; Certified Social Worker, 1984; Board Certified Diplomat in Clinical Work, 1988.

Professional/Community Involvement: Member, Adult Protective Community Advisory Board of the Department of Social Service; Community Advisory Board of the Volunteer Lawyers Association; and Community Advisory Board of the Greater Rochester Area Council on Aging.

Awards/Recognition: We Care Award for Outstanding Client Care from Park Ridge Hospital, 1987; Lee Fund, 1982, and Ely Whitney Scholarships, 1983.

Residence: Rochester New York.

POOLE, M. Bernadette, Ed.D

Education: Ed.D., Curriculum, Administration, Columbia University, New York, NY, 1973; MA, Teacher Education, Child Development, Columbia University, New York, NY, 1970; Inter-Group Relations Certification, Columbia University, New York, NY, 1969; Business Administration, Emmanuel College, Boston, MA, 1959.

Career: *President of AEDU-TECH Systems, Inc.*, providing Quality Management/Organizational Change/Strategic Planning Consulting and Training Services in the areas of Team Building, Problem-Solving, Cultural Diversity, Collaboration and Coaching/Counseling/Mentoring since 1990; Xerox Corporation, 1979-89: Design/Engineering CAD/CAM/CAE Technology Transfer Manager, 1986-89; Corporate Training Manager, Leadership Through Quality, The Xerox TQM Strategy, 1984-86; Organization Effectiveness Manager, 1982-84; Management Employee Involvement Internal Consultant, 1980-82; Manager, Customer Education, 1979-81; Associate Professor & Chair, School of Education, PACE University Westchester Campuses, Pleasantville, NY, 1976-79; Assistant Professor & Director, Competency-Based Teacher Education Project, Hofstra University, Hempstead, NY, 1970-76; Lecturer, Cultural Diversity in Education, Columbia University, NY, 1973-75; Community Relations Director, Columbia University Urban Center, NY, 1969-72; Program Evaluation Consultant, NY State Office of Economic Opportunity, NY, 1967-69; Director, Harlem Youth Unlimited Employment Office, NY, 1964-67.

Professional/Community Involvement: Trustee, Rochester Regional Library Council, elected June, 1996; Community Advisory Board Member, WXXI Public Broadcasting System since 1995; Trustee & Strategic Planning Chair, Monroe County Library System Board, Legislative Appointment, 1993-1998; 2nd Vice President & Strategic Planning Chair, Big Brothers/Big Sisters Board since 1992; Board Member & Program Chair, National Center For Missing and Exploited Children, NY since 1993; Board of Directors, Rochester Women's Network, 1996-1999; Chairperson, Citizens Advisory Committee on Information Technology, Town of Pittsford, 1994-1995.

Awards/Recognition: Keynote Speaker, SUNY Brockport Student Administration Retreat, 1997; President's Award, Big Brothers/Big Sisters, 1995; Volunteer Service Award, Hispanic Leadership Development Program, 1994; Certificate of Merit, City of Rochester, 1995.

Residence: Rochester, New York.

POUGH, Larry Clayton

Family: Married to Brenda-Murphy Pough; One daughter, Stephanie Janelle Pough.

Education: Bachelor of Arts, Chemistry, Dillard University, New Orleans, LA, 1969-1973; Diploma, Chemical Engineering (Program supervised by Iowa State University), 3M-International Correspondence School, 1975-1980; Executive Development Program, Business Management, St John Fisher College Program, Rochester, NY, 1986-1987; Certificate, Introduction to MRPII-American Production and Inventory Control Society; Certificate, Hazardous Materials Technician, Public Safety Training Center, MCC; Certified Instructor, OSHA Standard for General Industry, # 501, 1995; Certificate, OSHA Guide to Industrial Hygiene, #521; United Way African-American Leadership Development Program, 1995.

Career: *Safety, Health and Environmental Supervisor, 3M Tonawanda, NY since 1998;* Senior Process Engineer, 3M Tonawanda, NY, 1997-98; 3M Company, Printing Publishing System Division, Rochester, NY, 1973-1997; Safety & Environmental Supervisor (1994-1997), Senior Process Engineer (1993-94), Production General Supervisor (1984-93), Production Shift Supervisor (1980-84) and Process Engineer (1973-79).

Professional/Community Involvement: Secretary, Committee Chair, and Board Member, Urban League of Rochester; Board member, Theta Omicron Scholarship Foundation, Inc., Rochester, NY; Social Action Committee Chair and Past Trustee, Mt. Vernon Baptist Church, Rochester, NY; Past President, District Chairman, Committee Chair, Omega Psi Phi Fraternity, Inc., Rochester, NY; Company Coordinator, Classroom Volunteer, Junior Achievement of Rochester; Committee Chair, United Way Leadership Development Program; District Talent Hunt Chairman, Omega Psi Phi Fraternity for

Larry Clayton Pough
Photo, Mike F. Molaire. Copyright 1998, Norex Publications.

five states, New York, New Jersey, Pennsylvania, Delaware, and Maryland; Charter Member, Rochester Chapter Dillard University Alumni; President, Rochester chapter Dillard University Alumni, 1980-82; 3M Club Vice President, 1977; 3M Club President, 1978-1980; 3M Club Bowling League Treasurer, 1976; Served on the Steering Committee, AALDP Alumni Association 1996 Community Kwanzaa Celebration.

Award/Recognition: Outstanding Young Men of America, O.Y.M.A. Committee and Montgomery, Alabama.

Residence: Rochester, New York.

PRICE, Charles

Born: Rochester, NY, 1923.
Parents: Jennie and Charles Henry Price.
Family: Married to Pauline H. Price; Two children, Renee A. Price and Mrs. Charlene P. Scaife; Four grandchildren.

Education: Master's Degree Program, Industrial and Labor Relations for Managers, Cornell University; Industrial Relations and Supervisory Course, City of Rochester; First United States Army Intelligence School, Fort Rodman, New Bedford, MA; Boston Naval Yards, Boston, MA.

Career: First African American on the Rochester Police Department, sworn in, on December 1, 1947; Captain, Rochester Police Department since 1976; Retired in 1985; Commanding Officer, Internal Affairs, 1980-85; Commanding Officer, Genesse Section, 1978-80; Commanding Officer, Highland Section, 1977-78; Commanding Officer, Community Relations Division, 1975-1977; Commanding Officer, Juvenile Section Department, 1972-75; Promoted Detective Lieutenant., Criminal Investigation Section, Burglar/Larceny, 1970-72; Assistant to Commissioner of Police, 1968-70; Promoted to Detective Sergeant, Intelligence Officer, 1960-68; Police Officer, Police Athletic League, 1957-60; Police Officer, 1947-52.

Professional/Community Involvement: Advisory Board Member, Greater Rochester YMCA since 1995; Board Member, United Way of Greater Rochester, 1990-96; Member, American Association of Public Administrators, 1980-85; Southwest Kiwanis Club since 1963; Bill of Rights Committee, Kiwanis International, 1990-92; Pathway Houses of Rochester since 1992; President, Men's Service Center, 1992-1994; National Safety Council of the Rochester Chamber of Commerce (1975-85); Eureka Masonic Lodge #36 since 1951; U.S.A. retired Officer Association since 1985; NAACP (1950); President, Police Rosewood Club, 1970's; Sergeant of Arms, Locust Club Police, 1962; First Black Governor, NY State District, Kiwanis Club, 1987-1988; Lieutenant Governor, Genesee Division, Kiwanis Club, 1971-72.

Awards/Recognition: Black History Month Award, Rochester Board of Education, 1997; 9th Community Award, Eureka Masonic Lodge #36, 1981; Medal of Valor, Rochester Police department, 1981; Citizen of the Year, Monroe County Human Relation, 1960's.

RADNEY, Delores Jackson

Born: 1956, in Buffalo, New York; Moved to Rochester, 1987.
Parents: John and Carlene Jackson.
Family: Married George Radney; Three sons, Julian, Omar and Michael Radney.
Education : Bachelor's Degree, Dramatic Arts and Communications, SUNY Geneseo, 1978.

Career: *Coordinator, Family and Community Programs, of the Memorial Art Gallery*; Founder, Rochester Center of African American Culture; Consultant, Excellent People Productions; Director, Kuumba Kids Theatre Company; Account Executive, WDKX Radio, 1987; Sales Manager, WUFO Radio, Buffalo, New York, 1983-86; Publicity Director, African American Cultural Center, Buffalo, New York, 1985-86; Reservationist, American Airlines, Hartford, Connecticut, 1984-85; Research Writer, Surveys for Business, New York, New York, 1980-83; Production Assistant, New Federal Theater, New York, New York, 1978-80;

Professional/Community Involvement: Member, Rochester Kwanzaa Coalition.

Delores Jackson Radney
Photo, Mike F. Molaire. Copyright 1998, Norex Publications.

Awards/Recognition: Awarded the Partners of America Fellowship in International Development (six weeks of intensive training in community development and leadership), 1997; Award for Museum Leadership, Smithsonian Institution, 1992; Special Citation Award, Arts for Greater Rochester, 1992; White Rose of Friendship Award, Links Rochester Chapter.

Patents/Publications: "Community Connections in Rochester," *Journal of Museum Education*, Spring/Summer Issue.

Residence: Rochester, New York.

RAY, Andrew Anthony, Ph.D.

Born: Centreville, Mississippi, 1948; Moved to Rochester, 1968-69.

Parents: Ruby and Perry Ray.

Family: Married to Elizabeth R. Ray.

Education: Ph.D., Administration & Policy Development, SUNY Buffalo; MS Administration, University of Buffalo, NY; MS, Urban Education, SUNY Geneseo; BS, Economics, Southern University, Baton Rouge, Louisiana; Certificates Curriculum, University of California, Santa Cruz, CA; Education, University of Rochester, Rochester, NY; International Relations, Canisius College, Buffalo, NY; Administrative Leadership, University of Wisconsin, Milwaukee, Wisconsin; Special Education Administration, University of Buffalo, Buffalo, NY; Administrative Seminar, Loyola University, New Orleans, Louisiana; Administrative Leadership, SUNY Plattsburg, Plattsburg, NY; Governmental Studies, American University, Washington D.C.; School District Administrator, Advance Study, and Administration and Supervision, SUNY Brockport; Fellowships at Yale University, University of Ghana West Africa, American University, University of Wisconsin, University of California; Canisius College, Loyola University, SUNY Plattsburg & SUNY Brockport.

Caeer: *Principal, East High School, Rochester City School District since 1996*; Senior High Vice Principal, 1992-96; Senior High Summer School, 1987, 88, 95 and 96; Senior High Dean of Students, 1982-92; Career League and Counselor, 1982-84; Director, Adolescent Vocational Exploration Program, 1986; Urban Institute of Rochester, 1985-86; Teacher, Junior & Senior High, Social Sciences, 1969-82; Center Supervisor, Youth Tutors, Youth Program, 1971-72; University Tutor, Rochester Institute of Technology, 1973-74; Industry Intern, Singer Corporation, 1972.

Professional/Community Involvement: President (volunteer), Baden Ormond Federal Community Credit Union; Mentor, COMPEER & Big Brother Programs; Member, Phi Delta Kappa, School Administrators Association of New York (SAANYS), National Association of Secondary School Principals (NASSP), Association for the Study of Afro-American Life, Association of Supervisors and Administrators, Rochester (ASAR); Founder, Black Educators Association of Rochester (BEAR).

Awards/Recognition: John W. Thompson Community Service Award, Prince Hall Masonic Order, 1998; Dr. Charles Lunsford Community Service Award, Urban league, 1997; Omega Man of the Year (Local & District), 1993-94; New York State Outstanding Educator Award, 1993; Superior Service Award, 1992; New Bethel CME Church Man of the Year, 1992; Board of Education Citation, Friends of Frederick Douglass, 1992; Xerox CARI, Martin Luther King Award, 1991; New York State Outstanding Educator of The Year, 1991; District Parent Advisory Committee Award, 1991; Administrator of the Year Award, 1990; Founder's Award, 1990; Educator of the Year, Program to Interest Rochester Students in Science & Math ($PRIS^2M$), 1987; Community Service Award, Urban League of Rochester, 1980; Educator of The Year, Prince Hall Masonic Order, 1976; Educator of The Year, King Solomon Masonic Order, 1976; *Who's Who In Black America*, 1976 to present; Parent and Student Service Award 1975; Outstanding Teacher of the Year Award, 1973; Silver Medallist, Emory University Business Competition, 1968; Louisiana State Bronze & Silver Medallist in Academic Competition, 1963, 64.

Residence: Rochester, New York.

REAVES, Charles

Born: Rochester, New York, 1956.

Parents: Carrie and James Reaves.

Family: Married to Josanne C. Reaves; Three children, Cara Deanne, Toren Michael and Brennan James Reaves.

Education: BA, Communications/Public Relations, SUNY Brockport, 1980; AAS, Liberal Arts, Monroe Community College, 1976; Leadership Rochester, 1996; Currently working towards MPA at SUNY Brockport; Graduate of James Madison High School, 1974.

Career: *Center Director, YMCA, Arnett Branch since 1996*; Interim Director, Emergency Social Services, American Red Cross, 1995-96; Assistant Director, Emergency Social Services, American Red Cross, 1994-1995; Executive Producer and Host, *Rochester Talks*, a weekly cable TV talk show since 1993; Program Director, Summer Youth Employment Training Program, American Red Cross, 1994; Researcher/Educator, Rochester AIDS Prevention Project of Rochester, General Hospital of Rochester, 1992-1994; Coordinator/Case Planner, Monroe County Middle School Prevention Project, Rochester Society for Prevention of Cruelty to Children, Rochester, NY, 1991-92; Senior Community Educator, Planned Parenthood of Rochester and the Genesee Valley Inc., 1986-91; Assistant Director of Public Relations, Internship, Action For a Better Community, 1980.

Professional/Community Involvement: Vice President, Board of Directors, 19th Ward Community Association since 1997; Chair, Revenue Development Committee, Eastside Community Center since 1994; Member, African-American Unity Project to Combat School Violence, 1994; Mentor Program, Rochester City School, 1990-1994; COMPEER program, 1982-84; Member, Chili/Thurston Rd. Business Development Committee of 19th Ward, 1996.

Awards/Recognition: Certificate of Merit, Rochester Brainpower Hall of Fame, 1991; Commencement speaker at area high schools; Nominated for JC Penney Golden Rule Award for work with African-American youth, 1994.

Residence: Rochester, New York.

REFFEL, Zeporrah Conteh

Born: Sierra Leone, Western Africa; Moved to Rochester, 1974.

Parents: Honorable James Thomas Reffel, (an African tribal chief), and Mrs. Meneh Phekean Reffell (owner of The James Thomas Reffell French Memorial School, a private school for underprivileged children, started in 1940 Sierra Leone, West Africa).

Family: Divorced with a son, Abib Tejan M. Conteh.

Education: BS, Social Work, Rochester Institute of Technology; MS, Educational Administration, the State University College at Brockport; working on her doctorate degree in Education at the University of Rochester.

Career: *Counselor and part-time Teacher at Monroe Community College for six years*; founded Tejan's African Gift Shoppe at 1009 Genesee St, in 1990; Store moved to Village Gate Square in 1991; Another store opened at 468 Main Street in 1993.

Residence: Greece, New York.

RIDLEY, William, 1911-1986

Born: Oxford, NC, 1911; Moved to Rochester, 1944.

Family: Survived by his wife, Letha Ridley; A son, William Ridley III, and a brother, James Ridley.

Education: Doctorate, Education, SUNY Brockport, 1972; Technical Degree, Electrical Engineering, Illinois University; MS, Mathematics, Michigan University, 1937; Mathematics Degree, Shaw University, Raleigh, N.C.

ROBERTS, Norman L.

William Ridley, 1911-1986
Reprinted with permission of __about...time Magazine, Inc.__

Career: Taught in small Black colleges in North Carolina and Virginia; Civilian Instructor in radio communication, U.S. Army Air Force, 1942; Stromberg-Carlson, Rochester, NY, Research Engineer, 1944; Worked at Rochester Products Division, Sylvania Plant, Batavia; Became first Black teacher, Edison High School; taught there for five years; Taught at East High School; Night Instructor at Rochester Institute of Technology for 28 years; Counselor, School District Manpower Program; City-wide Planner for Cooperative Education; Retired, 1975.

Eulogies/Quotations:

"He was the finest teacher we ever had...He was brilliant in mathematics, but that wasn't all he taught us...Mr. Ridley really took a personal interest in his students."

Carolyn Conrow
Times Union, June, 23, 1986

"He was a persistent young man... He knew he was qualified whether others taught he should have the job or not."

Letha Ridley, Ridley's wife
Times Union, June, 23, 1986

"At a time when there were no obvious economic opportunities, Bill and his generation were the ones who achieved with the hope that things would change.... He was ready for the economic system but the economic system was not ready for him."

Walter Cooper, a research chemist at Kodak
Times Union, June, 23, 1986

ROBERTS, Norman L.

Born: 1952, Sylvania, Georgia; Moved to Rochester, 1963.
Parents: Willie and Doris Roberts.
Family: Married to Beatrice Roberts; Four daughters, Megan Louise, Shellie, Crystal, and Willie.
Education: BSW, SUNY Brockport, New York.

Career: *Program Manager, Homeless and Housing Program, Francis Center, Catholic Family Center since 1995;* Director of School #2 program/Youth Development, Society For The Prevention and Care of Children, 1994-95; Resource Development Associate, United Way of Greater Rochester, 1993-94; Operations Manager, Genesee Settlement House, 1992-93; Administrative Assistant, Genesee Settlement House, 1989-92; Manager, Truancy Prevention Program, 1986-89; Counselor/Intake Coordinator, 1984-86; Project Director, 1981-84, Youth Services Supervisor, 1979-1981; Candidate for School Board, in 1992; Presiding Elder, Triumph The Church and Kingdom of God In Christ.

Professional/Community Involvement:
President and Board Member, Neighborhood Housing Services, 1998; Former Board Member, Urban league of Rochester; The Advocacy Center; Teenage Parent Support; Chairman, 1994; President, Urban League Guild, 1994; Former Member, National Society for Fund Raising Executives; National Association of Social Workers since 1991; Budget Advisory Committee-Rochester City School District, 1990; Human Service Advisory Council-Rochester School District, 1986; Children's Service Subcommittee-Monroe County Department of Social Services, 1988; Chairperson, Community Task Force On Secondary Restructuring, 1987.

Awards/Recognition: Volunteer of The Year, Neiborhood Housing Services, 1998; Certificate of Appreciation, Urban League of Rochester; Service Award, Genesee Settlement House; Service Award, Triumph The Church and Kingdom of God In Christ; Dean's List, Brockport State College.

Residence: Rochester, New York.

ROBINSON, Suzette, MD

Born: Naturalized American; Moved to Rochester, 1990.
Parents: Rachel M. and Carl O. Robinson.
Family: Single.
Education: MD, SUNY Buffalo Medical School, 1986; BA, Magna Cum Laude, Natural Sciences, Fordham University, 1984; Residency, Obstetrics & Gynecology, Boston City Hospital, Boston, MA, 1990-1994; Certificates I-VII, Royal School of Music (London), 1965-1980.

Career: *Stone Gate OB/GYN, private practice since 1996;* Director of Continuing Education, St. Mary's Hospital, 1994-1996; Director OB/GYN, Family Health Associates, St. Mary's

Hospital, Rochester, NY, 1994-96; Clinical Instructor, University of Rochester since 1994; I.V. Team/Phlebotomist, Erie County Medical Center, Buffalo, NY, 1988.

Professional/Community Involvement: Hospital Representative of the Standards Committee of Rochester; Hospital Consortium of Greater Rochester C-Section Committee, 1995; Junior Fellow, American College of Obstetrics & Gynecology; Medical Society of the State of New York; Member of the Governor's Women's Task Force, 1996; Elected to Medical Records Committee, St. Mary's Hospital, 1994; Elected to Quality Assurance Committee, St. Mary's Hospital, 1994; American Medical Women's Association-Anti-Smoking Task Force, 1988; Annual Medical School Talent Show, 1987-88; Medical Society of the State of New York (representative to National Meetings, Caribbean Student Association, Caribbean Talent Show), 1988-89; Secretary, Student National Medical Association, 1988.

Awards/Recognition: Leadership Award, African-American Leadership Development Program, United Way, 1994; SUNY Brockport Medical School, Dean's Scholarship, Partners of America and New York Regents Scholarships; Fordham University, Dean's Scholarship, Dean's List.

SCOTT, Ruth H., The Honorable

Born: 1934, Albion, Michigan.
Family: Married William Scott; Three children, Gregory, June and Crystal.
Education: Master of Education Degree, Counseling, Kent State University, Kent. Ohio, 1961; Bachelor of Arts, Cum Laude, Albion College, Albion, Michigan, 1956; Certificate in Administration, SUNY Brockport, Brockport, New York, 1984; Mediation Certification, Center For Dispute Settlement, Rochester, New York, 1989.

Career: *President/CEO, Scott Associates* a consulting service for educational institutions, corporations, business, and government agencies since 1988; Secretary, Community and Legislative Officer/Compliance and Community Relations Officer (1977-1982), Branch Manager (1982-1985), and Regional Branch Manager (1985-1989), Rochester Community Savings Bank; English Teacher/Vocational Counselor/Community Resource, Rochester City School District, Rochester, New York, 1956-77; Developed the first ever African-American based curriculum in the Cleveland, Ohio Southernler and Caharagus County BOCES District ; The first woman elected to the City Council, serving in 1977-1989; Served on the Rochester Council's Community Development Committee; Was Chairperson of Council's Public Safety and Recreation Personnel Committees; Ran unsuccessfully for Mayor of Rochester in 1993; Public Affairs Officer, Community Savings Bank, 1977-1981: Public Affairs Officer, 1981; Personnel Consultant, 1978; Compliance Coordinator, 1980.

Professional/Community Involvement: Council Board Member, Memorial Art Gallery; Advisory Council to Health Insurance Companies; Member Akoma Choir, Memorial A.M.E Zion Church; Member, Board of Directors, National League of Cities; Chairperson of the NLC's Community and Economic Development Steering Committees; Member, Board of Directors, Women in Municipal Government; Member, Board of Directors, Rochester Area Chamber of Commerce; Member, Rochester Sales and Marketing Executive Club; Past Member, Board of Directors, Monroe County Water Authority; Past President, Rochester 19th Ward Community Association; Advisory Council, Women's Career Center of Rochester; Founding Member, Martin Luther King, Jr. Commission, Greater Rochester Area, Rochester Downtown Development Corporation, Rochester Fight Back Coalition on Drugs

The Honorable Ruth Scott
Photo, Mike F. Molaire.Copyright 1998, Norex Publications.

and Cultural Commission, Mayor/County Executive Committee on Rochester 2000 Vision Committee; Past Vice President, Board of Directors, Rochester Area Foundation; Past President, National Neighbors Association; Member, Advisory Committee for Eliminating the Deficit of the Rochester Philharmonic Orchestra; Hospital Services Analysis Committee, Genesee Region; Past Board Member, Social Concerns, United Methodist Church Buffalo Conference; Past Board Member, PRIS2M, WXXI-TV; A delegate at the 1976 Democratic Convention; The first woman and the first Black to head the 19th Ward Neighborhood Association.

Awards/Recognition: Include Leadership America Award; Chamber of Commerce Excellence in Politics Award; Listed in *Who's Who Among Black Americans*; *Who's Who Among Black Elected Officials*; *Who's Who In American*

College and Universities; *Who's Who Among Religious Leaders*; Albion College Distinguished Alumnus Award; Phi delta Kappa Education Honorary; Girls Scouts of America Community Service Award; Rochester Chamber of Commerce Women in Business Athena Award; Citations for contributions to the community, Monroe County Human Relations Commission; "Women Builders of Communities and Dreams," YWCA; Certificate of Recognition, United Church Ministry; Citizen of the Year, Omega Psi Phi Fraternity; Outstanding Christian Service Award, Colgate Rochester Divinity School; Doctor of Humane Letters, Honoris Causa, Alfred University; Nominated a Woodrow Wilson Fellow; Memorial A.M.E Zion Church Lay Leadership Award.

Quotations:

"She is pragmatic, studious, straightforward, articulate, and energetic. It is her energy, and concern for people that propel her into activism and politics."

> Valerie Elverton Dixon
> *about...time* Magazine, p14, June 1977.

"People expect government to handle things that government can't handle. Politicians don't have the time and can't do everything. People living in neighborhoods have to solve some problems. People have to be concerned with the quality of life where they live. Government can't do much without neighborhoods."

> Ruth Scott
> *about...time* Magazine, p18, June 1977

"I believe that underneath, people are basically the same...They want to think that someone cares and is willing to listen to them."

> Ruth Scott
> *about...time* Magazine, p18, 1977

"Ruth Scott is a piece of the sun on earth, full of energy, giving off warmth and light, but she thinks she's only a woman.:

> Valerie Elverton Dixon
> *about...time* Magazine, p18, June 1977.

"I'm a big picture person. I'm not a small detail person. I'm the kind of person who likes to stand back and say what's wrong with this picture and how can we make this work a little better than it is?"

> Ruth Scott
> *"Exemplars"* by Estelle Stark, in <u>Lake Effect</u> Magazine, Vol. VIII, Spring 1997.

"I'm proud of the fact I helped the council focus on quality of life in neighborhoods and the importance of having neighborhood input into our strategies...I also made people take a look at neighborhoods that were not as affluent. We have a civic responsibility for the street lights, the sidewalks, for things that are part of the public trust. I don't care who's living there, what they're doing or how they act."

> Ruth Scott, commenting on her contribution to the Rochester City Council
> *"Exemplars"* by Estelle Stark, in <u>Lake Effect</u> Magazine, Vol. VIII, Spring 1997.

SEALY, Annie Cockrell

Born: 1953, Macon, Ms.; Moved to Rochester, 1978.
Parents: Booker T. and Rhodia M. Cockrell
Family: Married to Trevor A. Sealy; Two children, Brooke Monet and Camille Nicole Sealy.
Education: AA, Accounting, Wayne County Community College, Detroit, Michigan, 1978; Business courses, Wayne State University and School of Business, Rochester Institute of Technology; United Way African-American Leadership Development Program (AALDP), 1996.

Career: Financial Analyst, US & Canada Finance, Rochester Area Operations Building Division since 1998; Financial Administrator, Kodak Park Site Services Buildings Division, Eastman Kodak Company, 1992-1998; Financial Special, Kodak Park Professional Film Sensitizing, 1991-92; Senior Cost Analyst, Copy Products Financial Planning, Equipment Manufacturing/Research & Development, 1991; Cost Accountant, Copy Products Materials Development & Manufacturing, 1985-1989; Cost Engineering

Assistant, Kodak Park Manufacturing/Finishing, 1981-85; Jr. Accountant, Clipper International Corp., Detroit, Michigan, 1977-78; Accountant, renaissance center Partnership, Detroit, Michigan, 1976-77; Accountant, Model Neighborhood/Inner City Drug Abuse Programs, Inc., 1972-76.

Professional/Community Involvement:Vice-President, AALDP Alumni Association, 1998-1999; Kodak United Way Campaign Sollicitor for small businesses and retirees; Member, Barbados American Club's Community Assistance Program; Served on committee to improve the West Irondequoit Central School District Health care Curriculum, 1995-96; Served on Steering Committee for AALDP Alumni Association 1996 Community Kwanzaa Celebration.

Residence: Rochester, New york.

SIMPSON, Lucille

Born: Sandford, Fla., 1935; Moved to Rochester, 1942.
Parents: Rosalie Johnson and Earl Nawkins.
Family: Married to Frank Simpson.
Education: Attended Sandford Coobs High School, but did not graduate.

Career: Executive Director and Founder, Green Acres Food Pantry and Neighborhood Center since 1996; Pick up donated food items from Wegmans several times a week to distribute to 200 seniors in four housing projects; Opened a food pantry for the hungry in St. Bridget's Church in the 1970s; Housekeeper and Nurse's Aid, Rochester's Jewish Home; Nurse's Aid, Highland Hospital; Day Care Worker, Monroe County Social Services.

Professional/Community Involvement: Member, Steering Committee, Action For a Better Community; Community Liaison For Partners For Food; Member, New York State Tenant Association.

Awards/Recognition: Rochester Safety Council Award, 1997; Faith In Action Award, Rochester Community of Churches, 1996; JC. Penney Golden Rule Award, United Way, 1998; Interracial Relations Award, American Association of Indians, 1997; President George Bush "Points of Lights" Award, 1996. The Green Acres endeavor was recognized in USA Weekend, April 13, 1997.

Quotations:

" We are all part of the human race and we are all God's children."
Lucille Simpson

SMITH, Thomas W., PH.D

Born: Portsmouth, Ohio, 1943; Moved to Rochester, 1973.
Parents: Henry A. Smith
Family: Married to Mary E. Smith; Three children, Natalie, Katherine, & Williams
Education: PH.D Organic Chemistry, University of Michigan, 1973. BS Degree, Chemistry, John Carroll University, 1969.

Career: *Research Fellow, Xerox Corporation Webster Research Center since 1990*; Manager, Quality and Technology Management, Xerox Corporate Research Group, responsible for the implementation of Xerox's Malcom Baldridge Award-winning quality initiative, "Leadership Through Quality," in the research organization, 1988-90; Research Fellow and Manager, Macro Organic & Surface Chemistry, Xerox Corporation, 1986-88; Manager Macromolecular Organic & Surface Chemistry Area, a 7-member research group engaged in the synthesis of polymers and photoactive materials and studies of chemistry at surfaces and interfaces, 1985-8 Manager, Chemistry of Materials ea, a 16-member research group engaged in the synthesis of polymers, photoactive, and electroactive materials, and studies of chemistry at surfaces and interfaces, 1983-85; Manager, Polymer Sciences Area, a 11 member group engaged in the development of optical recording media, 1979-83; Scientist, polymer Sciences Area, Xerox Corporation, 1975-78; Associate Scientist, Polymer Sciences/Photoreceptor Areas, 1973-75; Consultant, Environmental Research Institute of Michigan, 1972-73; Chemist, Lubrizol Corporation, Cleveland, Ohio, 1968-70; Research Technician, Lubrizol Corporation, 1963-1968; Adjunct Professor at the University of Rochester, 1984-85 and 1986/87; Taught a graduate level course, "Introduction to Polymer Science."

Professional/Community Involvement: Member, American Chemical Society, Inc. (ACS) since 1975; The Society for Imaging Science and Technology and Sigma XI; Chairman, Rochester Chapter of the ACS, 1992; Chairman, the ACS 25th Northeast Regional Meeting held in Rochester, NY, October 1995; At-Large Member, Executive Committee, Rochester Section, Inc., ACS, 1976, 77, 79; Treasurer, Rochester Section, Inc., ACS, 1980-81; Alternate Council, Polymer Division, ACS, 1980-81; ACS Polymer Division, Membership Booth Chairman/Board of Directors, 1979-80; Co-Advisor to Rochester Institute of Technology Master's Candidate, David Allen, 1979-80; ACS North East Region Meeting, Polymer Program Committee member, 1979-81; Domestic Membership Committee Chairman, Polymer Division, ACS, 1981-83; Chairman Elect, Rochester Section, ACS, 1981; Chairman, Rochester Section, ACS, Inc., 1982; Immediate Past Chairman, Rochester Section, ACS, Inc., 1983; Member, Advisory Committee for the hemical Technology Program, Monroe Community College, since 1983; Member, Polymer Science Advisory Board, University of Connecticut, since

1984; Member, Awards Canvassing Committee, Division of Polymer Chemistry Inc., ACS, 1985-86; North East Regional Meeting (NERM 17), Chairman, Polymer Program Committee, 1985-87; Member, Industrial Advisory Committee, University of Southern Mississippi, 1985-88; Co-Chairman, Symposium on Polyelectrolytes and Ionic Conducting Polymers, ACS, Division of Polymer Chemistry, 1989; National Science Foundation, Chemistry Division Triennial Oversight Review Committee, 1989; Member, ACS Board Special Committee on Corporate Associates since 1990; Member, Institute of Electrical Engineering Quality Advisory Board since 1991; Invited Expert Analyst, *CHEMTRACT, Macromolecular Edition, since 1991;* Chairman, National Awards Committee, Rochester Section ACS, Inc., 1991 92; Mentor, Career Planning Workshop for Under-represented Minorities, Perdue University, 1992; Co-Chairman, 1993 ACS Corporation Associates Symposium, "Diversity in the Chemical Workforce of the 21st Century: Building a Competitive Advantage," 1992-93; Chairman, Workshops Committee, ACS Division of Polymer Chemistry since 1992; General Chairman, ACS 25th Northeast Regional Meeting, October 1995, 1992-95; Alternate Councilor (1980 81), Workshops Committee Chairman, since 1992.

Awards/Recognition: Community Educators Award, Wilson Jr. High School, Rochester NY, 1975-76; Rochester Section ACS Award for Outstanding Service, Chairman, 1982; ACS Certificate of Recognition for Leadership of the Rochester Section; Winner of the 1983 Award for Outstanding Performance by a Local Section; Rackman Fellowship, 1971-72; Eastman Kodak Fellowship, 1971-72.

Patents/Publications: Author of (25) Scientific Publications in *Macromolecules, Xerox Disclosure Journal, Imaging Science, Encyclopedia of Polymer Science and Engineering, Journal of*

American Chemical Society; Journal of Polymer Science, Polymer Symposium Series, Optical Disk Technology; has made over 25 Invited Presentations from 1986 to 1993; Holder of 29 U.S. Patents, in polymeric materials, Organocarbonyl Compounds, Chalcogenide Alloys, Optical Disk, Toner Materials, Photoconductors: *U.S. Patent 3,896,073*; *U.S. Patent 4,122,030*, "Formation of Colloidal Dispersions of Selenium by the Locus Control Method," 1978; *U.S. Patent 4,252,671*, "Preparation of Colloidal Iron Dispersions by the Polymer-Catalyzed Decomposition of Iron Carbonyl and Iron Organocarbonyl Compounds," 1981; *U.S. Patent 4,252,672*, "Preparation of Colloidal Iron Dispersions by the Polymer-Catalyzed Decomposition of Iron Carbonyl and Iron Organocarbonyl Compounds," 1981; *U.S. Patent 4,252,673*, "Preparation of Colloidal Cobalt Dispersions by the Polymer-Catalyzed Decomposition of Cobalt Carbonyl and Cobalt Organocarbonyl Compounds," 1981; *U.S. Patent 4,252,674*, "Preparation of Colloidal of Cobalt Dispersions by the Polymer-Catalyzed Decomposition of Cobalt Carbonyl and Cobalt Organocarbonyl Compounds," 1981; *U.S. Patent 4,252,675*, "Preparation of Colloidal Group VI-A Transition Metal Dispersions by the Polymer-Catalyzed Decomposition of Carbonyl and Organocarbonyl Compounds Thereof"; *U.S. Patent 4,252,676*, "Preparation of Colloidal Group VII-A Transition Metal Dispersions by the Polymer-Catalyzed Decomposition of Carbonyl and Organocarbonyl Compounds Thereof," 1981; *U.S. Patent 4,252,677*, "Preparation of Colloidal Dispersion of Nickel, Palladium and Platinum by the Polymer-Catalyzed Decomposition of Carbonyl Compounds Thereof," 1981; *U.S. 4,252,678*, "Preparation of Colloidal Dispersions of Ruthenium, Rhodium, Osmiun and Iridium by the Polymer-Catalyzed Decomposition of Carbonyl Cluster Compounds Thereof," 1981; *U.S. Patent 4,432,841*, "Process for the Preparation of Chalcogenide Alloys by Electrochemical Coreduction of Esters"; *U.S. Patent*

Thomas Smith, Ph.D.
Photo Courtesy Thomas Smith

4,460,408, "Process for the Preparation of Chalcogenide Alloys by Solution Coreduction of Esters"; *U.S. Patent 4,484,945*, "Process for the Preparation of Chalcogenide Alloys by Solution Coreduction of a Mixture of Oxides," 1984; *U.S. Patent 4,496,957*, "Optical Disk," 1985; *U.S. Patent 4,548,800*, "Process For Selenium Purification," 1985; *U.S. Patent 4,592,989*, "Toner Compositions containing Complex ionophoric Polymeric Materials," 1986;; *U.S. Patent 4,618,551*, "Photoresponsive Imaging Members With Polysilylenes Hole Transporting Compositions", 1986; *U.S. Patent 4,624,701*, "Coreduction Process for Incorporation of Halogens Into Chalcogens And Chalcogenide Alloys," 1986; *U.S. Patent 4,645,619*, "Process for the Preparation of Colloidal Dispersions of Chalcogens and Chalcogenide Alloys," 1987; *U.S. Patent 4,638,335*,

"Optical Recording Member," 1987; *U.S. Patent 4,952,477,* "Toner and Developer Compositions With Semicrystalline Polyolefin Resins," 1990; *U.S. Patent 5,102,763,* "Toner Compositions Containing Colored Silica Particles," 1992; *U.S. Patent 5,166,026,* "Toner Developer Compositions With Semi-crystalline Polyolefin Resins," 1992; *U.S. Patent 5,314,778,* "Toner Compositions Containing Complexed Ionomeric Materials," 1994; *U.S. Patent 5,344,737,* "Polywax Toner Compositions and Processes," 1994; *U. S. Patent 5,424,160,* "Conductive Carrier Coatings And Processes for the Perfection Therof," 1995; *U. S. Patent 5,434,030,* "Toner Compositions Containing Complexes of Ionomeric Polymers," 1995; *U.S. Patent 5,461,580,* "Computer-aided Chemical Illustration System," 1995; *U.S. Patent 5,516,619,* "Conductive Composite Particles and Processes for the Preparation Thereof," 1996; *U.S. Patent 5,484,681,* "Conductive Composite Particles and Processes for the Preparation Thereof," 1996;

Residence: Penfield, New York.

SMITH, William D., 1919-1993

Born: Shreveport, La., 1919; Moved to Rochester, 1942; Died of an aneurysm at his Tremont Street home, Rochester, NY, Nov. 1st, 1993.
Family: Married to Christine L. Smith; three sons, Carl W. Smith, Warren C. Smith, Steven C. Smith; A sister, Ella Smith; Eight grandchildren; two great-grandchildren.

Career: Joined the Navy during World War II; served in the Pacific; Worked for the Regional Transit Service as a bus driver; Became RTS' Director of Training; retired in 1982; Democratic Leader from 1961-65; First African American to head a Rochester Ward; Elected to the Monroe County Legislature, 1966-71; Vice Chairman, County Democratic Committee, 1971(first Afri-

can American to hold that post); Served as Vice Commander of Pennington-Moye Post 9251 of the Veterans of Foreign Wars.

Eulogies/Quotations:

"For years he sponsored a lot of people, male and female, through that program (Alcoholics Anonymous) ... He'd take them to meetings and go to their home and counsel them. He treated everybody alike. He'd treat the alcoholic in the gutter the same way he'd treat the President of the United States."

Carl W. Smith, Smith's son.
D&C, Nov. 4, 1993

"He was dedicated and committed to the community... He served with a great deal of dignity and pride... He came to the legislature right after the (1964) riot. We were still going on with the healing process, and he was a true peacemaker."
Connie Mitchell, former Legislator, who was defeated by Mr. Smith.
Times Union, Nov. 4, 1993

SMITH-WALSH, Diana

Born: Jamaica, West Indies; Moved to Rochester, 1986.
Parents: Dennis and Linetta Walsh.
Family: Married Leroy Smith, Jr.
Education: MBA, Executive Development Program, William E. School of Business, University of Rochester, 1996; BBA, Finance & Accounting, PACE University, 1985.

Career*: President and Founder, SmithWalsh Management Group (since 1998),* a Rochester-based Management Consulting firm, providing services to a national client roster, including Action For a Better Community, Girl Scout of Genesee Valley, Vesid, Designer Touch, and many under $100,000 small businesses; Adjunct Professor at SUNY Brockport; President, Rochester Business Opportunities Corporation, 1992-

Diana Smith-Walsh
Photo, Mike F. Molaire. Copyright 1998, Norex Publications.

1997; Former General Manager, of the same organization; Former Director of Finance and Office Management, Girl Scouts of Genesee Valley; Former Senior Analyst, First Federal Bank of Rochester, and M&T Bank of Buffalo.

Professional/Community Involvement: Board Member, Black Business Association, Hispanic Business Association, Mary Cariola Children's Center, Alternative for Battered Women, Junior Achievement; Former Board Member, Rochester Chapter, American Red Cross, Rochester Business Opportunities Corporation; Member Rochester Entrepreneur Society, Micro Business Alliance, Rochester Rotary, Small Business Council, National Association of Beauty Culture Association, Minority Achievers Program; Former Member, Greater Rochester Women Funds, The Anthony L. Jordan Health Center, Educational Opportunity Center, Partners through Food.

Awards/Recognition: Hugh O'Brian Youth Foundation, 1997; International Black Employee Conference, 1996; Minority Business Students Association, 1996; Junior Achievement, 1994.

Residence: Rochester, New York.

SOUTHERLAND, Tyrone W.

Born: Rochester, New York, 1961.
Parents: Willie B. Southerland, Evelyn Wooten Southerland.
Education: BA Degree, History, University of Rochester; United Way's *African-American Leadership Development Program*, 1992; Graduate Student, Nazareth College, 1993.

Career: *Senior Driver, Catholic Family Center, since 1989*; Substitute Teacher, Rochester City School District since 1988; Telemarketing Sales Representative, Xerox Corporation, 1988; Commercial Account Representative, US Sprint, 1986-87; Direct Sales Representative, Greater Rochester Cablevision, 1987; Technical Sales Representative Candidate, Eastman Kodak Company, 1985-86;

Professional/Community Involvement: Presently: Member, United Church Ministries Community Coalition, National Association For African Descent, The Black Ministers Alliance, African-American & Hispanic Men's Alliance, The Aquinas Alumni Association, The United Teachers Association, The University of Rochester Black Alumni Association, The University of Rochester Alumni Association, Catholic Parish

Service Advisory Committee, The Shelter Shuttle Advisory Committee, Catholic Family Public Relations Committee, Ujima (The Association of the 1992 United Way's *African-American Leadership Development Program* Graduates); Counselor; played Varsity Football, Intramural Basketball, at the University of Rochester; Publicity Manager for the Association of Black Drama & Arts.

Awards/Recognition: Empire State Fellowship for Teacher.

Residence: Rochester New York

SPRATTING, Willis, 1924-1995

Born: June 11, 1924, Chicago Illinois.
Family: Married Margarett Spratting; Three children, Garreta Spratting Kipp, Rene Spratting-Mathies and Roderick Spratting; Three grandchildren.
Education: Master's Degree, Mechanical Engineering, University of Illinois, 1949; BS, Engineering, Bradley University, 1947.

Career: *Retired Vice President of Public and Community Affairs of Xerox Corporation's U.S. Marketing Group after 21 years, 1992*; Was employed by Aerojet-General Corporation, Sacramento, California; Served as Masters Sergean, U.S. Air Force, 1944 to 1946.

Professional/Community Involvement: Was Board Member, Keuka College, Public Broadcasting System, Rochester Museum and Science Center, Al Sigl Center, Margaret Woodbury Strong Museum and WXXI Public Broadcasting Council, Greater Rochester Metro Chamber of Commerce; Former President of the New York State Committee for Employer Support of the Guard and Reserve; founder of the Martin Luther King Jr. Greater Rochester Commission; Former

Chairman Education Committee for the Business Council of New York State.

Awards/Recognitions: Distinguished Alumni Association, University of Illinois, 1978; International Citizen Award, Rochester International Frienship Council; Civilian Patriot of the Year, reserve Officers Association of the United States; Civic Award for Commerce and Industry, Rochester Chamber of Commerce, 1989; Community Service Award, Masonic Service Bureau of Rochester, 1989; Charles T. Lunsford Distinguished Community Service Award, Urban League of Rochester, 1990.

Eulogies/Quotations:

"The man is a saint...He's given so much to this community. He liked everyone, he was interested in everyone, and he was always looking for ways he could help."

Bill Pearce, president of WXXI
D&C, March 15, 1995

"He's a catalyst... He stays the same throughout the process. He changes everyone around him."

Ruth Scott, former Rochester City Council member, at a dinner honoring Spratting, in 1992.

STEWARD, Austin, 1793-1869

Born: Prince William County, Virginia, 1793; Moved to Rochester, 1817; Died in Canandaigua, 1869.
Parents: Robert and Susan Steward.
Family: Married Miss Annie Brown, May 11, 1825.

Career: Rochester's earliest known Black businessman; Opened a meat market in a rented room in the Abner Wakelee building on Buffalo Street, 1817; Purchased a lot of land on the corner of Main and Mechanic; Built a two-story building for a store, 1818; Closed his business in Roches-

Austin Steward Memorial Sculpture
Placed in the Four Points Hotel, Downtown, site of his first owned property (unveiled in Feb, 1986, the full bronze-casted bust memorial was designed by sculptor Calvin Hubbard) Photo, Mike F. Molaire. Copyright 1998, Norex Publications.

ter, 1830; Moved to Canada, May 31, 1831; Came back to Rochester and bought a small variety store, 1837; Moved to a store at 86 Buffalo Rd. and partnered with John Lee, 1838; Fire destroyed the business, 1838; Moved to Canandaigua to teach school with his daughter, 1838 (for two years).

Professional/Community Involvement: Was a human rights advocate; Worked to abolish slavery and his aftermath; Assisted the Village Schoolmaster in teaching Sabbath School to Black youngsters, 1818; Attended the First National Negro Convention in Philadelphia, Ap-

pointed Vice President of the convention, 1830; closed his business in Rochester to help at the Wilberforce Colony, a settlement for fugitive slaves in Canada, 1831; Became an agent for the abolition newspaper, *Anti-Slavery Standard*, traveling around the country selling the paper, 1840; Was the president of a statewide convention held by Black abolitionists in Albany, 1840; Help organize the celebration of the West India Islands Emancipation Anniversary; The celebration was held at the Village Academy in Canandaigua; Frederick Douglass was a speaker, 1847.

Patents/Publications: Published his autobiography, *Twenty-Two Years a Slave and Forty Years A Freeman*, in Rochester, New York, 1857.

STOCKDALE, Harmon Earl

Born: Louisville, Kentucky.
Parents: Mr. & Mrs. Harmon H. Stockdale.
Family: Married to the former Johnnie Mai Morrison; Six children, Carlos Reginald, Bryant Gibbons, Rosa Yvonne (deceased), Rosalyn Yvette, Harmon, Jr., and Angela Yvonne.
Education: Doctor of Ministry, Vanderbilt University, Nashville, Tennessee, 1979; Master of Divinity, Vanderbilt University, Nashville, Tennessee, 1978; BA, Religion, Magna Cum Laude, Bishop College, Dallas, Texas, 1974; Attended Howard University; Licensed and ordained, Gospel Ministry, New Zion Church of Louisville, May 1969.

Career: *Pastor, Mt. Vernon Baptist Church, Rochester, New York since 1997*; Pastor, Mount Lebanon Baptist Church of Louisville, Kentucky, 1980-1997; Pastor of the historic Spruce Street Baptist Church, Nashville, Tennessee, 1975-1980; Minister in Charge, Junior Church activities, Good Street Church, Dallas, Texas; Served in various capacities at churches in the District of Columbia, and Florida; Bank of Louisville, Kentucky; Guaranty Bank, Dallas, Texas; U.S. Army, 1968-1971.

Community/Professional Involvement: Member, Urban League of Rochester; Assistant dean, National Congress of Christian Education of the National Baptist Convention, USA, Inc,; Past Moderator, Stones River District Association, Nashville, Tennessee; Past Member, Joint Board, Baptist Student Union, Nashville, Tennessee; Past Member, Board of Trustees, American Paptits College of ABT Seminary, Nashville Tennessee; Former Adjunct Professor of Preaching, The Southern Baptist Theological Seminary, Louisville, Kentucky.

Awards/Recognition: *Who's Who Among Students iI American Colleges and Universities*, 1974; Alpha Kappa Mu National Honor Society; Fellow , Fund for Theological Education, Rockefeller Foundation.

Residence: Rochester, New York.

Kathryn Terrell
Photo, Mike F. Molaire. Copyright1998, Norex Publications

TERRELL, Kathryn

Born: Ashville, North Carolina; Has resided in the Rochester Area for over three decades.
Parents: Rosa, Richard Brown
Family: One daughter, Janelle Beale; Two grandchildren, Karen, and Kevin Beale.
Education: A Graduate of Niagara Falls High School, N.Y. State Licensed Cosmetologist.

Career: *Owner of Kathryn's Beauty Bar, at 909 Jefferson Ave since 1960*; Retired from the City School District, as a field representative to Title I.; N.Y. State Examiner for Cosmetology; Co-Founder and first President of WDKX Radio; Hosted the Kathryn Terrell Show at WDKX for the past 13 years.

Professional/Community Involvement: The "Queen Mother" of Rochester's African-American community; Member of Community Child Care Board of Directors; Director, the Montgomery Center Advisory Committee; former Board Member, Action For a Better Community, 1964; Urban League of Rochester (Charter Member), Rochester Business Opportunity Corporation; Dr Paul Clinic, YMCA of Greater Rochester, Mental Health Association, Heart Association, Montgomery Neighborhood Center; Birthday of Rochester, 1980; State Board Examiner for Cosmetology; Member, Rochester Chapter Negro Business Women, Downtown Promotion Council, Mental Health Chapter, Concerned Citizens Group, Metropolitan Women's Club; was the first Black Republican N.Y. State Committee Woman.

Awards/Recognition: Civic Award, Genesee Valley Negro Business and Professional Women's Club; Salute from the Times Union; Citation from the Human Relations Committee; Service Award from parents at school No. 19; Service Award from the Mount Olivet Baptist Church Choir; the Forman Flair Award for Outstanding Volunteer Work in the Community; The Urban League's Community Leadership Award; the Rochester Area Chamber of Commerce Education Award; Special Salute by the Rochester Community, November 1st, 1991. Humanitarian Award, Project Care; President Bush "Points of Lights Award."

Residence: Rochester, New York.

THOMAS, Golden Era

Parents: Edsel, and Helen Thornhill.
Family: Single; Two children, Walter Jeffrey, and Nikki Giovanni; Three grandchildren, Golden Shaquanna, Terry Andriel, and Nide Tenaj.
Education: BA, Mass Communications, Wayne State University, 1980; AA, Liberal Arts, Highland Park Community College, 1977; African-American Leadership Development Program Graduate, Greater Rochester Area United Way, 1993.

Career: *Production Coordinator/Director, WXXI Public Broadcast Council since 1988*; Former employee, WROC TV8/NBC, 1981-88, and WUHF TV-31, 1980-81; Amrigon Enterprise, Detroit MI., 1979-80; Auston Professional, Modeling School, 1975-76.

Professional/Community Involvement: Board Member, Boys & Girls Club of Rochester, 1993-95; RC TV since 1998; William Warfield Scholarship Fund Inc. since 1998 Member, Action For a Better Community Steering Committee, 1990-

91; Community Partners for Youth, 1980-82; Member of National Association, Broadcast Engineering and Technicians (NABET); Former Member, Rochester Association of Black Communicators; listed in the Diversity Resource Directory of Rochester Area Volunteers Published, The Philanthropic Diversity Consortium of the Rochester (NY) Region, Publisher, 1993-1994.

Awards/Recognition: Certificates of Appreciation, Action For a Better Community, Community Partners for Youth, WROC PM News; New York State Broadcast Award, 1992; Certificate of Merit, New York State Assembly.

Residence: Rochester, New York.

THOMAS, Freddie, 1918-1974

Born: Norfolk, Virginia, Feb. 10, 1918; Moved to Rochester, 1952; Died at Rochester General Hospital, after a 2.5 years illness, Feb. 24, 1974.
Family: Married Midge Thomas; No children.
Education: BS degree, Wagner College, New York. Dr. of Humanity (Honorary), School of Common Sense, 1972.

Career: Research Technologists, Eastman Kodak Company for six years; Research Associate for the University of Rochester School of Medicine and Dentistry's Department of Radiation Biology and Biophysics, 1961; Had expertise in Tissue Culture, Photographic Science, African History, Eastern Philosophies and Cell Biology; Lecturer in African and African-American History; Visiting Lecturer in Black Studies at Howard University, Washington D.C.; Expert in Jewish culture.

Professional/Community Involvement
Tutored neighborhood youngsters, including high school and college dropouts, He encouraged to return to high school and eventually to college;

Was a member of 15 professional and scientific societies, including, The Royal Society of Health of London; The Royal Canadian Institute Tissue Association; The Mathematics Association of America; Rochester Academy of Science; The New York Academy of Science; University Archeological Society; Photographic Science & Engineering; Association Study Negro Life; History of Science Society; Phi Sigma Kappa; Pakistan Association for the Advancement of Science.

Awards/Recognition: Dr. of Humanity (Honorary), School of Common Sense, 1972; Outstanding Achievement Award, Rochester Chapter of the National Association of Negro Business and Professional Women, 1964; Recipient of numerous other awards; The Rochester Board of Education named the newly built Middle School at 625 Scio Street, "The Dr. Freddie Thomas Learning Center," May 4, 1995; The Triangle Square Center, 1180 East Main Street is a living memorial to Thomas; *Who's Who In American Education*; *Who's Who In American Science*; *Dictionary of International Biographies*; *Who Was Who Notable Americans*; American Association of Mathematics; Selected as one of the 84 Rochesterians for the Sesquicentennial "4 Score and 4" publications, 1984; The Freddie Thomas Foundation was founded in his memory, in 1974; The Freddie Thomas Foundation established the "Freddie Thomas Scholarships" for students excelling in math or science, May, 1991; Rhodes Scholar Nominee, Wagner College.

Patents/Publications: Publisher and Editor, The Evidence Newspaper; Editor, Rochester People Weekly; Has lectured in Sierra leone, Rio de Janieiro, Brazil; Paris, France; Siena, Milan, Italy; Brussels, Belgium; Copenhagen, Denmark; Tokyo, Japan.

Eulogies/Quotations:

"Everybody loved Freddie. He helped so many people during his life."

> John Griffin, president, Freddie Thomas Foundation's board of Directors and executive director, Triangle Community Center.
> D&C, Feb. 24, 1979

"I am just a natural man, one of the common folks who enjoys reading and studying and helping people. I like plain clothes, plain food and good friends."

> Freddie Thomas
> about...time Magazine, p12, July 1974.

"So many people only saw Freddie as scholar; they never looked past that to see the other part of him."

> Midge Thomas, Freddie Thomas' wife
> about...time Magazine, p12, July 1974

"...with his self mastery and yoga, he was able to control the pain even after he was bedridden."

> Midge Thomas, Freddie Thomas' wife, commenting on his rare bone disease.
> about...time Magazine, p13, July 1974.

THOMAS, Andrew

Born: Dawson, Georgia, 1948; Moved to Rochester, 1960
Parents: Susie M. and William W. Thomas.
Family: Married to Linda D. Thomas; Two children, Rosalynd and Andrew Thomas.
Education: MS, Public Administration, SUNY Brockport; BA, Criminal Justice, Rochester Institute of Technology; Certified Trainer in Mediation/Arbitration, New York State Office of Court Administration, Community Dispute Resolution Centers Program; Certified Trainer, New York State Unified Court System Domestic Relations Free Dispute Arbitration Program.

Career: *Executive Director, Center For Dispute Settlement, Inc. since 1979*; Director, Human Services Planning, City of Rochester, 1976-1979; Supervisor, Youth Services Systems, Rochester/Monroe County Youth Bureau, 1973--

76; Assistant Youth Director, Metro Center YMCA, Rochester, NY, 1971-73.

Professional/Community Involvement: Founding President, New York State Association of Community Dispute Resolution Centers; Member, Society of professionals in Dispute Resolution; National Institute for Dispute Resolution; International Association of Civilian Oversight of Law Enforcement Agencies; Board of Governors, Canadian Institute for Conflict Resolution; New York State Unified Court System ADR Task Force; Founding Board Member, National Association for Community Mediation; Past Vice President, New York State Forum on Conflict and Consensus; Consultant for Home Box Office (HBO), on the production of "Confrontation Attempted Murder," a documentary; Assisted in the Mediation and Conflict Resolution Training of Mohawk Indians on the Akwsasne Reservation; Participated in the focus group for the development of the Mediation/Arbitration Legislation in the State of Florida; Mediated disputes between the Peace and Justice Coalition and the Veteran's Memorial and Executive Council of the City of Rochester regarding Citizen's participation in the Memorial Day parade, Rochester, New York; participated in the mediation of property claims disputes on the Onondaga Indian Reservation, Syracuse, New York; Facilitated discussions between neighborhood residents and school district on the closing of a high school, Rochester, New York; Mediated disputes between Pro--Choice and Right--to--Life groups regarding public access to health care facilities, Rochester, New York; Mediated dispute regarding the reorganization of Ibero--American Action League of Rochester's Board of Directors; Mediated a tenant dispute at Hope Village in Wayne County, New York, involving local, state and federal agencies.

Awards/Recognition: Honored Member, *American Registry's Who's Who in Leading Professionals and Executives*, 1996; Community Leadership Award, Urban League of Rochester, 1988; Distinguished Alumnus of The Year, Rochester Institute of Technology College of General Studies, 1981; Outstanding Young Men of America, 1977.

Residence: Rochester, New York.

THOMAS, Midge Banks

Born: Rochester, New York.
Parents: Ethel and Milton
Family: Married Freddie Thomas (deceased); No children.

Career: *Executive Director, Triangle Square Center, 1993-98*; Assistant to Executive Director, Triangle Community Center, 1974-82; Owner, Original Creation Bridal Accessories, 1963-74; Owner, of Orchid Beauty Salon, 1947--59; President, Freddie Thomas Foundation, 1982-1997. Co-Founder, Freddie Thomas Foundation, 1974.

Professional/Community Involvement: Board Member, Ralph Bunche Scholarship, 1959-92; Member, Grantmakers Forum, 1994-96; Rochester Events Network, 1990-92; Coalition for Downtown, 1981-85; Vision 2000, 1991-92; American Red Cross, Rochester, 1990-98; The Freddie Thomas Foundation, 1990-96; Metropolitan Women's Network, 1983-85; Founder, Miss Jane Pittman Public Drinking Fountain, 1989.

Awards/Recognition: Duke Ellington Hall of Fame Humanitarian Award, FCD, Inc., 1995; Women of Greatness, Life Community Center, 1995; Community Service Award, Dr. Freddie Thomas Learning Center, 1997; Community Service Award, Omega Psi Phi Fraternity, Inc., 1996; Heart Award, Zonta Club of Rochester, 1993; Sojourner Truth Award, Rochester Gene-

Midge Banks Thomas
Photo, Mike F. Molaire. Copyright 1998, Norex Publications.

see Valley National Association of Black Professional Women, Inc., 1991; International Achievement Award, National Association of Negro & Business Profesional Women's Club, Inc., 1982; Honorable Mention, Times Union Gannett Newspapers, 1967.

Residence: Rochester, New York.

TOLBERT-BONDS, Josephine

Born: Coldwater, Mississippi; Moved to Rochester, 1984.
Parents: Ruby Tolbert and Robert L. Tolbert.
Family: Married to Anthony D. Bonds; No chil-

dren.
Education: B.S., Computer Science, Cum Laude, Jackson State University; Leadership Rochester, 1996.

Career: *System Analyst, Finance System, Distribution Systems, Marketing Systems, Eastman Kodak Company since 1987.*

Professional/Community Involvement
Kodak United Way Site Coordinator, (raised $1.2M, 30% over goal in 1993); United Way Campaign Coordinator for 8,000 Kodak Office employees (raised $1.4M, 43% over goal in 1994); Member Women's Forum of Kodak Employees, Links Incorporated, National Association of American University Women.

Awards/Recognition: National Dean's List.

Residence: Rochester, New York.

TUBMAN, Harriet 1821-1913

Born: Around 1821 as slave, Bucktown, Maryland; Moved to Rochester, 1849; Died from pneumonia, in Auburn, NY, March 10, 1913.

Life: Escaped from slavery on foot alone, 1849; Came to the A.M.E. Zion Church on Favor Street; Made 19 trips back to the south, freeing over 300 Negroes (family, friends and others) up from slavery to freedom; Served as a nurse and a spy during the Civil War; Braved every danger and overcame every obstacle; Settled in Auburn, NY in 1857; Lived there for 55 years.

Award/Recognition: A postage stamp bearing her image was issued in 1978.

Eulogies/Quotations:

"On my Underground Railroad, I never ran my train off the track and I never lost a passenger."
    Harriett Tubman

"I came here because I wanted to bring more attention to this remarkable woman whose story is one of personal trial and extraordinary courage..."
    Hillary Rodham Clinton, during her visit at the Harriet Tubman Home in Auburn.
    D&C, July 7, 1998

WADE Sr., George Franklin, 1932-1994

Born: 1932, Boston, Georgia; Moved to Rochester, about 1965; Died November 1, 1994.
Parents: Cass and Sarah Wade (deceased) Family: Married Bernice Elayne Whindleton; Three children, George Wade Jr., Cordelia Wade Beasley, and Galen F. Wade; Five grandchildren, Maria Annjanette, Brittany Nicole and Korey Aluan Beasley, Anthony Ronald and Kiara-Simone Wade.
Education: BS Degree, Building Construction, Florida A & M University, 1960; Related studies, Rochester Institute of Technology (1973) and Monroe Community College; Supervisor Training Phase II, Rochester Carpenters Apprentice and Journeymen Training Committee, 1993.

Career: Self-employed Contractor, Wades' Home Remodeling; Substitute Teacher, Carpentry, 1974-1976; Served in the Army, 1953-56.

Professional/Community Involvement: Unsuccessful Candidate for Rochester Legislature as a Democrat, 1985; Republican-Conservative Member, 1991; Member, Baden Street Settlement Board of Directors; Former Chairman of the Building and Ground at Baden Street Settlement; Former Leader of the 25th District Democratic Committee; Leader of the 25th and 27th Republican Committees; Member of the Executive Committee of the Rochester Republican Party; Former Trustee, Financial Secretary, Reynolds

George Wade Sr., 1932-1994
Photo Courtesy Bernice Wade

Street Church of Christ; Former Board President, South West Neighborhood Association and Third Ward Area; Former Chairman of the Board for the North East District Council.

Awards/Recognition: Certificate of Appreciation, Baden Street Settlement.

Residence: Rochester, New York.

Eulogies/Quotations:

"We pay taxes and don't get any benefits from them."
    George Wade F. Sr., claiming that the Democratic elected officials haven't helped African Americans.
    D&C, 1991

WALKER, Gregory Thomas

Born: Akron, Ohio, 1954; Moved to Rochester, 1988.
Parents: Janet R. Walker, Thurston L. Walker.
Family: Married to Sharon E. B. Walker; Two daughters, Gaelyn and Erryn.
Education: BA, Political Science, Miami University, 1976; Executive Development Program, Kellog School of Management, Northwestern University, 1996.

Career: *Eastman Kodak Company since 1988: Worldwide Category Manager, Cartridge Film Products, Consumer Imaging Division (responsible for $100M in revenue) since 1996;* General Manager, Marketing Communications & Support Services, Consumer Imaging Division, US & Canada Region (managed a staff of 25 and budget of $150M), 1993-96; Manager, Marketing Communications, Film Products, Consumer Imaging Division (managed staff of 10 and budget of $100M), 1988-93; Vice President and Group Advertising Director, Uniworld Group Inc. (managed a staff of 3 and billings of $10M), 1986-88; Account Manager, D'Arcy, Masius, Benton & Bowles (DMB&B), 1977-86.

Professional/Community Involvement: Board Member, Rochester Children's Nursery, 1996; Blue Cross/Blue Shield of the Rochester Area, since 1995; Rochester Ad Council, 1991-94; Locust Hill Country Club since 1996; Life Member, Alpha Phi Alpha Fraternity since 1980; Member, Photographic Information Council of the Photographic Manufactures and Distributors Association, 1990-95; Worldwide Marketing Leadership Panel, The survey Council Media & Marketing Decisions, 1989-95; American Association of Advertising Agencies (AAAA); Minority Advertising Internship Program Committee, 1982-86.

Awards/Recognition: *Outstanding Young Men of America*, 1980 & 1988; *Who's Who International,* 1996.

WALKER, Phyllis P.

Born: Jamaica, West Indies; Moved to Rochester, 1974.
Parents: Myrtle Brown and Philip Anglin.
Family: Married to Henry Walker; Two children, Lamar and Patricia.
Education: Candidate, Masters of Public Administration, SUNY Brockport; BS, Business & Economics, Empire State College, 1996; AAS, Human Services, Empire State College, 1993; Leadership Rochester, Class of 1996; Community Service Curriculum Development-DACUM, 1995; Intern Leadership Development-Economic Development, Pratt Institute, 1991; Citizens Police Academy, 1995; Licensed Real Estate Broker, 1992; Real Estate Certificate, SUNY Brockport, 1991; Certificate in Word Processing, Straford Business School, 1986.

Career: *Assistant Project Director, Rochester Americorps Program, Monroe Community College since 1994*; Executive Director, North East Block Club Alliance, 1989-94; Assistant Housing Director, Urban League of Rochester, 1989; Office Manager, Mars Associates, 1987-89; Assistant Graphic Artist, Eastman Kodak, 1980-86.

Professional/Community Involvement: National Youth Service Day Committee, Appointed by Mayor Johnson, 1995; United Way Conference Day Committee, 1995; Board Member, Neighborhood Based Alliance, 1993-96; Member, Gates Chili Middle School Parent Teacher Organization, since 1996; Parent/Student Science Fair Committee, 1995; VFW Women's Auxiliary, since 1994; School #39 and Edison Techni-

Phyllis P. Walker
Photo, Mike F. Molaire. Copyright 1998, Norex Publications.

cal High School Parent Teacher Association, since 1984; Planning Committee, Freddie Thomas Middle and Northeast Elementary School, 1992-94; Administrative Council/Finance Chair, Susan B. Anthony Cooperative, 1988-91

Awards/Recognition: *Who's Who Among Students in American Universities and Colleges*, 1995-1996

WALKER, Sherry Wanda

Born: Rochester, New York.
Parents: Margaret and Martin Lewis Walker.
Family: One daugther, Misteeke McEwen Walker.
Education: MA, Liberal Studies, Brockport, NY, 1996; BA, History, Keuka College, 1974; Diploma, Business, Madison High School, 1970; Certified New York State Mediator.

Career: *Executive Director, Eastside Community Center;* Former Director, Programs & Operations, Center For Dispute Settlement, Inc.; Community-based Agency Administration, Baden Street Settlement; Rochester City School District; Lemon Law Arbitrator; Honored Fellow Trainer with Canadian Institute on Conflict Resolution (Ottawa, Ontario, Canada); Trainer, Community Based Mediation, Cultural Awareness and Diversity, Community Conciliation.

Professional/Community Involvement: Board Member, Threshold Alternative Youth Services, Pre-Trial Services Corporation; Baden Ormon Federal Credit Union; Rochester Society for the Prevention of Cruelty to Children, Genesee Valley Chapter/NY Civil Liberties Union, Zoning Board for the City of Rochester, Police Department Civilian Review Board, County Sheriff Review Board; Member, Panel of Arbitrators, American Arbitration Association; Mediator, Arbritrator, Trainer with Center For Dispute Settlement, Inc.

Residence: Rochester, New York.

WALLACE Jr., Benjamin, Ph.D.

Born: Pineville, Louisiana, 1948; Moved to Rochester, 1980.
Parents: Benjamin and Pinkie L. Wallace
Family: Married to Saundra E. Wallace; One daughter, Ashley Y. Wallace.
Education: Ph.D., Organic Chemistry, University of Florida, 1979; MS, Organic Chemistry, University of Florida, 1977; BA, Chemistry Education, Dillard University, 1970.

Career: *Eastman Kodak Company: Research Associate, Manufacturing Research & Engineering since 1993*; Senior Chemist, Manufacturing Research & Engineering Organization,

Benjamin Wallace Jr., Ph.D.
Photo Courtesy Benjamin Wallace

1989-93; Senior Research Chemist, Chemical Conformance Group, 1985-89; Research Chemist, Innovation Facilitation, Office of Innovation, 1984-85; Research Chemist, Photographic Division, 1980-84; Served in the U.S. Army, Petroleum Army Specialist, 1970-73.

Professional/Community Involvement: Co-Founder of the Rochester Chapter of the National Organization of Black Chemists and Chemical Engineers (NOBCHE); Member of the American Chemical Society; President-Elect, Network Northstar, Inc., 1998.

Residence: Greece, New York.

WARFIELD, William, Ph.D.

Born: West Helene, Arkansas, January 22, 1920; Moved to Rochester, 1925; Living presently in Champaign, Illinois.
Parents: Robert E. Warfield, a Baptist minister (Former Pastor of Mt. Vernon Baptist Church, 351 Joseph Ave.).
Family: Married opera singer Leontyne Price, 1952; Divorced; No children; fFur brothers, Robert, Thaddeus, Murphy and Vern.
Education: Ph.D., Music, Boston and Milliken University; Bachelor's (1942), and Master's degrees (1946), Eastman School of Music; Attended Rochester public Schools; Graduated from the former Washington High School, then on Clifford Avenue.

Career: Four years in military service; "discovered" at Toronto's Club Norman by a wealthy Canadian, 1940; Made his concert debut at Town Hall, New York, March 19, 1950; Toured Australia under the invitation of the Australian Broadcasting Commission, (35 concerts from June through September; solo performances with 5 leading Australian symphony orchestras), 1950; Signed contract with MGM to play Joe the dock hand in Edna Ferber-Jerome Kern's musical *Showboat*, 1950; Singing lead with the national touring company of the Broadway hit *Call Me Mister; M*ade six separate tours for the US Department of State; Played the title role in George Gershwin's opera *Porgy and Bess*; Performances on NBC-TV's Hallmark Hall of Fame, Marc Connely's The Green Pastures, 1957 and 1959; Appointed Professor of Music, University of Illinois, Champaign-Urbana Campus since 1975; Chairman, Illinois Voice Department; Tour with the Jim Cullum Jazz Band, narrator of the band's concert presentation of Porgy and Bess since 1989; Live presentations of Showboat, 1996 and Harlem Rhapsody, 1997.

Community/Professional Involvement: President, National Association of Negro Musicians, 1985; Board Member, Opera Ebony, a company of Black singers based in New York and Philadelphia, 1985;

Awards/Recognition: The William Warfield Scholarship established in his honor, University of Rochester, 1977; Medal of Excellence, New York State Board of regents, Rochester, NY, Dec. 12, 1985; National Music Educators Competition, 1938; Grammy Award for best spoken word or no-musical recording for his narration of Aaron Copeland" A Lincoln Portrait, recorded in May 1984 with the Eastman Philharmonic Orchestra, 1984; first annual Youth Week Award, Youth Review, Genesee Valley park, Aug 26, 1951; William Warfield Scholarship Fund established in his honor, Eastman School of Music, 1980; Honorary Doctorate degree, Lafayette College, Easton, Pennsylvania, 1980; Hendel Medaillon, New York City's highest cultural award; Duke Ellington Medal; The Yale University'sitation to outstanding Black musicians.

Patents/Publications: *William Warfield: My Music and My Life*, William Warfield, Sagamore Publishing, 1991; Facade (Walton), narration by William Warfield, 20th-century; Soldier's Tale (Stravinsky), narration by William Warfield, 20th-century;

Quotations:

"I enjoy young people. I enjoy my students...I go over the literature of the song with them. Songs are in French, German, Italian, English, Russian and Spanish. I teach them the correct way to pronounce and give a translation of the words."

> William Warfield
> D & C, March 23, 1990

"The whole opera scene has changed dramatically for black artists...When I was starting out, that field was closed to me. Now many are making international ca-reers for themselves, as you can see from the Metropolitan Opera-though there are lots more needing help."

> William Warfield
> Times Union, Feb 20, 1985

"Back in my days, opera was not open to blacks...And to this day, it's easier for a black woman to get a foothold than for a black man. It's no problem to put make-up on a black Isolde. But when it comes to Siegfried, the epitome of bleu-eyed blondes... Most tenors are love objects, and when the waltzing and the kissing start, that's a problem for many directors who fear that audiences won't accept it."

> William Warfield
> D & C, Feb. 22, 1985

"Wow, that's terrific...did he really win? ...All of us are proud, very proud...He's a wonderful person. Since our father passed on, he's been a father to us all."

> Henry Warfield, Warfield's nephew, upon learning that Warfield won a Grammy Award.
> D & C, Feb. 29, 1984

"He's such a wonderful man...That is great...It's nice to have been part of it."

> David Effron, conductor of the Eastman Philharmonic Orchestra for the recording of Aaron Copeland's A Lincoln Portrait, upon learning that Warfield won a Grammy Award for his narration of that recording.
> D & C, Feb. 29, 1984

"Warfield is the greatest singing ambassador this town has ever had. It's difficult to realize how tremendously he is received wherever he goes..."

> Harry Watts Sr., Eastman School of Music
> D & C, Dec. 14, 1951

"Somebody introduced me as a legend in my own time recently, and it scared me half to death...But I'm still actively engaged in teaching and performing, and I'm so involved with that I don't have time to give it much thought. But if I think about it, I'm not comfortable."

> William Warfield
> Times Union, Apr 29, 1980

• *N.B. Dr. Warfield no longer lives in Rochester. The above information was completely compiled from public data. There was no corroboration by Dr. Warfield.*

WASHINGTON, Herb

Born: 1952, Flint Michigan; Moved to Rochester, 1980.
Parents: Reside in Flint, Michigan.
Family: Married Gisele Washington; One son, Terrell; One daughter, Arielle.
Education: Graduate of Michigan State University.

Career: *President, H. L. W. Fast Track Inc.; moved to Rochester from Detroit to open a McDonald's Family Restaurant, 864 N. Clinton Ave in 1980*; Opened second McDonald's franchise seven months later, 435 W. Main St.; bought the McDonald's, 3280 Monroe Ave., Pittsford in 1986; Became the first black McDonald's owner to operate a site in the predominantly-white suburb of Rochester; Presently owns five McDonald's in the Rochester area; Former World-Class Sprinter; Former Holder of World Indoor Record in the 50 and 60-yard Dashes; Designated Runner for the Oakland A's in 1974; Appeared in 105 games, scored 33 runs, stole 31 bases, and never went to the plate or caught a fly ball; *Left Rochester in May 1998 to buy 19 McDonald's restaurants in the Youngstown, Ohio area.*

Professional/community Involvement: Co-Chairman of the Small Business Committee of the United Way, 1988; Worked with the Urban League of Rochester to find dollars for Black Scholars; Member of the New York State Athletic Commission since 1990; Named Chairman of the Board of Directors, Buffalo Branch of the Federal Reserve Bank of New York in January, 1992; Vice President, National Black McDonald's Association; Director Federal Reserve Bank of New York.

Awards/Recognition: One of four Black members of Locust Hill Country Club.

Residence: Pittsford, New York. Moved to Ohio, 1998.

Quotations:

"It was about opportunity for really significant growth- nothing else...The city has been great. We've enjoyed it here. But the opportunity is such that when it comes, you have to be ready to seize it."

Herb Washington, commenting on his leaving Rochester to buy a larger McDonald's franchise.
D&C, May 27, 1998

WASHINGTON, Kathleen Eleanor

Born: West Point, New York, 1952; Moved to Rochester,1963/1989.
Parents: Corene Marie Washington and Percy Cecil Washington Sr.
Family: Married to Anthony C. Scott; Five children, Asa Scott, Adjowah Scott, Khari Garrett, Rashida Washington, and Wesley Washington.
Education: Music Education, Voice and Violin, Syracuse University, Syracuse, NY, 1975; Instrumental and Vocal Arranging for Jazz Course, Berklee College of Music, Boston, MA, 1981; Choral Conducting Techniques Course, Eastman School of Music, Rochester, NY, 1993; Public Administration, SUNY Brockport, 1996; Mediation and Conflict Resolution, Center For Dispute Settlement, 1995; Intervention With Children of Battered Women, Minnesota Board of Social Work, 1992; Intervention With Children of Battered Women, National Council on Family Relations; Graduate of the United Way's African-American Leadership Development Program, 1996; Graduate of Leadership Rochester, 1998.

Career: *President, Thalia Productions since 1993*; Providing Diversity Consulting and Training Services; Director, Women's Resource Center, YWCA of Rochester and Monroe County; 1993-96; Administrative Program Director, Awareness Theatre, Family Service of Rochester, 1992-95; Education Coordinator, Alternatives for Battered Women, Inc., 1990-93.

Professional/Community Involvement: Board Member, Women's Foundation of Genesee Valley since 1997; Middle School Committee, Hispanic Leadership Development Program, 1996; Mentor, YMCA Minority Achievers Program, 1996-98; President, New York State Coalition Against Sexual Assault (NYSCASA), 1996; Mediator, Center For Dispute Settlement; Member, *African-American Leadership Development Program* Alumni Association; Rochester Women's Network.

Awards/Recognition: Fulbright Fellowship, Fulbright Foundation, 1982.

Patents/Publications: *Blind Date*, Video and Educational Curriculum for Teenage Dating; *"Teaching Sensitivity to Cultural Issues in Women's Health Care in a Community Hospital Setting" in American Journal Preventive Medicine*.

WEBSTER-WHITE, Mary J., Reverend

Born: Elba, Alabama, 1945; Moved to Rochester, 1990.
Parents: Effie L. and Alto L. Horstead.
Family: Married John White; Four children, Kelvin, Martila and Jacqueline White; Five granddaughters; One grandson.
Education: BA, Psychology, State University of New York; Ordained Minister, Colgate Rochester Divinity School; Certified Alcoholism and

Substance Abuse Counselor (CASAC), New York.

Career: *Counselor, Finger Lakes Alcoholism Counseling and Referral Agency (FLACRA) Newark, New York since 1995*; Presently Interim Pastor, Potter Baptist Church, Potter, New York; Pastor, Rose Baptist Church, Rose, New York, 1993-96; Counselor, Community Alcoholism Service Clinic, Rochester, New York, 1991-94; Counselor, Mohawk Valley Council of Alcoholism, Whitesboro, New York, 1990-91.

Professional/Community Involvement: Long Range Planning Committee, American Baptist Churches in Central New York, 1995-96; Member, The Multi-Cultural Committee at Finger Lakes Alcoholism Counseling and Referral Agency since 1996.

Awards/Recognition: Appreciation Award, Boy Scouts of America, 1995.

Patents/Publications: *Soothing Words Make Good Medicine.*

Residence: Clyde, New York.

WHITE, Darlene Riggins, DDS

Born: New Orleans, Louisiana; Moved to Rochester, 1972.
Parents: Mr. Wesley and Mrs. Dorothy Riggins.
Family: Married to Ronald H. White; One son, Ronald H. White Jr., and a daughter, Verneda A. White.
Education: BA, Chemistry, Dillard University, 1972; Doctor of Dental Surgery, SUNY Buffalo, 1977; General Dentistry Resident, Eastman Dental School, University of Rochester, 1978.

Career: *Private Dental Practice since 1979*; Staff Dentist, Westside Health Services, servicing Brown Square, Fight Square, and Milbank Centers, 1978-80.

Professional/Community Involvement: Community Relations Spokesperson for the Seventh District of the Dental Society of the State of New York, featured on radio, television, and presentations at various classrooms in Suburban and City Schools; Annual Supporter of the Urban League Black Scholars Program.

Awards/Recognition: 1 1981; Second Baptist Church of Mumford Business and Professional Award, 1986; Negro Business & Professional Women's Clubs Award; First African-American Woman Graduate of SUNY Buffalo Dental Surgery Program.

Residence: Rochester, New York.

WHITT, Deborah Ham

Born: Manalapan, New Jersey; Moved to Rochester, 1983.
Parents: Joseph R. and Alma. L. Ham
Family: Married David W. Whitt, a Kodak research scientist (1992).
Education: BA, Personal Management/Business Administration, Rowan College, New Jersey, 1977.

Career: *Owner, Deborah Ham Whitt Agency*[2], Inc. (1992 sales $0.5-1 million); eight years in business; four employees.

Professional/Community Involvement: Member, Black Business Association of Greater Rochester, Wax Ski Club of Rochester, Rochester Area Chamber of Commerce, Rochester Alumnae Chapter, Delta Sigma Theta Sorority, Inc.; Mentor for high school students.

Awards/Recognition: 1993 Urban League Outstanding Businessperson Award; State Farm Insurance Companies Honor Agent, 1996; Agent Idea Award 1990, 1991; Black Business Association Business of The Year, 1997.

Residence: Greece, New York.

WHITIS, Almeta

Born: Buffalo, New York, 1947; Moved to Rochester, 1959.
Parents: Emma Mae Coles and John Whitis Jr.
Family: Two Children, Christopher Todd Brown, and Jonathan David Whitis.
Education: BS, Economics, SUNY Brockport, 1977; Certificate, Management of Social Organizations (Urban Administration), SUNY Brockport, 1977; Koine Greek Studies, RICE Institute, Rochester, NY, 1991-92.

Career: *President, Chantileer Productions and Inner Voice Theatre*; Worked for over 29 years as Actress, Dancer, Writer, Director, Stage and Television Producer/Show Host, Counselor, Choreographer, Storyteller, Motivational Speaker, Direct Salesperson, Administrator, Diversity and Staff Development, Trainer and Performing Arts Instruct; Venues include: Baden Street Settlement, University of Rochester, SUNY Brockport, Eastman School of Music, and Empire State College; Workshop Presenter, New York State Department of Education, The Sagamore, Bolton's Landing, Lake George, NY since 1993; Featured Artist: Visiting Artist Program, Monroe County Library System since 1994; University of Rochester Storytelling Conference, Corning Arts Festival, Corning, NY, American Institute of Graphic Arts, Rochester, NY, 1992-94; Eastman School of Music, Rochester, NY, 1991-95; Instructor, New York State Department of Educa-

Almeta Whitis at the Memorial Art Gallery, Feb., 1998.

Photo, Mike F. Molaire. Copyright 1998, Norex Publications.

tion, Staff Community School Improvement Center, 1989-91; Counselor, Drug Prevention Education, The Center for Youth Services, Rochester, NY, 1988-89; Artist-in-Residence, Rochester Chapter of Young Audiences, Inc., Rochester, NY since 1976; Consultant, Migrant Workers Program, Wayne County Rural Opportunities, Sodus, NY since 1986; Assistant to Placement Director, Educational Opportunity Center, Roches-

ter, NY, 1985-86; Artist-in-Education, The Institute for Arts-in-Education, Albany, Buffalo, and Syracuse, NY, 1985-86; Curriculum Developer/Task Force Member, Summer School of the Performing Arts, NY, NY, 1985-86; Artist-in-Residence, metropolitan School of the Arts, Syracuse, NY, 1985-86; Vice President, Operations, Video Power Productions, Syracuse, NY, 1984-86; Artist-in-Residence, Arizona Arts Commission, Phoenix, Arizona, 1981-84; Coordinator, Field Placement/Career Education Project, New York State Department of Education, Syracuse, NY, 1984; Choreographer-in-Residence, Paul Robeson Theater, Syracuse, NY, 1984-85; Supervisor, Community Reading and Job Training Program, City School District, Rochester, NY, 1980-81; Educational Consultant, SETREC Program, Artist-in-Residence, Teacher since 1976; Program Director, Southeast Community Center, Rochester, NY, 1976-1978; Performing Arts Director, Allofus Art Workshop, University of Rochester, Rochester, NY, 1972-76; Principal Dancer, Bottom of the Bucket... But, Dance Theatre, Rochester, NY, 1971-75.

Professional/Community Involvement: Board Member, William Warfield Scholarship Fund, 1998-2001; Steering Committee Member, Association of teaching Artists, 1998-1999; Cultural Resource Committee, City of Rochester since 1996.

Awards/Recognition: Best of Rochester, City Newspaper, Rochester, NY, 1998; Rochester Area Foundation, Inner gardening Award, 1998; Artist of the Year Award, National Chapter of Young Audiences, Inc., 1997; Helen E. Quinn Service to Education Award, Alpha Alpha Chapter of Delta Kappa Gamma Society, 1996; Distingusihed Scholar Public Service Award, SUNY Brockport Alumni Association, 1996; Rochester Area Foundation, "Youth Are Resources" Grant, 1994-95; Decade of the Child Award, Governor of New York State, 1993; Appointee, New York Foundation for the Arts Review Panel, 1992; Hong Kong Arts Commission, Peace Art International, Artist-in-Residence, 1994-95; Outstanding Teacher, Madison High School, Rochester, NY, 1977; Professional Merit, St. Bonaventure University, Olean, NY, 1977; New York State Council on The Arts (NYSCA) and WXXI Artist Grant, 1975; New York State Regents Scholarship, 1971-76.

Patents/Publications: *I Give You The Dawn*, an Historical Perspective of African-American Women, Producer, Writer, Director, Nazareth College, RCSD STREC (an original play); *The Reading Way*, Talent for Nationally Syndicated Public Television Series, WXXI, Rochester, NY; *The Africa African-American Connection*, Weekly Cable Program, Creator, Producer and Show Host; *Through a Child's Eye*, Weekly Cable Program, Creator, Producer and Show Host; *Black Woman of Central New York*, Producer, and Show Host, Weekly Cable Program, Video Power Productions, Syracuse, NY.; *Spotlight on You*, Producer, and Show Host, Weekly Cable Program, Video Power Productions, Syracuse, NY.; *Getting It Together*, Producer, and Show Host, Weekly Cable Program, Video Power Productions, Syracuse, NY.;

Original Plays: *Edmonia Lewis Speaks, I Give You The Dawn, In the Beginning the Drum... the Word... the People..., Women's Peace, An Evening With Almeta: A Celebration of Spirit and Life, The Harvest Season, Historic African-American New Yorkers Pay a Visit, One Voice, Spotlight on Jonah Wade.*

WILLIAMS, Mingon G.

Born: Long Branch, New Jersey; Moved to Rochester, 1991.
Family: One daughter, Jocelyn
Education: BS Degree, History, Monmouth College, West Long Branch, New Jersey; Attended Howard University.

Career: Vice President Field Operations for Supplies marketing and Sales, Xerox Corporation's United States Customer Operations since 1991; Joined Xerox in 1977 as a Sales Representative in the Central New Jersey District; Later held positions as Major Account Sales Manager, District Sales Manger, Fort Washington, Pennsylvania;

District Manager of Sales for Wisconsin and the Upper Peninsula of Michigan; Region Marketing and Planning Manager, Chicago; Most recently, Major Account Operations Manager.

Professional/Community Involvement: Board Member, Center for the Improvement of Child Care, Los Angeles, California, and Hillside Children's Center, Rochester New York; Recently inducted into the YWCA Academy of Women Achievers; Member of the Black Women's Leadership Council, and belongs to numerous women and minority focused organizations.

Residence: Rochester, New York.

WILLIS Frank B.

Born: March, 13 1947; Moved to Rochester, 1958.   **Parents**: Harry and Mattie Willis.
Family: Married Bobbie M. Henderson; One son, Oji Camara
Education: BS Degree, Dyke College, Cleveland, OH, 1971;

Career: *Rochester School Board Member; served on the board since 1980*; Current term expires December 13, 1995. Worked for the City of Rochester Urban Renewal, 1972 74; The County of Monroe Dept of Social Service, 1974.

Professional/Community Involvement: One of the founders of Communicade Newspaper from 1972 1986.

Residence: Rochester, New York

WILSON, Sr., Johnny Myles

Born: Fairbanks, Louisiana, 1928; Moved to Rohester, 1969.
Parents: Christel J. Wilson and Phillip Wilson.

Johnny Myles Wilson, Sr.
Photo Courtesy Johnny Wilson

Family: Married to Nathalie C. Wilson; Three children, Johnny, Jr., Ruperd and Yolanda Wilson.

Education: MS, Logistical Science, US Army War College, Fort Leavenworth, Kansas, 1978; MS, Education Administration, Indiana University, Bloomington, Indiana, 1957; BS, Education, Gambling State University, 1950; Additional Higher Education Studies at Northeast State University, Monroe, Louisiana, University of California, Santa Clara, California, and Syracuse University, Syracuse, NY, 1969-1974; Certificate of Logistical Science, United States Logistics Management Center, Fort Lee, Virginia, 1975;

Career: Supervising Principal for Student Teachers and Administrative Interns, State University of New York, Brockport, NY, 1975; Secondary School Principal, Benjamin Franklin High

School, Rochester City School District, 1971-80; Secondary School Principal, Benjamin Franklin High School, Rochester City School District, 1969-71; Secondary/Elementary School Principal, State of Louisiana, 1960-1969; Class Room Teacher and Elementary School Principal, State of Louisiana, 1949-1959; Served 30 years of active and reserve military service as Instructor, Company Commander, Assistant Chief of Staff G-4, and Brigade Commander; a Commissioned Officer with the permanent rank of Full Colonel (O-6); A Notary Public; An ordained Baptist Deacon.

Professional/Community Involvement: Member, Board of Deacons, Mt. Vernon Baptist Church since 1971; Past Member, New York State Department of Education, State Regents Examination Board, Albany NY Governor's Education Committee; Member, Task Force For Alcohol Prevention for New York State, 1980-1983; Board Member, Wilson Commencement Park, 1990-95; Center For Dispute Settlement, 1983-85; Program For Rochester to Interest Minorities in Science and Math (PRIS^{2}M), 1979-81; Otetiana Council Boy Scouts of America, 1976-78; Urban League of Rochester, Inc., 1974-75; Strong Memorial Hospital, Adolescent Clinic Inner Satellite Clinic, 1971-72; Northaven Adoption Agency, 1971-72; Baden Street Settlement House, 1969-70; Rochester Community Saving Banks, 1971-73; Committee Member, Rochester School District, Budgeting, 1985; Reorganization of Schools, 1980-81; Personnel Selection, 1976-89; Building Utilization, 1975-78; Schools Feeder Pattern, 1975-76; Instructional Council (1975-77); Commissioner for Civil Defense, 1970-77; Rochester Telephone Scholarship Committee, 1970-71; The Ralph Bunch Scholarship Committee 1958-59; The National Association of Secondary Schools and Colleges, 1958-59; Committee for Evaluative Study of Secondary Schools, 1958-59; State Department of Education, Baton Rouge, Louisiana, 1958-59; Member, Phi Delta Kappa, Association for Secondary Schools and Curriculum, School Administrators Association, State of New York Omega Psi Phi Fraternity, and the United States Army Retired Officers Association.

Awards/Recognition: United States Army Meritorious Award; Army Commendation Award; Appreciation Award for Service Rendered, New Bethel, CME Church, 1982; Distinguished Contributions Recognition Award, 1980; Project Upward Bound Appreciation, 1980; 12th Annual Civil Award for Outstanding Contributions to Education, Chamber of Commerce, City of Rochester, 1976; Fourth Annual Community Award, Eureka Lodge # 36 F and AM Prince Hall Masons, 1975; Man of The Year, National Association of Black Professional Women, 1975; Dr. Charles Lunsford Award, Urban League of Rochester; Cited in the United States Congressional Records Proceedings and Debates of the 92nd Congress, Second Session, Vol. 118, No. 37, PP E2404, Washington, D.C., March 13, 1972; Listed in *Who's Who in American Education*, in the 70's, ISBN 0-914328.

Residence: Rochester, New York.

WIMS, Rosa

Born: Lake City, Florida; Moved to Rochester, 1939.
Parents: Mary and George White.
Family: Married Edward Wims; Six children.
Education: LPN, Nursing, Rochester Urban School of Practical Nursing, 1971; Certificate, Environmental Services, SUNY Brockport, 1981.

Career: *Founder, The Faith Community Health Awareness Center, formerly known as the Jefferson Avenue Health Awareness Center, 1987*; Served as unpaid Director of the Center since its foundation; Worked as a LPN for Rochester General Hospital for 28 years.

Professional/Community Involvement: Board Member, Arthritis Foundation, Urban League of Rochester, Main Street West Attorneys, Mercy Center with Aging Advisory, Progressive Neighborhood Federal Credit Union, Maranatha Human Services, Heart Association Advisory, St. Mary's Hospital Health Advisory.

Awards/Recognition: Urban League Community Leadership, Urban League of Rochester, 1983; Heart Association for Outstanding Service, Heart Association, 1983; President's Volunteer Action Award, George Bush, President of the United States, 1990; African Americans of Distinction, presented by NY State Governor, Mario Cuomo, 1994; Certificate of Merit, William Johnson Jr., Mayor of the City of Rochester, 1995.

WINTERS, Joseph Richard, 1950-1997

Born: Washington, D.C., 1950; Died of a massive heart attack, Nov. 5, 1997 at home in Perinton.

Parents: Survived by his mother, Angeletta Winters; Two brothers, Romande and Lawrence Winters; Two sisters, Jonetta Winters, and Marjorie Karim.

Family: Married to Mary Frances, President, The Winters Group; Two children, Joseph Jr., and Mareisha.

Education: BA, Statistics, University of Rochester, 1973. MBA, Accounting/Finance University of Rochester, 1975; New York State Certified Public Accountant, 1977.

Career: *Senior Financial Analyst, Corporate Finance, 1997*; Director, Earnings Reporting, Eastman Kodak Company; Has been with Kodak since 1978, as Estimator, Sales Reporting Analyst, Product Earnings Analyst, Financial Reporting Director; Was with Peat Marwick & Main, as Staff Accountant, then Senior Auditor, 1975-1978.

Professional/Community Involvement: Member American Heart Association of Rochester and Eastside Community Center, Boards of Directors; Treasurer of Kappa Alpha Psi, Service Fraternity, Perinton African-American Heritage Committee; Member of the Urban League of Rochester, Opportunities in Accounting for Minority Students Committee, the Urban League Finance Committee, 1982 89; President , University of Rochester River Campus Alumni Board of Directors, 1983 86; Assistant Treasurer, Association of Retarded Citizens Board of Directors, 1980 85; Eastman Kodak Professional Liaison with National Association of Black Accountants since 1988; Member, National Association of Black Accountants, & the National Black MBA Association.

Quotes/Eulogies:

"He was a very outgoing person...He extended himself to everyone and had a phenomenal number of friends."

> Essie Calhoun, family friend.
> *D&C*, November 6, 1997

"Joe believed in the word of God...He was a very good husband and father and his stewardship of the community was remarkable. I never heard him say no."

> Reverend Errol E. Hunt, pastor of Memorial A.M.E. Zion Church where Mr. Winters was a member.
> *D&C*, November 6, 1997

"The father has to take a different role today, because things have changed in the workforce. Someone has to help with the washing, the shopping, etc. You have to share the workload because women shouldn't be expected to do that alone."

> Joseph Winters
> ***about...time*** Magazine, p19, Dec. 1988

Mary-Frances Winters
Photo, Fred Tanksley.Ccopyright 1994,98, Norex Publications.

WINTERS, Mary-Frances.

Born: Niagara Falls, New York, 1951.
Parents: Lawrence and Gladys (deceased) Smith.
Family: Married to Joseph Winters; Two children, Joseph Jr. , and Mareisha.
Education: MBA, University of Rochester's William E. Simon Executive Development Program, 1982; BA, English & Psychology, University of Rochester, 1973.

Career: *President and Founder of The Winters Group Inc., 1984,* a Rochester-based research consulting firm providing Organizational Development, Human Resources, Diversity and Research services to a national client roster, including blue chippers Xerox Corp., Bausch & Lomb, Eastman Kodak Co., Avon Corporation, E.I. du Pont de Nemours & Co; Previously Senior Market Analyst and Affirmative Action Officer at Eastman Kodak Co for 11 years.

Professional/Community Involvement:
Serves on the following Boards: Greater Rochester Metro Chamber of Commerce Inc., Blue Cross and Blue Shield of the Rochester Area, Chase Manhattan Bank, McQuait Jesuit High School; became the First African-American Woman Trustee of the University of Rochester School of Business, 1986; Past President, Black Business Association of Rochester; Past Board Member, Girl Scouts of U.S.A., Rochester Area Educational Television Association Inc., Eastman Dental Center, Eltrex Industries, the Governor's Council on Management and Productivity; Former Chairperson of the Advisory Committee of the Greater Rochester Women's Fund; Past President, Girl Scouts of Genesee Valley, Inc.; Member, Alpha Kappa Alpha Sorority, Inc., the Perinton African-American Heritage Committee, The Links Incorporated, and an active Member of the A.M.E. Zion Church.

Awards/Recognition: University of Rochester Hutchinson Medal, highest honor bestowed upon an alumnus of the University, 1998; Small Business Person of the Year, US Small Business Administration, Rochester Branch Office, 1997; Frederick H. Minett Professor, Rochester Institute of Technology, 1995-96; Special Minority Enterprise Development Week Recognition, Small Business Administration (SBA), 1993; Women in Enterprise (National) Award, Sponsored by Avon Corporation, & the U.S. Small Business Administration, 1992; Athena Award by the Women's Council of the Greater Rochester Metro Chamber of Commerce, 1991; included in the 1989 *Edition of Marquis Who's Who in American Women*; Minority Business Person of the Year by the Rochester Minority Enterprise Development Committee, 1988.

Residence: Fairport, New York.

WOODWARD, Kenneth W., MD, 1928-1996

Born: 1928, Columbus, Ohio; Moved to Rochester, 1960; Died of cancer at Genesee Hospital, April 4, 1996.

Parents: Charles (deceased) and Delight Woodward.

Family: Married Elizabeth Elaine Woodward, RN; Seven children,Charles, Linda, Cynthia, Kenneth, Krista, Timothy, and Matthew; 13 grandchildren.

Education: MBA, University of Rochester, 1972; M.D. Medicine,University of Rochester, 1953; Bachelor's Degree, Pre-medical, Ohio Wesleyan University, 1950; Licensed in the State Of Connecticut since 1990; Licensed in the State of New York since 1959; Professional Board Certified; American Board of Pediatrics since 1959.

Career: *University of Rochester School of Medicine: Associate Dean for Minority Affairs, 1992-96*; Professor of Pediatrics 1992-96; Strong Memorial Hospital, Clinical Associate Professor of Preventive, Family and Rehabilitation Medicine, 1980-92; Clinical Associate Professor of Pediatrics, 1980-92; Senior Associate-Pediatrician since 1974; Associate Pediatrician, 1968-74; Assistant Pediatrician, 1960-68; Genesee Hospital: Senior Attending, Pediatrics, 1979-1995; Attending Pediatrician, 1965-79; Assistant Attending Pediatrician, 1960-64; Attending Pediatrician, Highland Hospital, 1960-89; St Mary's Hospital: Attending Pediatrician, 1960-86; Director of Pediatric Education, 1961; Pediatric Cardiology Consultant, Meyer Rehabilitation Hospital, Omaha, Nebraska, 1959-60; Pediatric Cardiology Consultant, SAC Air Force Base, Omaha, Nebraska, 1959-60; Pediatric Cardiologist, University Hospital, Omaha, Nebraska, 1959-60; Pediatrician, Miners' Memorial Hospital, Williamson, West Virginia, 1958-59; Xerox Corporation: Manager of Medical Support and Screening Programs, 1991-92; Manager, Clinical & Disability Services, 1986-91; Manager,

Clinical Services, 1981-85; Executive Director, Rochester Health Network (RHN) and RHN Plan, 1972-81: Played major role in the building of the Anthony L. Jordan Health Center, North East Health Center, the Genesee Health Service, and the Westside Health Services Centers; Private Practice, Rochester General Pediatrics, 1960-72; Rochester Neighborhood Health Center (Anthony L. Jordan Health Center): Project Director, 1970-72; Project Director/Medical Director, 1969-70; Medical Director, 1967-69; Medical Director, Baden Street Settlement Health Center, 1965-68; Monroe County Health Department: Medical Supervisor of Child Health, 1960-65; Director of Rheumatic Fever Diagnostic Clinic, 1961-65; Clinical, Associate Professor Pediatrics, Preventive and Community Health, 1974-92; Academic Associate Professor Pediatric, Preventive Medicine and Community Health, 1973-74; Academic Assistant Prior Preventive Medicine and Community Health, 1970-72; Academic Assistant Professor Pediatrics, 1968-72; Clinical Senior Instructor Pediatrics, 1965-68; Clinical Instructor in Pediatrics and Assistant Pediatrician, 1960-65; Academic Assistant Professor Pediatrics, University of Nebraska School of Medicine, Omaha, Nebraska, 1959-1960.

Professional/Community Involvement: Member, Rochester Academy of Medicine, 1960-1996; Monroe County Medical Society, 1960-1996; Medical Society of the State of New York since 1978; American Academy of Pediatrics, 1961-1996; National Association of Community Health Centers, 1973-1996; Board of Trustees, Rochester Institute of Technology, 1974-1996; Board of Trustees, Ohio Wesleyan University, 1985-1996; Board of Managers, University of Rochester Medical Center, Strong Memorial Hospital, 1982-1996; New York State Public Health Council, 1976-1996; Rochester Pediatric Society, 1960-80; New York State Medical Association, 1960-80; American Public Health Associa-

Dr. Kenneth W. Woodward
Photo, Fred Tanksley. Copyright 1994, Norex Publications.

tion, 1974-82; National Medical Association, 1973-83, 1992; Board of Trustees, Rochester Academy of Medicine, 1983-88; Board of Directors, United Way of Greater Rochester, 1983-87; United Way Planning Committee, 1979-81; Board of Directors: Boys and Girls Club of America, 1975-85; Rochester Rehabilitation Center, Inc., 1975-79; Neighborhood Health Centers of Monroe County, Inc., 1969-72; Health Association of Rochester and Monroe County, 1965-68; Monroe County Cancer and Leukemia Association, 1965-68; Monroe County Cancer and Leukemia Association, 1965-67; Rochester Branch of National Urban League (Founding Member), 1965-67; Action For a Better Community, 1965-68; Police Advisory Board, City of Rochester, 1965-68; Board of Directors, Eastman Dental Center, 1974-85; Board of Health Care Services, Institute of Medicine, National Academy of Science, 1981; Committee for a Study of Community Integration of Federally-Supported Health

Services, Institute of Medicine, National Academy of Medicine, 1980-82; National Primary Health Care Advisory Committee, Department of Health and Human Services, 1980-84; National Health Maintenance Organization, Management Development Advisory Board, Department of Health and Human Services, 1979-84; National Association of Community Health Centers, Inc. (NACHC), Health Policy Committee since 1978; U.S. Presidential Appointment to the Health Industry Advisory Committee on the Cost of Living Council, Advisory Committee, the Community Health Connection Initiative for Health Promotion, Disease Prevention, National Association of Community Health Centers, 1983-88; National Institute of Health, Research Review Committee, January 1977; National Institute of Health, Research Review Committee, May 5-7, 1976; New York State Health Department, Commission on Graduate Medical Education, 1984-86; New York State Communities Aid Association, Board of Managers, 1980-82; Project HOPE Institute for Health Policy Study, 1979-81; New York State Senate Health Committee Advisory Council, 1975-85; New York State Health Advisory Council, 1975-86; Governor-elect Hugh Carey's Task Force on Health, 1974.

Awards/Recognition: Edward Mott Moore Award, Medical Society of Monroe County, 1973; Certificate of Merit, Rochester Academy of Medicine, 1973; Man of the Year Award, Genese e Valley Club of the National Association of Negro Business and Professional Women's Club, 1973; Distinguished Community Service Award, 1980; New York State Governor's Health Education and Illness Prevention Citation, 1981; Samuel A. Rogers Award, presented at the 12th Annual Conference of the National Association of CommunityHealth Centers, Inc., 1981; A new Health Center developed by Westside Health Services, was named the Kenneth W. Woodward Center, 1983; Distinguished Service to Alma

Mater, Medical Alumni Council, The University of Rochester, 1984-86; Distinguished Achievement Citation, conferred by Ohio Wesleyan University, 1988; Sesquicentennial Year, Ohio Wesleyan University, chosen as the Sesquicentennial Alumnus, representing the field of Medicine, 1992.

Patents/Publications: Author of a chapter in Rosalind S. Miller, Editor, *Primary Health Care, More Than Medicine,* Engle Cliffs, New Jersey, Prentice Hall, Inc., 1983; Over eight publications in The New England Journal of Medicine, Pediatrics, and various Proceedings Publications; Over six presentations in national conferences.

Eulogies/Quotations:

"I think he was proudest that he had not allowed the circumstance of race to place limitation on what he could do as a human being...He was able to see first in all people their humanity and treated every person with the dignity and respect all human beings rightfully deserve."

Dr. Walter Cooper, a friend of 48 years.
D&C April 9, 1996

YEADON, III, George

Born: *Washington D.C., April 23, 1953.*
Parents: Clara C. Yeadon, and George H. Yeadon II. Family: Engaged to Faith D. Adams.
Education: MBA, Operations Management, University of Rochester, 1983; BA, Engineering and Applied Physics, Harvard University, 1975.

Career: *Manager, Negotiated Sales Administration Xerox Corporation*; Formerly an Administrative Manager in Line and Staff positions for Xerox Corporation in US Operations; Formerly a product design engineer for Xerox, and Westinghouse Electric Corporation in Pittsburgh, Pennsylvania.

Awards/Recognition: Harvard College Scholarship; Outstanding Young Men of America; Xerox Special Merit.

Residence: Rochester, New York.

YOHANNES, Tesfamicael

Born: Asmara, Eritrea, 1955; Moved to Rochester, 1983.
Parents: Amete Negassi and Yohannes Habton.
Family: Married Nigisti Yohannes; Four children, Themas, Feven, Helen and Nathnael Yohannes
Education: MS, Public Administration (MPA), SUNY Brockport, 1994; BS, Social Work, Nazareth College, Rochester, NY, 1989; AS, Human Services, Monroe Community College, Rochester, NY, 1987; fluent in English, the Eritrean languages of Tigrinya and Tigre, and the Ethiopian language of Amharic; Familiar with Arabic.

Career: *Monroe County Government of New York State since 1989*; Probation Officer, Department of Public safety since 1994; Case Worker-Youth Opportunity Unit, Department of Social Services, 1991-94; Job Developer-Employment Unit Rehab Team, 1990-91; Examiner-Housing Unit 1989-90; Refugee Resettlement Program, Sudan, Africa, 1982-1983; Coordinator, assisted up to 50,000 Eritrean refugees, Political Administrator, 1978-1982; Eritrean Resistance Movement Member/Organizer, Eritrea, Africa, 1974-78.

Professional/Community Involvement: Chairperson, Eritrean Relief Committee, Rochester Branch since 1989; Chairperson, Rochester/Asmara Committee, International Sister Cities of Rochester since 1993; Chairperson, Eritrean Community of Rochester, 1984-1987; Scholl-based Planning Team, Monroe Middle School, Rochester, New York since 1994; Vice President,

Association of Africans in Upstate New York, since 1991; Action for Peace and Justice, Rochester, New York, since 1991; Secretary, Job Developers Network, Rochester, New York, 1990-91; Refugee Advisory Committee, Catholic Family Center, Rochester, New York since 1985; Nominating Committee, Presbytery of Genesee Valley, 1992-94;

Residence: Rochester, New York.

Who's Who Politics & Government

City Administration

BAKER, M. Renee

D&C, Dec. 29, 1993

Appointed Director of Employee Relations, City Goverment, Dec. 1993. Former Director of Personnel and Labor Relations for Syracuse for eight years; previously Affirmative Action Officer for State University College of New York at Brockport.Holds a Master's Degree in Counseling Education from SUNY Brockport and a Master's Degree in Public Administration from the Maxwell Graduate School of Public Affairs at Syracuse University.

BURCH, Bridgette D.

D&C, Aug 1, 1997; Frederick Douglass Voice, Vol 59, N

Appointed Director of Communications, City Government, Dec. 1993. She was Staff Director of Mayor Johnson's Transition Team. Previously, Director of Development of Public Affairs at the Urban League of Rochester, 1987--1990; Public Relations Manager, Blue Cross/Blue Shield. A 1977 graduate of St. Agnes High School, she is a native of Rochester. She attended Fisk University double majoring in English, Speech and Drama. She received a MS in Telecommunication with emphasis on Radio and Broadcasting.

GOOD, Ronald J.

First African American elected to Rochester City Council,1975. He was previously a member of the old Monroe County Board of Supervisors and the Monroe County Legislature.

(see Who Was First)

D&C, Aug 1, 1997

JOHNSON, Loretta

First woman to be named Acting Superintendent of the Rochester City School District in July 1994.

(see Who Was First)

D&C, Aug. 1, 1997

SCOTT, Loretta C.

Commissioner of Parks, Recreation and Human Services. She was hired by Tom Ryan.

WHITE, Van

Appointed Crime and Violence Czar by Mayor Johnson. In 1998, he left the administration to join the law firm Nixon & Hargrave.

WILSON, Laval

He became the first African-American Superintendent of Schools for the city of Rochester in Oct. 1980.

(see Who Was First)

County Administration

CARSON, Loftus C.

He was appointed the first Executive Director of The Monroe County Human Relations Commission. The Commission was created by resolution No. 115 by the City Council of Rochester in May 1960. Mr. Carson held that position for 20 years.

(see Who Was First)

COLES, Truman E.

The first Black Assistant Dstrict Attorney in Monroe Country.

(see Who Was First)

MAXWELL, Maxie

The first Black to join the County Public Defender's Office in a position other than clerical (as an investigator).

(see Who Was First)

D&C, Nov 6, 1968; *Times Union*, Nov 22, 1969.

Democrats

ASHFORD, Laplois "Lakey"

The first Black to win a city-wide office in 1968. He was elected to the Rochester Board of Education. He lost a bid to become Rochester's first Black City Councilman in 1969. First African-American President of the Rochester Board of Education.

(see Who Was First)

Times Union, Nov.3, 1971

BEST, Wyoma

The first Black woman elected to the Rochester School Board in 1971.

(see Who Was First)

D&C Oct. 29, 1995; *D&C* Nov., 1995.

BODDIE-NEAL, Lydia

Elected to the Rochester City School Board in 1995.

(see Biographies)

D&C ,July 27, 1993, *D&C*, Nov. 6, 1991.

CHILDRESS-Brown, Maxine, The Honorable

Rochester City Council since 1983, representing the South District ; served as a Vice President; Chairwoman, Jobs and Economic Development Committee. Ran unsuccessfully for Democratic Nomination for Mayor, 1993.

D &C, Sept 4, 1991

BULLARD, Herbert Todd, The Honorable

Elected to the Monroe County Legislature in 1991; Represents the 27th District.

(see Biographies)

D&C, Oct 30, 1991

CURRY, Archie C.

Elected to RochesterCity School Board in 1977; Lost re--election; Appointed in 1982; Re-elected in 1983, and in 1987; Former Board President; Equal Opportunity Representative, Monroe County Affirmative Action/Human Relations Department. Bachelor's Degree, Urban education, Empire State College, 1976.

(See Biographies)

DAVIS, Reuben K., The Honorable

Rochester City Court Judge, 1974. Davis was unsuccessful in 1967. He was appointed to the judgeship in March 1967 and again in 1973. He was elected a N.Y. Supreme Court Justice for the 7th Judicial District in 1982.

(see Who Was First)

GANTT, David, The Honorable

he first Black to represent Monroe County in the New York State Legislature. His district is the 133rd Assembly. He is presently the Dean of the Monroe County Delegation.

(See Who's Who and Who Was First)

D&C, Nov 3, 1993

GAYLE-JONES, Jewelle

Rochester City School Board Member since 1992. A Monroe Community College Professor.

(see Who's Who)

GORDON, Elmer L.

He was elected the first Black President of the Monroe County School Board Association. Became the first Black member of the Rush-Henrietta School Board in June 1970. He served for 10 years.

(see Who Was First)

HENDRICKS, Robert

D&C, Nov, 1995

The first Black to run for City Council.

(see Who Was First)

JACKSON, Marvin

Elected to the Rochester School Board in 1995. Former Parent Council President. Mr. Jackson is an Eastman Kodak Manager.

(See Who's Who)

JOHNSON, Teresa L., The Honorable

First African-American woman to serve as Rochester City Court Judge, 1990. The first Black female Deputy Attorney in Monroe County.

D&C, July 27, 1993

about...time *Magazine, p32, Feb.*
1980

(see Who Was First and Who's Who)

JOHNSON, William A., The Honorable

Mayor, City of Rochester, first term, 1994-1997; Second term, 1998-2001; First political experience.

KING, Glenn F., The Honorable

Elected Northeast District City Councilman and sworn in January 2, 1980. He was Assistant to New York State Assemblyman Gary Proud for three years. He was a member of the Rochester Black Political Caucus.

D&C. Sept.7, 1991

LEE III, Jesse

Ran unsuccessful against Ben Douglas for the Rochester City School Board (primary) in 1991. Bachelor's Degree, Business Administration, Stayer College, Washington, D.C.; Master's Degree, Business and Public Administration, Southeastern University, Washington, D.C. Project Coordinator at the Association for the blind and Visually Impaired of Greater Rochester Inc; Former Program Analyst for the U.S. Department of Health and Human Services; Former Construction Worker and President of a laborers union in Washington, D.C.. President of the Rochester Chapter of the National Federation of The Blind of New York State; Member of the Rochester Area Council for the Disabled; Fund-raising Chairman of the National Association for the Advancement of Colored People and Member of the Executive Board.

D&C, Oct. 30, 1991; *D&C*, Aug, 28,
1995

LIGHTFOOT, Willis W., The Honorable

Monroe County Legislator in 1978-1980, 1986 to present, representing the 25th District; Unsuccessful candidate 1979, 1981. Ranking minority member on the Public Safety Committee; Member Human Services Committee; Has served on the National Association of Black County Officials. Founder and Executive Director, Southwest Area Neighborhood Association; President of Action For a Better Community, 1968-1971; Officer, Jefferson Avenue Business Association. A graduate of Madison High School, 1959.

MITCHELL, Constance, The Honorable

She ran for Supervisor of the Rochester Third Ward, the first major political campaign by a Black in the Rochester area. She felt short by 150 votes. Constance Mitchell became Monroe County Supervisor, the highest elec-

D&C, July 20, 1993; *D&C*, Sept. 29, 1991; Nov. 3, 1993

tive office held by an African-American woman in the United States at the time. She became the First African--American woman elected to Monroe County Board of Supervisors

(see Who Was First)

NORWOOD, Wade, The Honorable

A Rochester City Councilman since 1990; Legislative assistant to Assemblyman David Gantt since 1985. Bachelor's Degree, Political Science, University of Rochester, 1985. Born, Oct. 29, 1964, in Genesee Hospital.

Quotations:

"We expected quite frankly that Wade would fulfill his own prophecy: that he would become the first black president...We all figured that when he ran for City Council, it was step one."

> Laurence Kanner, principal of Rush-Henrietta High School about former student Wade Norwood
> *D&C*, Sept. 29, 1991

PAUL, Beatrice

She was elected to the Rochester School Board in 1975. She became the first Black to serve as President of the Board in 1978.

D&C, November 12, 1991

(see Who Was First)

PORTER, Darryl

Ran for Rochester School Board in 1991; Past President of Neighborhood Group 14621; Served on the school district's values committee; Active in the district since 1982; A facilitator at Eastman Kodak.

D&C, Aug. 10, 1993

REED, Anthony, The Honorable

Monroe County Legislator.

SMITH, William D.

D&C July 27, 1993

The first Black person to head a Rochester Ward in the Democratic Party. He led the Third Ward from 1961 to 1985. First African-American Vice Chairman of the Monroe County Democratic Committee, 1970.

(see Who Was First)

D&C, Oct. 30, 1991

SCOTT, Ruth, The Honorable

Ran unsuccessfully for Democratic Nomination for Mayor, 1993; Rochester City Council 1977-1989; First Black woman on City Council; First woman and first Black President of the 19th Ward Neighborhood Association.

(SeeWho's Who and Who Was First)

THOMAS, Ronnie, The Honorable

Monroe County Legislator since 1983; Represents, the 22nd District; Chairman of Public Works Committee; Former County Legislature President, 1986-87; Former Project Director, Minority Business Development Center; Executive Director, Baden Street Settlement; Former General Manager of Erwin's Coin--Op and Dry Cleaning Centers. Bachelor's Degree, Astronomy/Aeronautical engineering, Ohio State University, 1972.

about...time Magazine, p32, Feb. 1980.

(see Who Was First)

THOMAS Sr., Stanley J.

The first African American to run for public office in Rochester; He ran unsuccessfully for Supervisor of the Third Ward.

(see Who Was First)

WILLIS, Charles L., The Honorable

about...time Magazine, p14, Oct. 1980; D&C, Nov 6, 19

Sworn in as Monroe County Family Court Judge by City Court Judge Ruben K. Davis on December 27, 1979. He was appointed City Court Judge in 1971. In 1963, he was regional Director of the New York State Commission of Human Rights. Served as Assistant District Attorney in 1967; First Public Defender of the City of Rochester, 1968; Corporation Counsel for Rochester, 1970; Appointed First Deputy Counsel for the McKay Commission.

WILLIS, Frank B.

D&C, Sept 7, 1991

Member, Rochester School Board since April 1980. A graduate of Monroe High School; Bachelor's Degree, Behavioral Science/Business Administration, Dyke College, Cleveland, Ohio, 1971; Was President of Okang Communications Corp. and publisher of Communicade newspaper.

DOUGLAS, Benjamin L., The Honorable

Elected to City Council Legislature in 1991, representing the Northeast District. Rochester School Board Member, 1986-1991; Board President, 1988-89; Ran unsuccessfully against Councilman F. Glenn King in 1983; Past President of Group 14621 Neighborhood Association.

(see Who's Who)

D&C, Nov 3, 1993; Oct 29, 1995.

Republicans

DULANEY, Mark L.

Ran unsuccessfully against William A.Johnson Jr. for Mayor of Rochester. Dulaney is a chemical technician at Eastman Kodak Company. His platform included cuts in city property taxes, reduce the cost of city parking, and a push for a school choice program. He ran unsuccessfully for the Monroe County Legislature in 1992 against incumbent Democrat William J. Benet. He switched to the Republican Party in 1992. He grew up in New York City, attended Bronx Community College, Medical Laboratory Science.

Quotations:

"I want to be known: Mark Dulaney--lower taxes, school choice and teaching people how to be more successful."
> Mark Dulaney, GOP Mayoral Candidate
> *D&C* Sept. 16, 1993

"My foundation comes from being a black man and watching the Democratic Party make us dependent on the Government."
> Mark Dulaney, GOP Mayoral Candidate
> *D&C,* Sept. 16, 1993

D&C, Sept. 13, 1991

"As a 32--year old black man, I am tired of blacks being at the top of every negative statistic and at the bottom of every positive statistic."
> Mark Dulaney, GOP Mayoral Candidate
> *D&C,* Oct. 28, 1993

(see Who Was First)

D&C, April 12, 1993; *D&C,* March 8, 1993.

HEDMAN Sr., Roy

Ran for Tte City School Board in 1991. Ran unsuccessfully against County Legislator Charles J. Eber in 1985. Planner for the Monroe County for more than 21 years. He is Past President of the Franklin Parent and Community Group; Former Parent Representative of City School Board Finance Committee. Board Member of Baden Street Settlement.

JACKSON, Beverly

She was Co-Chair of the Monroe County chapter of the Black Republican Council and a Board Member of the National Black Republican Council. She lost a Rochester City Council seat in 1985, by 11 votes, the closest a Republican had come to winning a city office since 1969.

KING Sr., Roy, The Honorable

D&C, Oct 30, 1991

He was Executive Committee man of the Third Ward Republicans. He is believed the first Negro to ever sit as a Ward leader on the influential executive committee of either party.

(see Who Was First)

STEWARD, Lewis, Reverend

D&C, Oct. 9, 1998

Ran for the State Senate against Democrat Rick Dollinger in 1998. Reverend Steward was born on Feb. 3, 1946. He is married to Jan Steward with a daughter, Nicole. He attended SUNY Brockport (Bachelor's Degree in Political Science. He received a Master's Degree in Divinity from Colgate Rochester Divinity School/Bexley Hall/Crozer. He was a Minister of the New World Tabernacle Church,1989-93; Chaplain, Groveland Correctional Facility, 1982-1992; Assistant Minister, Chritian Friendship Church since 1988. He is the president of the Congress of African-American Unity since 1993.

THOMPSON, John W.

D&C 7/29/98

The first President of the Western New York League of Colored Republican Clubs. The league included in its membership every colored Republican voter in the counties of Broome, Cayuga, Chenango, Chautauqua, Cortland, Delaware, Erie, Genesee, Herkimer, Livingston, Lewis, Monroe, Jefferson, Niagara, Oneida, Onondaga, Ontario, Orleans, Seneca, Schuyler, Steuben, Renselear, Fulton, Franklin and Clinton.

(see Who Was First)

WADE, George F.

Unsuccessful candidate for Monroe County legislature, 1985; Ran against Willie Lightfoot, in 1991.

(see Who's Who)

School Administration

JANEY, Clifford

Superintendent of the Rochester City School District. He received BS Degree in Sociology, Northeastern University in 1969, Masters Degree in Reading and Elementary Education from Northwestern; Ph.D., Boston University, Educational Policy Planning and Administration with minor in Health Policy and Administration. He was Director of Black Studies at Northeastern University, Boston, 1969. Twenty one years with the Boston Public School: Reading Teacher, Principal, elementary, middle and high School, and Chief Academic Officer, 1969-1990.

Who's Who Churches & Religion

ALLEN, Keith J., Pastor
His Way Church of God
230 Hudson Ave
Rochester NY 14605   *232-5180*

ANDERSON, James, Elder
Bethseda New Life Fellowship
48 Cameron St.
Rochester NY 14606   *458-4080*

ASHFORD I, Fleming W., Reverend
Tried Stone Mission Church of God in Christ
21 Ritz St
Rochester NY 14605   *458-8453*

BAILEY, Alimon, Bishop
Church of Jesus Christ
16 Helena St.
Rochester, NY 14605   *325-7108*

CHEATHAM, Randolph, Bishop
Shekinah Glory Holy Body of Christ Church
901 Joseph Ave
Rochester NY   *266-2808*

CHERRY SR., James L., Reverend.
Aenon Baptist Church
175 Genesee St.
Rochester NY 14611   *436-0990*

COKER, Rosetta G., Pastor
Emmanuel Church of Jesus Apostolic Faith
295 Gregory St.
Rochester NY 14620   *244-6253*

COOK, Dwight E., Reverend
Mount Olivet Baptist Church
141 Adams St.

Rochester, NY 14608   *232-6742*

CROCKER, John, Pastor
Friendship Baptist Church
44 Columbia Ave
Rochester, NY 14608   *328-6591*

DONALDSON, Sarah, Reverend
Faith Deliverance Church of Jesus Christ
94 Central Park
Rochester, NY   *426-5761*

EVANS Sr., Lawrence Lee, Minister
First Community Interfaith Institute
219 Hamilton St.
Rochester, NY 14620   *461-0379*

FLAUNDERS, Willie J., Reverend
God's Temple of Holy Praise
59 Prospect St.
Rochester   NY 14611   *464-0900*

FORBES, Albert W., Reverend
Goodwill Missionary Baptist Church
111 Clifton St.
Rochester,NY 14611   *436-2683*

FRANCIS, Orpah, Reverend
Triumph the Church and Kingdom of God in Christ
1025 N. Clinton Ave.
Rochester, NY 14621   *544-9540*

GARY, General Grant, Reverend
Holy City Church of God in Christ
292 North
Rochester, NY 14605   *232-9350*

Gavin, Clarence C., Reverend
First Genesis Baptist Church
292 Hudson Ave.
Rochester, NY 14605   *454-7418*

GENTRY, Conklin, Pastor
Breath of Life Seventh-day Adventist Church
1410 Clifford Ave
Rochester, NY 14621   *467-7120*

GOFF SR., Novell, Reverend
Baber African Methodist Episcopal Church
550 Meigs St.
Rochester, NY 14621   *461-1395*

GRAVES, Raymond L., Reverend
New Bethel CME Church
270 Scio St.
Rochester, NY 14605   *232-3815*

HARRIS, Maggie, Deacon
Community Lutheran Church
942 Joseph Ave.
Rochester, NY   *338-2420*

HILL, Willie Ray, Minister
East Henrietta Road Church of Christ
285 East Henrietta Rd
Rochester, NY   *256-0190*

HOSTON, Ronald J., Reverend
Bethseda Church of God in Christ
120 St. Bridgets Drive
Rochester, NY 14605   *232-3414*

HUNT, Errol E., Reverend
Memorial A.M.E. Zion Church
549 Clarissa St.
Rochester, NY 14608   *546-5997*

JOEL, Darius, Reverend
Restoration Church of God
595 Frost Ave.
Rochester, NY   *328-5414*

JONHSON, Denis, Pastor
Community Bible Church
248 Andrews St.
Rochester, NY 14604   *232-4575*

KINER, Ethel M., Reverend
First Zion Tabernacle
371 Lake Ave
Rochester. NY 14608   *254-3490*

LOWE, JR., Simon, Reverend.
United Missionary Baptist Church
606 Bay St.
Rochester, NY 14609   *482-3985*

MCCLOUD, Altamease, Pastor
Jesus Apostolic Faith Healing Temple
30 Lowell St.
Rochester, NY 14605   *548-7806*

MCCREE Sr., Rufus W., Elder.
Outreach Temple Church of God in Christ
218 Murray St.
Rochester, NY 14606   *254-3820*

MCCREE, Jr., Samuel, Reverend
Zion Hill Missionary Baptist Church
250 Bronson Ave
Rochester, NY 14611   *328-4660*

McGill, Raymond A., Reverend
New Life Fellowship Church
362. Columbia Ave.
Rochester, NY 14608   *436-0085*

MEEKS, Warren E., Reverend
New Born Fellowship Church
123 Barberry Ter
Rochester, NY 14621   *342-5020*

NELSON,. Eluah M., Reverend
Bibleway Healing Assembly
660 W. Main St.
Rochester, NY 14611   *328-9734*

PARKER, Abraham, Reverend
St. Paul Holliness Church
63 Thomas St.
Rochester, NY 14605   *232-2448*

PARRIS, Gregory, Reverend
Church of Love Faith Center
100 Brooks Ave.
Rochester, NY 14619   *328-5022*

PORTER, Madeline, Reverend
Graves Institutional C.M.E. Church
372 Flint St.
Rochester, NY 14611   *436-2663*

POUNCY, John E., Reverend
United Methodist Church of the Resurrection
537 Post Ave
Rochester, NY 14619   *328-6432*

ROUK, David C., Elder
Church of God by Faith
230 Adams St.
Rochester, NY 14608   *235-4950*

SMITH, Douglas, Reverend
Emmanuel Missionary Baptist Church
60 Grove St.
Rochester, NY 14605   *263-3390*

THOMSON, James, Deacon
Antioch Baptist
144 Baden Street
Rochester, NY 14605   *454-6096*

THURMAN, Charles A., Reverend
Second Baptist Church of Mumford
957 George St.
Mumford, NY 14511   *538-4490*

TURNER Clarence J., District Elder
Christ Temple Apostolic Faith Church
766 W Broad St
Rochester, NY 14608   *458-5808*

WHITE, Ira, Reverend
Full Gospel Tabernacle Gospel Church
614 Clifford Ave
Rochester, NY 14621   *266-8540*

WHITE, Lloyd, Pastor
End Time Deliverance Miracle Ministry
144 Edinburgh
Rochester, NY 14608   *328-1090*

WILLIAMS, Raymond, Reverend
Mount Zion Baptist Church
131 Bronson Ave
Rochester, NY 14608   *436-4366*

YOUNG, Darryll H., Reverend
Trinity Emmanuel Presbyterian Church
9 Shelter St.
Rochester, NY 14621   *235-5967*

***

Index

Index

Index

Index

Index

Index

Index

Index

Index

Index

Nomination Form

Feel free to photocopy this form to nominate people you believe should be part of this book. To help us evaluate your nomination, please describe in a couple of sentences why you think your candidate should be included. Thank you for your input.

African-American Who's Who™ Nomination

Name (nominee)	
Address	
Zip/Tel	
Your justification for the nomination	
Your name	
Telephone	

African-American Who Was First™ Nomination

Name (nominee)	
Address	
Zip/Tel	
Describe the "FIRST" (include a reference that documents it, such as a newspaper article)	
Your name	
Telephone	

Norex Publications P.O. Box 25333 16 Cardogan Square Rochester, NY 14625
Phone/Fax (716) 671-5164 * E-mail: NOREXpub@ix.Netcom.com

Order Form

Please Feel free to photocopy this page to request information or order more books. Mail to:

Norex Publications

P.O. Box 25333, 16 Cardogan Square Rochester, NY 14625
Phone/Fax (716) 671-5164 * E-mail: NOREXpub@ix.Netcom.com

☐ Please include me in your mailing list. Keep me informed of any opportunity or any new product.

☐ Please send me _____ additional copies of your book. I am enclosing a check or money order in the amount of $32.86($29.50 + $2.36 (tax), and $3.00 for shipping) for every copy I order.

☐ I am interested in buying a large quantity of your book for our fund raising effort. Please send information.

☐ I want to become a distributor for your book (s). Please send me information.

Name_____

Address_____

City_____State_____ZIP_____

Telephone_____Occupation_____

Organization_____

Comments _____

_____